ALL REAL ESTATE IS LOCAL

ALSO BY DAVID LEREAH

Are You Missing the Real Estate Boom?

ALL
REAL ESTATE
IS LOCAL

**WHAT YOU NEED TO KNOW TO PROFIT IN REAL ESTATE—
IN A BUYER'S AND A SELLER'S MARKET**

DAVID LEREAH

CURRENCY · DOUBLEDAY

NEW YORK   LONDON   TORONTO   SYDNEY   AUCKLAND

A CURRENCY BOOK
PUBLISHED BY DOUBLEDAY

Published in the United States by Doubleday, an imprint of The Doubleday
Broadway Publishing Group, a division of Random House, Inc., New York.
www.currencybooks.com

CURRENCY is a trademark of Random House, Inc., and DOUBLEDAY is a
registered trademark of Random House, Inc.

All trademarks are the property of their respective companies.

Book design by Tina Henderson

Library of Congress Cataloging-in-Publication Data
Lereah, David A.
All real estate is local : what you need to know to profit in real estate—in
a buyer's and a seller's market / by David Lereah. — 1st ed.
p. cm.
1. Real estate investment—United States. 2. Real property—Purchasing—
United States. 3. House buying—United States. 4. House selling—United
States. 5. Business cycles. I. Title.

HD255.L464 2007
332.63'2430973—dc22
2006037698

ISBN: 978-0-385-51922-9

PRINTED IN THE UNITED STATES OF AMERICA

SPECIAL SALES
Currency Books are available at special discounts for bulk purchases for sales
promotions or premiums. Special editions, including personalized covers,
excerpts of existing books, and corporate imprints, can be created in large
quantities for special needs. For more information, write to Special Markets,
Currency Books, specialmarkets@randomhouse.com

10 9 8 7 6 5 4 3 2 1

First Edition

To Wendy with love . . .

. . . and to the memories of my Grandpa,
David Arditti, and my uncle, Fred Arditti,
who inspire what I do

CONTENTS

PREFACE

Buyers beware. All things are not created equal, especially real estate. As of this writing, the median price of a home in San Francisco was over $750,000, while the median price of a home in Decatur, Illinois, was almost $90,000. It is not overstatement to say that the American dream of homeownership is more difficult to obtain in San Francisco than in Decatur.

A real estate expansion or contraction has never been fair and equitable. Some regions, cities, and towns experienced great property-value gains during the 2001 to 2005 real estate boom, while others were left untouched. Similarly, the 2006 real estate contraction inflicted pain in markets primarily located on the East and West Coasts of the United States, while most cities and towns located in the middle of the nation were spared. Depending on where you lived or where you purchased property during those years, you either did well or not so well in real estate. Life is not fair in the real estate markets.

My own experiences help explain why you can't take the "local" out of real estate. As a nationally known real estate economist, I constantly get asked by the media to explain why prices are up in Washington, D.C., but down in Baltimore; or down in Naples, Florida, but up in Fort Myers, Florida. It is human nature to generalize—all of us do it from time to time—but it could be a costly mistake to do it in real estate. The cumulative home-equity gains for someone owning property in the Washington,

D.C., metropolitan area during the 2000 to 2006 period totaled an amazing $262,000, but owning property in Detroit, Michigan, during that same period generated a meager $2,000 in equity. I could provide similar equity-gain contrasts between towns and between neighborhoods within metropolitan areas as well. Where you purchase real estate is as important as when you purchase real estate. All real estate is local is a mantra that should be constantly repeated by anyone contemplating purchasing property.

I have benefited from property investments where I took advantage of local activity and information, and failed in real estate where I have ignored the local marketplace. I will share some of my successful and failed stories with you in this book. I will also share stories told to me by other successful real estate investors about how they took advantage of local market activity to make profitable property purchases. It becomes increasingly clear that investigating the local market before purchasing property pays large dividends. That is the purpose of this book—to provide information and guidance on what you need to know, locally, to make the right choices and profit in real estate.

This book would not be possible without the meaningful contributions of a number of colleagues and friends. I would like to extend heartfelt thanks to my Doubleday editor, Roger Scholl, who prodded and encouraged me to write a book that emphasized that all real estate is local. Roger helped shape and edit the entire manuscript. I would like to pay special thanks to Talia Krohn from Doubleday and to Kate Anderson, who also provided valuable editing assistance. I would also like to thank Dale Mattison, Owner/Broker of the Mattison Group at Long & Foster, Washington, D.C., and Linda Rheinberger, Owner/Broker of One Source Realty and Management, Las Vegas, Nevada, for providing valuable insights and real-world experiences from the real estate community. A special thanks to Lawrence Yun and Ken Fears, colleagues from the National Association of Realtors, for providing critical data and analysis in many sections of this book. I could not have completed this book under the demands of preparation and my business schedule without my assistant, Cassandra Sims. I am also grateful to my agent, Alice Martell, for her constant encouragement and to my family, particularly my wife Wendy, for their support and patience throughout the entire writing process. If I have inadvertently omitted someone who contributed to the completion of this book, I apologize for the empty acknowledgment. Of course, I alone am responsible for the contents of this book and for whatever misuse I might have made of the suggestions from others.

Finally, I owe a great deal to the Realtors, lenders, and other real estate practitioners and to the many homebuyers and investors across the nation who have shared their concerns and experiences in purchasing real estate with me.

(Please note: The contents and views expressed in this book do not necessarily reflect the views of The National Association of Realtors.)

ALL REAL ESTATE IS LOCAL

Chapter One

A NEVER-ENDING STORY

My grandfather was not a gifted storyteller by any means. But there was one particular story he told with an emotion that captivated me every time I heard it. While I am sure that over the years his tale grew in size and hyperbole, it really doesn't matter. It is the lesson of the story that is important.

My maternal grandfather was twelve years old when he, his mother, and his younger brother, like so many European immigrants in the early 1900s, anxiously crossed the Atlantic Ocean seeking a better life in America. Grandpa, as I affectionately called him, was born Dario Arditti, but an official at Ellis Island Americanized his name to *David* Arditti (in fact, I am named after Grandpa). He held several odd jobs in his teenage years, learning English and getting what education he could. His first job as an adult was sweeping floors for a company in the garment district in New York City. Over time, he worked his way up and took on greater responsibilities. By early 1928, he was the company's bank courier. One of his tasks was to deposit the company's overflow of operating funds every Thursday morning at a branch office of the Bank of Italy, located in Manhattan.

As his courier activities became routine, the bank manager grew particularly fond of Grandpa. Perhaps he felt an affinity for the struggling young Arditti, who was regularly depositing money in the Bank of Italy. After several weeks of exchanging pleasantries, the bank manager took a greater interest in Grandpa, opening a savings account for my grandfather and convincing him to deposit one-third of his salary every week in the account. The manager began giving Grandpa tips on the stock market, recommending specific companies in which to invest. Grandpa followed his advice. Curiously, the value of every company Grandpa invested in climbed dramatically over the next two years. In fact, by the summer of 1929, Grandpa had accumulated significant wealth for someone twenty-seven years of age.

Because he followed the advice of the bank manager, Grandpa was one of the few investors who avoided financial ruin in the Crash of 1929. He liquidated most of his stock holdings before the crash and invested in "real" hard assets. One of his largest investments was the purchase of a gift/furniture store: the International Gift Shop. The shop was located on what was then perhaps the busiest retail intersection in America, Thirty-fourth Street and Eighth Avenue, near Macy's department store and across the street from Madison Square Garden. By the time Grandpa was thirty-six years old, he had become a relatively wealthy man—as well as a shrewd equities investor. My grandfather owed a great debt of gratitude to the bank manager who nurtured and guided him both financially and emotionally.

It was years later that Grandpa realized what had really happened. The Bank of Italy was founded in San Francisco. The garment company for which Grandpa worked dealt with Bank of Italy's New York branch office. Sometime in 1929, the Bank of Italy merged with the Bank of America. The chairman and founder of the Bank of Italy, Amadeo Giannini, became the chairman and CEO of the new and larger Bank of America. It was a name Grandpa had heard his bank manager mention from time to time; as fate had it, the bank manager was the son-in-law of Amadeo Giannini!

My grandfather realized that Giannini's son-in-law was investing Grandpa's savings funds in stocks of companies that the bank manager knew had applied for large loans to the Bank of Italy in order to expand their businesses. They were loans that would soon be approved by the bank. The company's stock price usually rose after a large bank loan was approved. Of course, using inside information was more prevalent in the twenties; not until the establishment of the Securities and Exchange Act of 1934, which created the Securities and Exchange Commission, did the practice become unlawful.

My grandfather was one of the fortunate few during the Great Depression who had financial assets left after the 1929 stock market crash. But he had to make some hard choices with his money. His younger brother (my great-uncle) had lost some of his savings, and the import business he had founded was struggling financially. Grandpa loaned his brother the money to keep the business alive. But Grandpa faced a more important financial decision in the mid-1930s. The owner of the skyscraper on Thirty-fourth Street that housed my grandfather's International Gift Shop was desperately cash-poor. Knowing that his tenant had significant funds, the owner offered Grandpa the opportunity to purchase the building for $1 million, with a down payment of a mere $100,000. Now Grandpa could make the ultimate investment—real estate. It was the hardest of hard assets in a time of economic uncertainty. The $100,000 price tag was not an obstacle—Grandpa had the money. And the $1 million price tag was a deep discount for a building that was about 55 percent occupied during the Depression. But because the real estate markets had been down across the country as a result of the Depression, rather than purchase the building, Grandpa offered instead to pay for a low-priced, three-year lease up front. This seemed a sound decision—it would give the property owner sorely needed cash and at the same time reduce the leasing costs for the International Gift Shop over a three-year period. It seemed like a win/win deal for both parties.

But it turned out to be the biggest mistake my grandfather ever made. Thirty years later, in 1969, the property owner sold the fifty-story building for $150 million! Moreover, the new owner of the building tripled Grandpa's rent, forcing the International Gift Shop to close its doors shortly afterward. Grandpa retired that year and moved to Florida.

Grandpa told me this story every year until the day he died, and he always ended the story with the same advice: Never ignore the local marketplace. What Grandpa didn't appreciate at the time was that Thirty-fourth Street was one of the busiest and most popular streets in the world. Grandpa didn't research the local real estate market. He made his decision about purchasing the skyscraper based on what he read in the newspapers and heard on the radio: Across the nation, jobs were scarce and families were struggling to make ends meet. He relied on national trends as well as on his experience of what was happening to those closest to him up in the Bronx, where he lived—businesses along the Grand Concourse struggling to survive. This was what was uppermost in his mind as he made his decision. He didn't realize at the time that Manhattan was where the action was—indeed, it was the center of America at that time. Grandpa allowed the ills of the nation and the neighborhood where he lived—which he read and heard about every day—to blind him to the activity and prospects of the local marketplace in which his business was located. He had an opportunity to purchase a fifty-story building on one of the most sought-after retail streets in the world for a deep discount, and he missed it. He ignored the rich potential of Manhattan because he was so focused on the nation and the Bronx. He ignored the gravity and pull of Manhattan because of the dismal stories he heard about Newark, New Jersey, and Philadelphia. He learned the hard way that *local* real estate values are determined by *local* activity. He had made a mistake that he would not let himself, or me, ever forget.

In this book, I am following Grandpa's lead. My objective is to offer you some valuable lessons on purchasing real estate. My grandfather was not the only person to make a mistake in real estate. Mistakes are made by many households and investors every year. The common thread among them is that they did not pay attention to local influences and activity.

Over the years, I have worked diligently evaluating local, regional, and national real estate markets, and I want to pass on some of this knowledge to you. I am also an active real estate investor, and I have built a modest but successful portfolio of investment properties of my own. I guess you could say I have come to understand what makes real estate tick. I believe that if you master the lessons that I have learned over the years on how to evaluate and purchase real estate the local way, you will become a successful real estate investor—and make Grandpa proud.

Chapter Two

THERE IS NO PLACE LIKE HOME

Several years ago, an old college friend called me and asked why his investment in a two-year-old town house in Dallas, Texas, had not generated big returns. I asked him what he had expected to realize from his investment when he purchased the property. He replied that he wanted to earn what everyone else was earning from the real estate boom—annual double-digit price increases. In response, I told him: *All real estate is local*.

The legendary Speaker of the House Thomas P. "Tip" O'Neill made famous a similar phrase about politics. But it applies equally to real estate. My college buddy made a mistake common to many people who buy real estate. He assumed that properties in his own neighborhood and city would perform as well as properties in all other areas of the country. He ignored local influences on property values. What he did not realize was that the great real estate boom of the twenty-first century discriminated. Not every state, city, and neighborhood experienced the same highly publicized property-value increases; not every homeowner realized the same wealth gains from property ownership as others did. Dallas was left out of the boom, and so was my friend.

All real estate is local. I have found that home buyers and real estate investors who ignore these five potent words eventually make costly and avoidable mistakes. They either purchase real estate in the wrong location, like my college friend, or purchase property too late. Sometimes you also have a difficult decision to make even after gathering information about a local market.

In 2002, a neighbor of mine was looking to purchase a second home—a beach house in Virginia Beach, Virginia. Beachfront homes had already appreciated by 30 percent during the previous two years. My neighbor might have just decided that the price was already too high and postponed a purchase. Instead, he examined the local Virginia Beach area economy and the then-current influences in the local real estate market. Spurred by what he learned, he made an offer on a $900,000 beach house. That house is currently worth about $1.5 million. Yes, he was lucky, but he earned his luck by becoming comfortable with the dynamics of the local market. And finally, he had the nerve to make the deal happen.

The performance of real estate—that is, how properties appreciate in value and how that price appreciation translates into household (or investor) wealth—is almost never evenly distributed. Even as I write this, the nation is a tale of two real estate markets. Most of the metropolitan areas that experienced the real estate boom during the first five years of the twenty-first century cooled immediately after the boom; other metros that did not experience the boom stayed the course or actually gained momentum. For example, in March 2006, Naples, Florida, which had been a well-publicized boomtown, reported a 30 percent drop in home sales for the month, increasing the inventory of homes in that local market to nine months' supply (anything over six months is considered excess). During the same month, Cincinnati, Ohio, which never really participated in the boom, reported a 24 percent increase in home sales. No matter what time period we choose, there will always be regions (or metros) of the nation that fare well while other regions (or metros) of the nation do not.

Translation: There are always buying opportunities in the real estate markets. You just have to *keep your focus on local activity* in the regions and neighborhoods in which you are interested in buying.

I spend a great deal of my professional life talking to reporters, real estate professionals, housing analysts, and many other audiences about events and trends in real estate markets. The one thing I consistently and repeatedly emphasize is that real estate is local. The Washington, D.C., market for home sales is booming—why isn't Baltimore's market as healthy? Naples, Florida, experiences a double-digit drop in home sales—will Fort Myers, Florida, be next? These questions and more require a local analysis. When you purchase any property—your home, a vacation home, an investment property—you are not just purchasing that particular property. You are also investing in the local marketplace in which that property resides. In real estate, the property and its local market are joined at the hip. They are one and the same.

Let me give you a rather loose analogy. When you marry, you not only establish a very intimate relationship with your wife or husband, but you also "inherit" her or his family as well. So it is with purchasing property—you establish an intimate relationship with your property, but at the same time you "inherit" the local market. You are buying the downtown, the theaters, the professional sports teams, the education system, the local university, and so on. To purchase property wisely, you need to know your property's surroundings. You need to understand the local politics, the local economy, and the local businesses.

Every local real estate market is decidedly different from another. That is due in large part to the fact that each real estate property is unique in some way. Let's face it—there is nothing more local (to you) than your own home. Property is not a homogeneous commodity. While a builder may construct identical four-bedroom, two-bath homes in a particular development, once a family moves into one of those homes it takes on its own personality. Decorating, landscaping, and upgrading are all personal choices that affect the home's value. This uniqueness flourishes throughout real estate markets from coast to coast. Every home is different, every neighborhood is different, and every town and city is different.

A good illustration of the unique character of real estate can be seen by comparing the pricing of a used home with the pricing of a used automobile. An automobile is a commodity that can be relocated anywhere. Its value is determined by the supply and demand for a particular model, based on upgrades and condition. For example, if two 2004 Lexus RX 330s were available for sale and had identical upgrades, color, and mileage, the only differentiating factor would be condition. If one vehicle was in poor condition (e.g., a tear in the leather seats or an engine leaking oil) and the other vehicle was in excellent condition, the vehicle in poorer condition would be priced lower.

A home's value is also determined by the supply and demand for the home based on the model of the home (colonial or ranch, condominium), upgrades (Formica or granite or marble countertops), and the current state of the home—in other words, whether it is in good shape. But there is one large difference between a car and a home. A home cannot travel. It is firmly entrenched where it is built (except, of course, with a mobile home). Thus, a home's value, unlike the automobile's, is as dependent on its location as on its characteristics and amenities. Even if a home is in excellent condition, if the neighborhood in which it resides deteriorates, so will the value of the home.

Most people view the value of their home in a simplistic way—add a bathroom, renovate your kitchen, and value goes up. Or be lucky enough to be in a real estate market where there are not many homes available for sale, but many buyers, and your price will probably go up. Or when mortgage rates go down, there are usually more households looking to purchase homes, so there may be some upward pressure on prices. But most households believe that if you hold on to your home for a long enough time, values eventually go up.

But it is not that simple. There are many times when you do not control the value of your home. You can make as many home improvements as you want, but if your neighborhood is deteriorating, home values could stagnate or even fall. Similarly, you can have a great house in a great neighborhood, but if your metropolitan area is losing jobs (as happened in Detroit—see below), values may stagnate or drop. If your neighborhood is experiencing high crime rates or your local government decides to build a highway through your neighborhood, home values are destined to decline.

And there are positive influences on home values that you might not suspect. If Major League Baseball decides to bring professional baseball to your city or if the local government works with some big developers to revitalize the downtown, property values will probably rise over time. Or let's say CBS decides to air a popular television show that is set in your city, or Oprah dedicates one of her shows to her favorite towns and your town makes the list. The increased exposure is likely to raise your town's popularity, attracting both visitors (thus helping the local economy) and households looking to move there permanently. Do not underestimate the influential reach of Oprah (see Chapter Six).

As you can see, determining the value of a property is not as simple as supply and demand. There are so many factors and influences beyond your control. That is what makes real estate unique. You buy your home, but you are also buying the neighborhood and the city. You are buying the local property tax rate, the state income tax, and the Democrats or Republicans who are running your town and the political decisions they make. Some of those decisions will affect the value of your home. And because your home is probably your largest and most expensive asset, you need to pay attention. You may not be able to control some of the events and factors that influence property values, but the more you are aware of, the more successful you will be in purchasing and investing in real estate. This is the fate of real estate. Because of its uniqueness and inability to relocate, all real estate is local. It is a mantra you will hear throughout the pages of this book.

ROAD TRIP

To illustrate the local nature of real estate, let's take a road trip and visit three metropolitan real estate markets. Two of them virtually exploded during the recent real estate boom; one was bypassed by that same boom. Their stories may raise some eyebrows, but they will also tell a tale of the importance of local influences.

First stop—Las Vegas. In the early 1700s, Spanish traders traveling to the West Coast referred to the then-unexplored Las Vegas valley as *jornada de muerta,* journey of death. For these early travelers, the only local real estate in demand was, unfortunately, six feet under ground. A lot happened to "The Meadows" (the English name for Las Vegas) during the next two centuries. The Meadows created one of the most explosive and robust real estate markets in America today.

During Las Vegas's early history, two important local political decisions provided the foundation for its eventual ascent to real estate stardom: the legalization of gambling in the state of Nevada in 1911 and the building of the Hoover Dam in 1931. The construction of the Hoover Dam brought an influx of construction workers to the city, creating a strong demand for housing. But not until the 1960s—with the help of two of America's most famous icons, Howard Hughes and Elvis Presley—did the gambling and entertainment industry take hold in Las Vegas.

The eccentric billionaire Hughes invested in hotel and casino properties during the 1960s. That jump-started a long series of investments by other corporations and investors, providing substantial funding for the gambling business. Then, in 1969, "The King" opened at the International Hotel (now the Las Vegas Hilton), confirming Las Vegas as a gambling and entertainment mecca in the United States.

Unique local events such as these may seem unrelated to real estate at the time they occur but are often the impetus for a swell in home buying. These events were a favorable portent for steady population growth in the

1970s and unprecedented growth in the 1980s. Between 1985 and 1990, the city's population almost doubled, from 186,000 to 368,000 households, setting the stage for a real estate explosion during the subsequent twenty years.

In recent years, the Las Vegas real estate market did more than expand—it boomed. And many households purchasing Las Vegas real estate were the beneficiaries of the boom's crazed pricing adventure. According to Las Vegas broker/Realtor Linda Rheinberger, her clients Joe and Nancy Farkes from Naperville, Illinois, purchased a home in Las Vegas for $292,000 in 1991. They used the Vegas property as a second home until Joe officially transferred jobs with Lucent Technologies in 1996, when he began working out of his home on his computer. When Lucent's business turned sour, Joe took an early retirement package. Nancy worked in various retail establishments before she was permanently hired by Walgreens in the bookkeeping department. The Farkeses had put down 15 percent ($43,800) on the Las Vegas property in 1991; today they own it free and clear. As of May 2006, the property was worth $700,000! Joe now works at the Station Casinos (geared toward locals) on a temporary basis; he no longer needs a long-term, permanent job. Las Vegas was good to the Farkeses.

Annual home-price appreciation peaked in 2004 at 49 percent (as measured by the median sales price of an existing home). In fact, from 2001 to 2005, Las Vegas experienced a remarkable 122 percent home-price gain! (Indeed, the big winners in Vegas during that time were homeowners, not the big-time casino players.) This attracted investors and speculators to the Vegas real estate market and pushed prices even higher. That led many Wall Street analysts and many in the media to believe that the Las Vegas real estate market was a bubble ready to burst. They predicted that the Las Vegas "house of cards" would eventually tumble.

But those analysts and reporters were looking at only half of the story. On closer inspection, it was apparent that both external (regional) and local (city) factors were influencing Vegas home values. Households in California (Nevada's neighbor) were facing skyrocketing home prices. In 2004, the $720,000 median home price in San Francisco was significantly greater than the $280,000 median home price in Las Vegas. The huge price differential convinced some households to look for a better life (at least financially) in Las Vegas. Many California households moved to places like Las Vegas and Phoenix, Arizona, where housing was more affordable. Las Vegas gained an additional 49,000 households in 2005.

The increased *demand* for housing in Las Vegas exerted upward pressure on home prices.

And the local factor? Las Vegas had become a major wholesale distribution hub, providing warehouse space for many companies and products. Moreover, with many retirees moving to Vegas, both the health care and professional business service industries (accountants, lawyers, financial services) also grew dramatically. Together, these industries helped raise the level of local economic activity and created jobs in the area. The number of jobs grew by 69 percent from 1980 to 1990 and by 87 percent from 1990 to 2000. It expanded by another 25 percent from 2000 to 2005. Amazingly, Vegas's annual job-growth rate of 5.7 percent from 1990 to 2005 was nearly four times the national average job growth of 1.5 percent. Job creation is a key ingredient in healthy home sales and price appreciation.

With favorable migration trends and job creation, Las Vegas was ripe to occupy housing's center stage. And given that Las Vegas's median home prices were substantially below those in California, the Vegas real estate market was not a bubble at all. Rather, the Vegas market—like most of the hot housing markets across the country—was better characterized as a balloon. What's the difference? A balloon can expand and contract; a bubble bursts. The Vegas balloon expanded from 2001 to 2004; then it deflated somewhat in 2005, with home-price appreciation slowing to 12 percent. But there was no bubble and no bubble popped.

With such positive local and external influences, the Las Vegas real estate market is expected to have a long-term promising future, although its near-term prospects are not as promising. As the nation's hot markets cooled in 2006, so did Las Vegas; the city experienced a drop in home sales, home inventory building, and a price correction. Like other hot boom markets (e.g., Miami) toward the end of the boom (2004–2005), Las Vegas was inundated by investors speculating on property rising to levels not supported by market fundamentals, driving prices up too quickly. Despite favorable market fundamentals for an expanding real estate market, Vegas real estate became vulnerable, subject to the speculative whims of out-of-town investors. Predictably, as interest rates rose in 2006, speculators pulled out of the Las Vegas market, sending home sales and values downward and deflating Vegas's balloon.

In the longer run, Nevada should continue to be one of the top destinations among retirees and wealthy households for several reasons. First, Nevada has no state income tax. Second, the nation's gambling capital has been mentioned as a potential home for a Major League Baseball team in the near future. And third, the National Basketball Association has selected Vegas as a site for its annual all-star game in the near future. Paying attention to the local events and local fundamentals provides an accurate road map for Las Vegas real estate. Even with air coming out of the Vegas housing market balloon, it is clear that the fundamentals are favorable for a continuing long-term real estate expansion.

Next stop—Miami. When Ponce de León first sailed into Biscayne Bay in 1513, little did he know that almost 500 years later this rural area juxtaposed between the bay and the Miami River inhabited by the Tequesta Indians would become one of the world's great international cities. Because of its proximity to Latin America, Miami serves as the headquarters of many multinational corporations and has the largest concentration of international banks in the nation.

Miami's rise to real estate riches began in 1959 with an event outside of the United States—the Cuban Revolution. The revolution unseated Fulgencio Batista and brought Fidel Castro and communism to power. Soon after, Castro eliminated individual freedom and rights, prompting many middle- and upper-class households to flee their homeland for the United States. The Miami area welcomed most of the Cuban exiles, and by the end of the 1960s, more than 400,000 Cuban refugees were living in Miami–Dade County. That set the stage for a renaissance in Miami real estate, and the city/county's real estate markets were running at a good clip in the 1960s and 1970s. In the 1980s, Miami experienced another wave of immigration—this time, poorer immigrants from Cuba as well as from other Latin American nations such as Haiti. These new residents helped fuel demand for housing in and around Miami, and the local real estate market benefited from that activity.

At the turn of the twenty-first century, all the real estate stars were aligned for a further boom in the local Miami real estate market. Foreign funds targeted for property were flowing in steadily from Latin America and Europe. Wealthy and aging boomers were seeking second and retirement homes in Miami's pleasant, sunny climate (as well as being attracted by a zero state income tax). And the city's local economy was bursting with job growth from a well-diversified business sector.

As a result, the Miami metropolitan area experienced an astonishing 160 percent growth in home prices from 2001 to 2005. In fact, Miami posted four consecutive years (2002 to 2005) of better than 20 percent home-price appreciation. And this boom was not only due to U.S. buyers or investors from Latin America. The Europeans, too, purchased Miami real estate in a large way in the 2000s. What made Miami so attractive to our friends across the North Atlantic? The currency exchange. The U.S. dollar fell by nearly 40 percent against the euro during the real estate boom. This attracted both European investors and families desiring vacation property to South Florida. Europeans purchased property at virtually a 40 percent discount. According to a National Association of Realtors International Survey (2005), international home buying accounted for 15 percent of all home sales in Florida in 2005 (and probably a lot higher in Miami).

In addition, Miami's job market remained very strong, generating 67,000 jobs in 2004 and 90,000 jobs in 2005. Miami also had and still has one of the highest net-migration trends in the nation—38,000 households moved into the Miami area in 2005. Price appreciation climbed to double digits because the inventory of existing single-family homes available for sale remained relatively lean throughout this period (the result of steady demand). The months' supply registered 1.9 months in 2001 and 6.1 months in 2004.

Examples of Miami-mania were plentiful during the boom years. A good friend of mine, a well-respected real estate executive, told me how he got caught up in the Miami real estate boom. In early 2004, he flew to Miami to visit his company's Florida real estate operations. He was standing by a window in one of his company branches admiring a tall, slender, high-rise condominium basking in the Miami sun. Someone from his Miami staff told him that two-bedroom condos on the top floors were selling for $800,000 and, based on recent price trends, they were sure to top $1 million within three months. He immediately went across the street to visit one of these units. For whatever reason, he did not have the nerve that day and declined to make an offer. Four months later, he visited his Miami office again and was told that the same two-bedroom condos were now selling for $1.2 million! Now infected with the boom hysteria, he purchased a two-bedroom condo for $1.22 million that day. Six months later, that condo was worth about $1.8 million! He sold it and booked more than a $500,000 gain after selling costs.

But things do change. Soon after that sale, the Miami market cooled and the inventory of condos increased. The inventory for condominiums available for sale soared by 2006, exerting downward pressure on condo prices.

Clearly, overenthusiastic developers built too many condos during the boom. By the end of 2006, the price for a two-bedroom condo was back down to about $1.2 million. My friend was one of the fortunate ones.

Looking to the future, the Miami real estate market is doing more than catching its breath. Inventories are building, and the months' supply (including single-family homes and condos) in August of 2006 was hovering near fourteen months—a sign of excess inventory. Air has leaked out of Miami's housing balloon. In the short term, home values are falling. A price correction is what the doctor ordered for Miami. Like Las Vegas, investors speculated on real estate, disrupting the local fundamentals of Miami's market. It may take a while longer to correct the current downturn in Miami real estate.

But if you are in it for the long run, remember: All real estate is local. Most local measures of Miami's economic and housing activity and events indicate that the area's real estate market will eventually settle down and plateau at a more reasonable (and sustainable) level of activity. The city is still a magnet for retirees and international capital. Because Miami has to work down its excess inventories, investing in properties in 2006 and the early part of 2007 may not be prudent. But I would not bet against Miami property values for the longer term. Miami has some favorable local influences that should provide eventual price support for the latter years of this decade.

Last stop—Detroit. Let's end our travels with a visit to a metro that the real estate boom passed by. America's automotive center has had its share of ups and downs over the years. The "Motor City," as Detroit is affectionately called (or Motown, for music lovers), was established by fur traders in 1701 but grew to become the center of industry in the American Rust Belt.

Located along the Detroit River and convenient to the Great Lakes waterway, Detroit emerged as a key transportation center. The city enjoyed steady growth throughout the 1800s, focusing on shipbuilding and manufacturing industries. Henry Ford introduced the first automobile in 1896, and Detroit was bound for auto stardom. By 1904, Ford built its first factory, on Piquette Avenue, and produced the Model T. From then it was off to the races—the Ford company spread its wings with more manufacturing plants along the outskirts of Detroit (Highland Park), while other automotive pioneers surfaced, including William Durant, the Dodge brothers, and Louis Chevrolet. Soon after, Detroit became the automotive

capital of the world, creating jobs and attracting new residents.
back, the first half of the twentieth century was Detroit's glory
growth and prosperity.

Several local events contributed to Detroit's demise during the second
half of the 1900s. There were bitter battles between the United Auto
Workers union and the auto manufacturers that divided the city. Stiff
competition from abroad (particularly Japan) narrowed profit margins of
the major U.S. auto manufacturers, creating employment problems. The
city was also stricken with racial tensions and high drug use, tearing at
Detroit's inner core. The city's population plummeted, while crime and
violence soared. Needless to say, property values stagnated throughout
this period.

Detroit missed the recent real estate boom (2001–2005) because it
was still hungover from its ills of the 1950s, 1960s, and 1970s. Although
the city began to experience a "renaissance" in the 1970s with the construction of the Renaissance Center, it was not until the 1990s that the
Motor City experienced a meaningful rebound in economic activity. In
1996, a Michigan referendum legalized gambling, bringing to the area the
MGM Grand Detroit, the Motor City Casino, and the Greektown Casino.
These attractions increased tourism, and with it, revenue for the city.
Other notable developments included the construction of Comerica Park
in 2000, the new home of the Detroit Tigers, and the construction of Ford
Field, bringing the NFL's Detroit Lions back into the city from Pontiac,
Michigan.

But even these positive developments were too little and too late.
Detroit still does not have a well-diversified economy and is highly dependent on the auto industry. The big three automakers—General Motors,
Ford Motor Company, and DaimlerChrysler—continue to lose market
share to their foreign counterparts. On October 8, 2005, the General
Motors spin-off parts company Delphi filed for Chapter 11 bankruptcy. In
the summer of 2006, Ford announced it was reducing the number of vehi-
cles it would produce by 25 percent.

And what happened with Detroit real estate? By the end of 2005, the
median price of an existing home in Detroit was only $156,200, one of the
lowest median home prices in the nation. Home prices grew by only 0.7
percent in 2005. Detroit experienced a relatively sharp (for Detroit) 6.2
percent rise in home values in 2001, but averaged only 1.4 percent price
gains in 2002 and 2003 before tumbling 2.1 percent in 2004. Unlike Las

Vegas and Miami at the turn of this century, Detroit suffered job and population losses, a death knell for real estate. In 2001 and 2002, Detroit lost a total of 117,600 payroll jobs. The rate of job losses fell to roughly 20,000 per year in 2003 and 2004, and to 4,600 in 2005. More than 25,000 people migrated out of the Detroit area in 2005.

While Detroit-area home prices are affordable and housing supply remains relatively lean, there are few healthy drivers of local housing demand. Without employment growth and population growth, real estate prospects continue to look dim. More recently, there have been several closures of auto plants and auto-parts suppliers in the area. Unlike most of the Midwest region of the United States, where affordability and job growth remain strong, Detroit and most of Michigan continue to struggle.

TRIP REPORT

Regardless of what transpires in the national real estate market, our three-metro tour suggests that local market activity is far more influential on local home values and sales than are national trends. Each metro faced the same national market changes during the boom period—solid U.S. economic growth, a favorable mortgage-rate environment (rates fell), rising oil prices, and a widening federal budget deficit. But locally, Detroit experienced a sluggish economy and lost population, while Las Vegas and Miami both had robust economic activity and gained population. Local events explained each market's real estate fate.

More specifically, Las Vegas and Miami experienced a real estate boom because they each had a healthy, local, diversified economy that generated jobs. They also had a lean inventory of available homes for sale, exerting upward pressure on home values. And both metropolitan areas attracted many types of households due to favorable state tax incentives and favorable living and entertainment conditions (warm weather and water for Miami; warm weather and gambling for Las Vegas). Detroit, on the other hand, had none of these favorable characteristics. In fact, Detroit's market environment was the antithesis of Las Vegas's and Miami's—its state tax was not favorable; weather conditions varied with the seasons—hot in the summer, cold in the winter; its economy was not well diversified and jobs were being lost; and households, seeking steady jobs, were moving to other states. On a positive note, Detroit has taken some first steps—it has brought in gambling à la Las Vegas, and it has brought its NFL team back into the city. In Detroit's situation, local politics are probably more important than other influences to get Motown back on its real estate feet.

But Las Vegas and Miami also experienced the hangover of the boom. As of this writing, both metropolitan areas are experiencing a local downturn in real estate. Detroit stayed stagnant throughout this period, while Vegas and Miami experienced the highs of a boom and the lows of a downturn.

The experiences of Las Vegas, Miami, and Detroit can be applied to most metros across the nation. Every region or metropolitan area has its own distinct local events, trends, and characteristics. No matter what the national averages are for home-price appreciation, home sales, and housing supply, in any given year there will always be metros that perform below the national average, at the average, and above the average. Even though real estate appreciates in value over the long term, in the shorter term, property values can go up, down, or sideways, depending on the location.

All real estate is local, and this is apparent when you look at the different real estate performances among metropolitan areas across the nation. Let's look at year-over-year sales growth by state during the first quarter of 2006 (the most recent data available as of this writing):

EXISTING-HOME SALES GROWTH
(2006 Q1 vs. 2005 Q1)

State	Sales Growth (%)
New Mexico	26
Louisiana	21
North Carolina	16
Arkansas	16
Utah	12
Indiana	10
Tennessee	10
Nevada	−16
Florida	−17
Washington, D.C.	−19
California	−20
Arizona	−22

As you can see, the states with the highest growth (10 percent and greater) in existing home sales were New Mexico, Louisiana, North Carolina, Arkansas, Utah, Indiana, and Tennessee. The states with the highest *negative* sales growth were Nevada, Florida, Washington, D.C.,

California, and Arizona. Certainly there are marked differences in sales performance as areas that had boomed from 2001 to 2005 cooled off and states that for the most part had experienced less-rapid price appreciation from 2001 to 2005 made gains.

Looking at the metropolitan areas, we see stark differences in housing performance. The days-on-market measure, presented in the table below, is probably the best indicator of a local market's real estate activity level. As days-on-market lengthens, activity stalls; as days-on-market shortens, activity picks up. The point is that each metropolitan area has its own unique set of market circumstances that explains why days-on-market is either lengthening or shortening.

For example, in March 2006, Boston was a relatively high-priced real estate market (as measured by median prices) and was experiencing some local economic problems (job gains were sluggish or down). The result was a sharp drop in home buying and thus lengthening of days-on-market. During the same first quarter of 2005 to first quarter of 2006 period, Dallas was a relatively inexpensive real estate market, and its local economy was expanding (probably due to higher oil prices). The result for Dallas was a sharp gain in home buying and thus a shortening of days-on-market. Knowing the current state of each of the 150 major metropolitan areas across the nation is necessary to determine whether that market is likely to go up or down in the future.

DAYS-ON-MARKET LENGTHENING
(March 2005 to March 2006)

Metro	March 2005	March 2006
Boston	73	126
Los Angeles	49	53
Miami	55	70
Phoenix	28	47
Reno	42	70
Washington, D.C.	38	54

DAYS-ON-MARKET SHORTENING
(March 2005 to March 2006)

Metro	March 2005	March 2006
Charlotte	109	89
Dallas	82	74
Raleigh	98	89
St. Louis	81	55
Wilmington	74	68

Again, it is the location of a property that generally determines whether properties lose or gain value. As of the second quarter of 2006, there were 124 metropolitan areas with annual price increases and 27 with price decreases. The magnitude of the price increases and decreases varied widely, depending on the location. Purchasing real estate in Miami is quite different from purchasing real estate in Spokane, Washington. Each location has its own local influences that affect home values. From Portland, Maine, to Portland, Oregon—all real estate is local. If you are still not convinced about property-price differences and price-performance differences across local real estate markets, review the following tables before proceeding to the next chapter.

METROPOLITAN STATISTICAL AREA	2006 (SECOND QUARTER) % CHANGES
Baton Rouge, LA	27.3
Ocala, FL	25.3
Virginia Beach-Norfolk-Newport News, VA-NC	23.6
Gainesville, FL	19.7
Portland-Vancouver-Beaverton, OR-WA	19.1
Jacksonville, FL	18.8
Tampa-St.Petersburg-Clearwater, FL	18.8
Spokane, WA	18.6
Beaumont-Port Arthur, TX	18.3
Eugene-Springfield, OR	18.3
Orlando, FL	17.0
Farmington, NM	16.7
Gulfport-Biloxi, MS	16.6
New Orleans-Metairie-Kenner, LA	16.6
El Paso, TX	16.3
Los Angeles-Long Beach-Santa Ana, CA	14.6
Richmond, VA	14.6
Bismark, ND	14.1
Salem, OR	13.5
Dover, DE	13.4
Jackson, MS	13.4
Montgomery, AL	13.1
Cumberland, MD-WV	12.9
Corpus Christi, TX	12.6
Salt Lake City, UT	12.5
Elmira, NY	12.4
Raleigh-Cary, NC	12.1
Glens Falls, NY	11.8
Phoenix-Mesa-Scottsdale, AZ	11.8
Spartanburg, SC	11.5
Hagerstown-Martinsburg, MD-WV	11.4
Nashville-Davidson-Murfreesboro, TN	11.4

Philadelphia-Camden-Wilmington, PA-NJ-DE-MD	11.4
Norwich-New London, CT	11.0
Honolulu, HI	10.8
Amarillo, TX	10.4
Charleston-North Charleston, SC	10.4
Trenton-Ewing, NJ	9.9
Albany-Schenectady-Troy, NY	9.6
Chattanooga, TN-GA	9.0
Shreveport-Bossier City, LA	8.8
Birmingham-Hoover, AL	8.7
Deltona-Daytona Beach-Ormond Beach, FL	8.6
Tulsa, OK	8.6
Columbia, SC	8.5
New York-Wayne-White Plains, NY-NJ	8.4
Oklahoma City, OK	8.4
Riverside-San Bernardino-Ontario, CA	8.2
Tucson, AZ	8.2
Albuquerque, NM	8.0
Boulder, CO	7.8
Little Rock-N. Little Rock, AR	7.8
St. Louis, MO-IL	7.8
Baltimore-Towson, MD	7.7
Syracuse, NY	7.5
Waterloo-Cedar Falls, IA	7.4
Charlotte-Gastonia-Concord, NC-SC	7.2
Houston-Baytown-Sugar Land, TX	7.2
Newark-Union, NJ-PA	7.1
Mobile, AL	7.0
Tallahassee, FL	7.0
Knoxville, TN	6.6
Las Vegas-Paradise, NV	6.3
Pensacola-Ferry Pass-Brent, FL	6.0
Austin-Round Rock, TX	5.9
Champaign-Urbana, IL	5.9
Greenville, SC	5.7
Palm Bay-Melbourne-Titusville, FL	5.7
Reading, PA	5.7
Springfield, MA	5.4
Colorado Springs, CO	5.3
Atlantic City, NJ	5.1
Milwaukee-Waukesha-West Allis, WI	5.0
New Haven-Milford, CT	5.0
Chicago-Naperville-Joliet, IL	4.9
Wichita, KS	4.9
New York-Northern New Jersey-Long Island, NY-NJ-PA	4.6
Atlanta-Sandy Springs-Marietta, GA	4.4
Peoria, IL	4.4
Anaheim-Santa Ana-Irvine, CA	4.3
Rochester, NY	4.2
Omaha, NE-IA	4.1

Erie, PA	3.9
Springfield, MO	3.9
Canton-Massillon, OH	3.8
Lexington-Fayette, KY	3.6
Fargo, ND-MN	3.5
San Francisco-Oakland-Fremont, CA	3.4
Durham, NC	3.3
Washington-Arlington-Alexandria, DC-VA-MD-WV	3.3
Dallas-Fort Worth-Arlington, TX	3.2
Akron, OH	3.0
Kennewick-Richland-Pasco, WA	2.9
Springfield, IL	2.8
Denver-Aurora, CO	2.7
NY: Nassau-Suffolk, NY	2.2
Kankakee-Bradley, IL	2.0
Miami-Fort Lauderdale-Miami Beach, FL	2.0
Barnstable Town, MA	1.9
Des Moines, IA	1.9
Sioux Falls, SD	1.9
Topeka, KS	1.9
Appleton, WI	1.8
Cape Coral-Fort Myers, FL	1.8
Greensboro-High Point, NC	1.8
Bridgeport-Stamford-Norwalk, CT	1.7
Hartford-West Hartford-East Hartford, CT	1.7
Pittsburgh, PA	1.5
Cedar Rapids, IA	1.4
Charleston, WV	1.2
San Diego-Carlsbad-San Marcos, CA	1.2
Kansas City, MO-KS	1.1
Dayton, OH	1.0
Louisville, KY-IN	1.0
Pittsfield, MA	0.9
Sacramento—Arden-Arcade—Roseville, CA	0.8
Boston-Cambridge-Quincy, MA-NH	0.6
Madison, WI	0.6
Cincinnati-Middletown, OH-KY-IN	0.4
San Jose-Sunnyvale-Santa Clara, CA	0.4
Allentown-Bethlehem-Easton, PA-NJ	0.3
Lincoln, NE	0.3
Sarasota-Bradenton-Venice, FL	0.2
Reno-Sparks, NV	0.1
Columbus, OH	−0.1
NY: Edison, NJ	−0.1
Providence-New Bedford-Fall River, RI-MA	−0.2
Binghamton, NY	−0.5
Buffalo-Niagara Falls, NY	−0.7
Kingston, NY	−0.8
Gary-Hammond, IN	−0.9
Lansing-E.Lansing, MI	−1.5

South Bend-Mishawaka, IN	−1.5
Decatur, IL	−1.7
Indianapolis, IN	−1.8
Portland-South Portland-Biddeford, ME	−1.8
Fort Wayne, IN	−1.9
Grand Rapids, MI	−1.9
Minneapolis-St. Paul-Bloomington, MN-WI	−2.0
Worcester, MA	−2.3
Toledo, OH	−2.6
Memphis, TN-MS-AR	−3.0
Bloomington-Normal, IL	−3.1
Yakima, WA	−3.4
Green Bay, WI	−3.6
Youngstown-Warren-Boardman, OH-PA	−5.1
Cleveland-Elyria-Mentor, OH	−5.2
Davenport-Moline-Rock Island, IA-IL	−5.5
Rockford, IL	−5.5
Detroit-Warren-Livonia, MI	−8.0
Danville, IL	−11.2

METROPOLITAN STATISTICAL AREA	2006 (SECOND QUARTER) MEDIAN PRICE ($THOUSANDS)
San Francisco-Oakland-Fremont, CA	751.9
San Jose-Sunnyvale-Santa Clara, CA	748.2
Anaheim-Santa Ana-Irvine, CA	726.2
Honolulu, HI	640.0
San Diego-Carlsbad-San Marcos, CA	613.1
Los Angeles-Long Beach-Santa Ana, CA	576.3
New York-Wayne-White Plains, NY-NJ	549.2
Bridgeport-Stamford-Norwalk, CT	495.5
NY: Nassau-Suffolk, NY	478.0
New York-Northern New Jersey-Long Island, NY-NJ-PA	473.7
NY: Newark-Union, NJ-PA	443.8
Washington-Arlington-Alexandria, DC-VA-MD-WV	443.4
Boston-Cambridge-Quincy, MA-NH	421.2
Barnstable Town, MA	406.3
Riverside-San Bernardino-Ontario, CA	395.7
NY: Edison, NJ	393.6
Sacramento-Arden-Arcade-Roseville, CA	380.6
Miami-Fort Lauderdale-Miami Beach, FL	376.2
Boulder, CO	373.2
Reno-Sparks, NV	353.4
Sarasota-Bradenton-Venice, FL	350.9
Las Vegas-Paradise, NV	319.1
New Haven-Milford, CT	292.6
Providence-New Bedford-Fall River, RI-MA	291.1
Trenton-Ewing, NJ	290.4
Worcester, MA	285.7

Baltimore-Towson, MD	285.1
Portland-Vancouver-Beaverton, OR-WA	283.4
Chicago-Naperville-Joliet, IL	278.5
Norwich-New London, CT	274.0
Phoenix-Mesa-Scottsdale, AZ	272.2
Orlando, FL	271.7
Cape Coral-Fort Myers, FL	271.6
Atlantic City, NJ	257.3
Hartford-West Hartford-East Hartford, CT	256.6
Denver-Aurora, CO	255.2
Kingston, NY	248.6
Tucson, AZ	247.3
Allentown-Bethlehem-Easton, PA-NJ	243.4
Portland-South Portland-Biddeford, ME	242.7
Virginia Beach-Norfolk-Newport News, VA-NC	237.3
Philadelphia-Camden-Wilmington, PA-NJ-DE-MD	235.1
Minneapolis-St. Paul-Bloomington, MN-WI	233.0
Tampa-St. Petersburg-Clearwater, FL	231.6
Hagerstown-Martinsburg, MD-WV	229.4
Milwaukee-Waukesha-West Allis, WI	227.7
Eugene-Springfield, OR	227.6
Richmond, VA	227.3
Madison, WI	221.4
Colorado Springs, CO	218.3
Palm Bay-Melbourne-Titusville, FL	215.7
Gainesville, FL	214.1
Charleston-North Charleston, SC	213.8
Pittsfield, MA	213.8
Deltona-Daytona Beach-Ormond Beach, FL	210.7
Springfield, MA	208.6
Raleigh-Cary, NC	207.7
Dover, DE	200.0
Jacksonville, FL	198.0
Salem, OR	195.3
Albany-Schenectady-Troy, NY	193.0
Charlotte-Gastonia-Concord, NC-SC	191.4
Salt Lake City, UT	191.2
Albuquerque, NM	185.4
Spokane, WA	179.0
New Orleans-Metairie-Kenner, LA	178.0
Durham, NC	177.9
Nashville-Davidson—Murfreesboro, TN	177.9
Farmington, NM	177.1
Austin-Round Rock, TX	176.7
Tallahassee, FL	174.7
Atlanta-Sandy Springs-Marietta, GA	173.9
Baton Rouge, LA	172.3
Birmingham-Hoover, AL	169.7
Ocala, FL	169.5
Pensacola-Ferry Pass-Brent, FL	169.0

Kansas City, MO-KS	158.8
Glens Falls, NY	158.7
Kennewick-Richland-Pasco, WA	157.1
Columbus, OH	155.7
Detroit-Warren-Livonia, MI	155.7
Dallas-Fort Worth-Arlington, TX	153.9
St. Louis, MO-IL	153.0
Knoxville, TN	152.9
Houston-Baytown-Sugar Land, TX	152.7
Green Bay, WI	152.6
Greenville, SC	151.4
Bloomington-Normal, IL	151
Montgomery, AL	150.7
Greensboro-High Point, NC	150.6
Lexington-Fayette,KY	150.0
Jackson, MS	149.3
Cincinnati-Middletown, OH-KY-IN	149.1
Des Moines, IA	147.8
Memphis, TN-MS-AR	145.6
Columbia, SC	145.1
Gulfport-Biloxi, MS	144.6
Champaign-Urbana, IL	143.5
Omaha, NE-IA	142.9
Chattanooga, TN-GA	142.3
Reading, PA	141.9
Lansing-E.Lansing, MI	141.5
Sioux Falls, SD	140.3
Cleveland-Elyria-Mentor, OH	139
Lincoln, NE	138.7
Bismark, ND	138.6
Corpus Christi, TX	138.5
Mobile, AL	138.2
Louisville, KY-IN	138.1
Fargo, ND-MN	137.2
Grand Rapids, MI	136.4
Shreveport-Bossier City, LA	136.1
Tulsa, OK	135.0
Kankakee-Bradley, IL	134.9
Cedar Rapids, IA	133.4
Spartanburg, SC	132.3
Appleton, WI	131.9
Yakima, WA	130.2
Gary-Hammond, IN	128.4
Little Rock-N. Little Rock, AR	128.2
El Paso, TX	126.7
Oklahoma City, OK	125.4
Akron, OH	123.4
Charleston, WV	123.1
Indianapolis, IN	122.4
Springfield, MO	122.1

Dayton, OH	120.6
Pittsburgh, PA	120.3
Amarillo, TX	118.6
Davenport-Moline-Rock Island, IA-IL	118.5
Syracuse, NY	116.8
Rockford, IL	115.9
Toledo, OH	115.8
Peoria, IL	115.4
Rochester, NY	115.3
Canton-Massillon, OH	114.4
Beaumont-Port Arthur, TX	114.2
Springfield, IL	112.1
Wichita, KS	111.5
Waterloo/Cedar Falls, IA	108.2
Topeka, KS	105.1
Erie, PA	102.3
Fort Wayne, IN	100.8
South Bend-Mishawaka, IN	100.6
Cumberland, MD-WV	100.0
Buffalo-Niagara Falls, NY	96.8
Binghamton, NY	92.8
Elmira, NY	87.3
Decatur, IL	85.3
Youngstown-Warren-Boardman, OH-PA	78.7
Danville, IL	65.2

Chapter Three

ANATOMY OF A REAL ESTATE MARKET

Property values, including those of your own home, usually fluctuate in an upward direction. There are times when this statement may sound a bit far-fetched for some households. But if you hold on to a piece of property long enough, you will come out okay.

Those property owners in Boston in 1990 who are still property owners there today understand this better than anyone. An old high school friend of mine, Jerry, set up a medical practice in a suburb of Boston back in 1988. He purchased a four-bedroom, three-bath home for about $300,000. By 1990, the market value of his property was near $330,000. Then the roof caved in. Boston experienced a sharp economic recession in late 1990 and 1991; that led to home prices plummeting in Boston and its suburbs. Jerry's home lost about 30 percent of its value over the next eighteen months, bringing the estimated market value of his home down to about $231,000. It took almost four years for the home's market value to rise to the $330,000 level registered in 1990. The good news is that this story has a happy ending for Jerry. By 2006, Jerry's home was worth approximately $900,000. Although home values usually fluctuate in an upward direction, you must have patience.

Most properties are considered appreciating assets; other assets, like automobiles, refrigerators, boats, and so forth, are depreciating assets. The new car you buy today loses value with each passing day (actually, the minute you drive it off the lot) and with every mile driven. But its depreciation can be reasonably predicted. The Blue Book for used automobiles lists used-car prices categorized by excellent quality, good quality, and poor quality over many years. The used-car price tables are very consistent from year to year because, in the end, automobiles wear down and are less useful over time.

Property values, on the other hand, usually fluctuate up or down in the short term, depending on local market conditions, and appreciate over the longer term. So if you are not planning on staying in your property for the long term, you could be exposed to some downside risk. In the short term, local property values fluctuate up and down, and some of those changing conditions can be structural—in other words, may be more permanent. For instance, a Fortune 500 company decides to open a large regional office complex in your town, bringing 10,000 jobs to the local area. That has a very positive influence on local property values that extends far beyond the next twelve months. Whether changes are structural or short-term, fluctuating real estate values reflect an ever-changing economy and local housing marketplace.

MARKET REALITIES

Understanding local market behavior is essential not only for being able to grasp how property values are determined, but to help you become a smart buyer of real estate. Depending on the market's current condition (i.e., the balance between demand and supply), property values are either headed upward, going downward, or staying flat. From a buyer's perspective, you are negotiating for a property from either a position of strength, weakness, or somewhere in between. Moreover, local property markets are always changing. What may be balanced today might be a seller's market tomorrow, and a buyer's market a year from now.

When the demand for homes in a particular area increases, there is upward pressure on market prices. In other words, when demand is more robust than supply, prices increase. But often the supply of available housing does not immediately change in response to increased demand. This is due either to time lags between a change in price and an increase in the supply of new properties becoming available (builders cannot react instantaneously), or to homeowners delaying putting their properties on the market. When demand increases and supply has not had time to respond, the resulting excess demand exerts upward pressure on home values. As inventories increase over time—from the construction of new homes and homeowners putting their homes on the market—one can expect to see downward pressure on prices.

A BALANCED MARKET

In the ideal local real estate market, there should be a balance between the demand for homes and the supply of homes available for sale. Although there is no exact benchmark to measure balance, there are ways of knowing if a local real estate market is close to being a balanced one.

A local market has an adequate supply of homes for sale if houses on the market sell within five to seven months (some locations may be on the low end of this range and others on the high end). This means that at the current sales pace, the entire inventory of homes would be sold within five to seven months.

Of course, demand for home buying depends on a variety of factors, including local job growth, income growth, mortgage rates, and net migration. In a balanced market, neither the buyer nor the seller has the upper hand in negotiations. Examples of balanced local markets in recent years include Charlotte, North Carolina, and Houston, Texas. Neither area participated in the real estate boom, but neither stagnated either. During 2001 to 2005, the supply of homes in Charlotte averaged a respectable 5.7 months, while the area's annual price appreciation averaged 4 percent. The months' supply in Houston averaged 6.1 months during the same period, while annual price appreciation averaged 3.5 percent. I'm sure homeowners in Charlotte and Houston were envious of property owners in Miami, Las Vegas, and other boom regions and cities that posted annual double-digit price appreciation as a result of a tight supply. But those boom market rates were not sustainable. They were seller's markets—where demand exceeded supply. Eventually, those boom markets had to cool, and they began to do so in late 2005. Charlotte and Houston, however, maintained their steady but modest climb in home values even after the boom began to wane. The fact is, a well-balanced local market is a more sustainable market.

To be sure, it is difficult to determine the exact amount of housing demand and housing supply that creates a balanced local marketplace. That is because each local market is unique. One practical way to identify a balanced market is to look for home values that produce a 3 to 5 percent price appreciation. The goal of any housing market should be to generate healthy and sustainable price appreciation. A 3 to 5 percent appreciation rate satisfies this criterion. If a local market generates a sustainable 3 to 5 percent home-price appreciation rate, and if there is a balance between demand and supply, then the current months' supply is almost certainly appropriate.

A SELLER'S MARKET

When the market demand for homes in a particular area is high and there is a shortage of homes available for sale, the balance of power in the market shifts toward the seller. With excess demand in the market for homes, sellers can wait for offers on their property to reach (or exceed) their minimum selling price.

We were in a seller's market in early 2005 at the height of the real estate boom in most of our nation's housing markets. Housing was "hot," particularly in ocean resort towns. This prolonged excess demand for properties exerted substantial upward pressure on prices. I can recall more than a few instances where buyers of beachfront properties earned hundreds of thousands of dollars within just a year or two of their initial purchase.

In Topsail Beach, a small beach town in North Carolina, during the height of the real estate boom (2003–2005), investors could purchase a beachfront property for $700,000 and a year later sell it for close to $1 million. This story is not unique to Topsail. The same thing occurred in coastal markets from Miami to Boston and California for both resort and primary residences in the very hottest local markets. Each local market presented a similar picture: a frenzied market in which multiple bids on a home resulted in a sale price significantly higher than the listing price. Some owners who had not even listed their home for sale received bids in their mailboxes. Such a frenzied market is caused by excess demand in the midst of a tight supply. But these kinds of markets are unsustainable.

A BUYER'S MARKET

When demand for new and existing homes is weak and there is a glut of properties available on the market, the upper hand in negotiations switches to buyers. Buyers now have a much wider choice of properties from which to choose and are often able to negotiate a price that is lower than the listed price.

From 1983 to 1992, the average supply of homes available for sale registered a lengthy 9.2 months. There was an excess supply of homes in the nation at large, and housing demand fell due to a slowdown in the U.S. economy and double-digit mortgage rates. One local market that was particularly hard hit during this period was Boston. The months' supply of homes in Boston rose to an unthinkable sixteen months. At the same time, the local Boston economy experienced a sharp recession and lost 15 percent of its jobs. That created a serious imbalance between weak housing demand and excess supply. Predictably, home values plummeted, creating a buyer's market in Boston during the early 1990s. Sellers did all they could do to sell their homes—even offering to pay some of the upfront costs of the buyers, reducing the listing price, and offering other incentives to attract buyers.

TRANSITIONING MARKETS

Many times, local markets are in transition—switching over from a seller's market to a buyer's market, or vice versa. In transitioning markets, the balance of (negotiating) power is in flux. This transition is what occurred in many of our nation's previously hot local markets when the real estate boom slowed in late 2005 and then cooled in 2006. *Both buyers and sellers need to beware when negotiating in a transitioning market.*

Usually, in the early stages of a market transitioning from a seller's to a buyer's market, sellers remain stubborn and continue to list their properties at high prices. At the same time, buyers have lost their appetite to bid at such lofty prices. If you are a seller, you need to carefully read the market. Listen to your Realtor—that is what he or she is there for. To sell more quickly, list your home at a more reasonable price that reflects current market conditions. If you list your house at a price that reflects last year's market, your property will remain on the market longer, costing you lost opportunity money. Most real estate agents will tell you that in a softening market, you need to present a reasonable listing price in order to sell the property. Usually, most serious interest from buyers is generated in the first few weeks a property is listed. If the listing price is too high, the property will sit, lose its luster, and force you to lower the price even more to attract potential buyers.

If you are a seller, the lesson you should learn from a market that is transitioning from seller to buyer is to forget about the "good ole days" of high-price growth. You are no longer going to get top dollar. *Price your property correctly.* In fact, during market transitions, your real estate professional will likely recommend staging—where you "window-dress" your home to attract prospective buyers to want to live there. You will find many ways to spruce up your home on the HGTV cable channel: eliminating clutter, removing some furniture to create a spacious appearance, repainting rooms in neutral tones, eliminating personal items like family photos, and so on. Curb appeal—such as landscaping—is equally important.

If you are a buyer, you need to be more sensitive to your strengthening negotiating position. If days-on-market time lengthens for the seller (your Realtor can tell you this), you are in a better position to make demands. For example, you can bid a lower price, ask the seller to pay points, and negotiate the timing of the transaction, to name a few options. If you are bidding on a new home, the builder may be willing to make concessions. While the builder may not reduce price because he does not want to anger recent buyers, he may be willing to add upgrades to the deal. The list of possible upgrades can include landscaping, free washers and dryers, crown molding, upgraded window treatments, paying down the mortgage rate, or paying the first six months of mortgage payments.

When the market is transitioning in the opposite direction—from a buyer's to a seller's market—the roles are reversed. If you are the seller, you will be calling the shots. There will be less need for staging and you will probably not have to offer buyers incentives. If you are a buyer in a seller's market, flexibility is a key in negotiations. You may need to bid higher than the listing price, depending on the number of bids and interest. You may also need to bid quickly—you may not have the luxury to think about the offer. You may also have to be more flexible in the timing of the transaction.

WHAT DRIVES DEMAND AND SUPPLY

So what actually drives the demand for and supply of property? Purchasing real estate is sometimes like purchasing shares of IBM. Should you buy at $100 per share or wait, hoping it will fall to $90 per share? Before making such an investment decision, most of us try to get a "feel" for the value of IBM shares. We read research reports on the company, we examine the company's earnings, we look at IBM's management team, its competition, its products, and so forth.

Similarly, in preparing to make an offer on a home, we should ask ourselves this question: Should we bid the listing price, underbid, or overbid? Part of the answer will be determined by what type of market we are in—seller's, buyer's, or balanced market. But the other part of the answer will be determined by our "feel" for the value of the home that we want to purchase. That is based primarily on looking at comparables (also called "comps"—similar homes recently sold).

But the real key to successful real estate purchasing is to anticipate where prices are headed and then purchase in those neighborhoods or towns that have favorable prospects for property values. We need to understand what factors influence the demand and supply for real estate *in a local marketplace* to better project future values. Let's take a ten-minute tour of those influences.

DEMAND FOR PROPERTY

People purchase homes for a variety of reasons. Some households want larger homes, so they trade up from a smaller one. Perhaps a person has received a big promotion or has inherited a sizable sum, and now desires a larger home with additional amenities. Or a young couple living in a small one-bedroom apartment in the city learns that they are expecting twins and now seek to purchase a three-bedroom home in the suburbs. Other households may want to downsize: for example, empty-nesters whose children have grown and started their own families and who want to purchase smaller homes or condominiums. Some households have relocated to another city due to new job opportunities or for family reasons. Whether you are a first-time buyer, a trade-up or trade-down buyer, a second-home buyer, or a real estate investor, there are a variety of reasons why and where you purchase property. Put all these households and factors in a mixing bowl, stir them up, and you have *the local demand* for property. Demand for real estate influences the willingness and ability of households to make home purchases. All factors influencing demand can be grouped into four categories: population factors, home-buyer where-withal factors, investment factors, and purchase-cost factors.

POPULATION FACTORS

Population growth is *the* primary fuel behind home buying. The more people (households) living in a neighborhood or city, the greater the demand for homes. The operative adage is that high population-growth rates are good for housing, while low population-growth rates are not. Households in West Palm Beach, Florida, know the happy side of this adage. Retired households are moving to West Palm Beach from all over the country seeking a warmer climate. At the other end of the spectrum, households in Detroit, Michigan, know the downside: People are leaving Detroit in search of more stable employment opportunities, and "out-migration" from Detroit is inhibiting home-price growth.

California has had it both ways. Beautiful beaches, fertile land, wineries, agriculture, and Hollywood stars brought explosive population growth throughout the twentieth century. But at the beginning of the twenty-first century, the cost of living in California skyrocketed. Many of the state's cities were no longer affordable to the average household earner. Affordability problems have driven some households to seek less costly living arrangements in other states.

The population of a local market influences property values through:

- Internal population growth
- Household formation
- Net migration
- Demographic trends

Internal population growth is the difference between birth rates and mortality rates in a local market. Young metropolitan areas (those with a low average age for its total population) are likely to have high *internal* population-growth rates compared with older metropolitan areas (those with a high average age). This is because a young community with, let's say, a median age of thirty-two years is more likely to have children and so increase the internal population of that community than an older community where the median age is fifty-five. Thus, without any other influences on the population, a younger metropolitan area should experience a more robust demand for housing (trade-up buying) vis-à-vis an older one.

Household formation also influences property values. Households range from a single person living by him- or herself, to a married couple, to a mother and/or father living with children. A married couple is considered one household because they live in a home together. Change in the trend of household formation impacts the demand for housing. When a couple divorces, for instance, they are now considered two households, because they will be living separately. Thus, divorce rates influence household formation and housing *demand* increases: The higher the divorce rate, the greater the number of households looking to purchase a home.

Net migration. Even if the total population stagnates, the magnitude and pace of migration will keep certain housing markets active. *Migration* is the term for people moving from one location to another. In-migration represents the number of people moving *into* an area; out-migration is the number of people moving out of an area. The difference is the net migration. If more people move into than out of a metro area, you have a positive net migration.

Our visit to Las Vegas in the previous chapter revealed the importance of migration patterns. We learned that a primary reason Las Vegas experienced substantial price appreciation over the last several years was its high migration rate.

There are other metro areas across the United States that possess "gravity" in attracting households. Pleasant-climate locations like Florida, Nevada, and Arizona are attracting aging baby boomers from the North seeking warmer weather. There are some projections that forecast a doubling of Nevada's population within the next twenty years due to high net-migration rates. Florida is expected to add population equaling the total populations of Pennsylvania and Maryland within the next forty years due to current migration trends.

Demographics are perhaps the best-known influence on the demand for home buying. The largest demographic player right now is the baby boomer population group. We saw their impact on the housing market in the 1990s, when boomers entered their peak earning years and home sales exploded. There are about 78 million boomers, and they are fueling the purchase of larger homes (trade-up buying), second homes (vacation and/or investment), and condominiums (downsizing). Because analyzing demographic trends is crucial in understanding future home values by location, following the footprints of the boomers will help identify the robust housing markets during the next decade. I'll go into more detail about this in Chapter Seven.

Tracking trends in the five major population groups is also critical for identifying healthy and profitable local markets. Focusing on the life-cycle trends of these groups—retirees, boomers, the baby bust, immigrants, and echo boomers—will allow us to better anticipate future real estate values.

HOME-BUYER WHEREWITHAL FACTORS

I was in Macy's department store several years ago with my daughter, who was ten at the time. As we made our last purchase and prepared to leave, the clerk handed my daughter a lollipop. "What do you say?" I prompted my daughter. She replied: "Charge it."

I tell this story to better explain what I mean by financial wherewithal. Financial wherewithal is your capacity to service your living expenses, including your mortgage payments, based on your actual income/wealth. Financial wherewithal means not resorting to credit cards and zero-down-payment loans. You need to have the necessary income and savings to purchase property you wish to buy. If you have never owned a home before but you have saved a sufficient amount of money to purchase a home, you will likely do so. If you are a current homeowner and want to purchase a larger home and you have the funds to do so (from either personal savings and/or home-equity gains), you will likely purchase a trade-up home. The greater a household's financial wherewithal, the greater the demand for home buying.

There are many ways to raise your financial wherewithal through income growth, favorable employment opportunities, consumer confidence, and stored wealth.

As a household's income rises, so does its demand for housing. Similarly, increased income raises the demand for more expensive properties as people enter the trade-up market. The typical homeowner spends about 20 to 30 percent of disposable income on housing (mortgage payments and housing-related goods and services—e.g., furniture, landscaping). The greater your income, the more likely you can purchase the property you desire.

It follows that local markets with relatively high average or median household income levels may experience healthier real estate markets than do those local markets with low household income (for instance, there may be a higher percentage of renters in a low-income market). It is also true that markets with higher median home prices relative to median incomes may have lower homeownership rates than do more affordable markets.

For example, California has the highest median home price in the nation—$524,000—making it the least affordable state, as measured by the National Association of Realtors Housing Affordability Index. Not coincidentally, California also has the lowest homeownership rate in the nation, at 59.7 percent (2005).

Local markets with high unemployment rates will inhibit property purchasing, while markets with low unemployment rates and job creation are likely to promote home sales, exerting upward pressure on property values. Detroit's unemployment rate is 7.1 percent, while Las Vegas's unemployment rate is 2.1 percent. It is not surprising that Detroit's homeownership rate is 59.7 percent, substantially lower than Vegas's 73 percent rate.

Confidence is more vital in the purchase of property than almost any other good or service sold. This is because purchasing a home is probably the biggest financial transaction most of us will ever make. If people see their local (or national) economy deteriorating, they may become less optimistic about their own financial circumstances. A drop in their confidence may end their search for a new home or delay entry into the existing home marketplace. Similarly, when their local economy (or the national economy) is experiencing sustained growth and improving prosperity, confidence builds, increasing a household's likelihood of purchasing a home.

In some cities, you can just feel the confidence in the air. Look what happened in Las Vegas and Phoenix during the height of the real estate boom. Those cities attracted thousands of households from other cities and states. You can also observe confidence steadily building in cities like Houston and San Antonio. Both those Texas cities experienced a more modest job creation and net migration, applying steady but modest upward pressure on property values. Conversely, one can observe confidence falling in a local market. A good example is San Diego toward the end of the real estate boom in early 2006, which suffered a severe housing-affordability problem.

In addition to income, people store or accumulate wealth through savings, inheritance, existing home equity, investments, or gifts. Obviously, the greater your wealth, the greater your demand for home buying.

The amount of your perceived wealth, too, can influence the demand for housing. If the value of the home in which you currently reside is

$400,000 and it jumps 50 percent in value, giving you a $200,000 unrealized price gain, you may feel a bit wealthier and may be more inclined to purchase a larger home or a second home in the near future. Or you might purchase an automobile or use the funds to pay for your children's education. During the recent real estate boom, many homeowners spent unrealized home-equity gains—by cash-out refinancings and home equity lines. A cash-out refinancing refers to a homeowner who refinances his or her existing mortgage and takes out cash from the transaction. Establishing a home equity line is essentially opening a line of credit on the equity in your home. It is like having a checkbook on your home's equity. With a line of credit, homeowners have cash available when they need it.

INVESTMENT FACTORS

Momentum at the turn of the century's real estate boom brought renters into the homeownership circle, encouraged existing homeowners to trade up, and spurred investors to speculate on property values. The common thread contributing to some of these "boom-led" purchases was the expectation of higher future home prices. Quite simply, the boom highlighted the investment potential in property purchases. Amazingly, 28 percent of all home purchases in 2005 were investment homes (rental properties), while 12 percent of all home purchases in 2005 were vacation homes, resulting in second-home purchases that totaled 40 percent of all home purchases in 2005. Whether you were a renter, homeowner, or investor, the boom convinced many households that a real estate property meant not only a place to live but an investment as well. Such thinking affects housing demand in two ways—by raising price expectations and through speculative investing.

Property owners expect the value of their property to rise over time; this is what is referred to as **price expectations**. The fact is, *real estate is America's number-one vehicle for building wealth*. Total homeowner equity in the United States at the end of 2005 was almost $14 trillion. The majority of wealth for almost 80 percent of all households is derived from the real estate market, not from stocks or bonds. For many, real estate equity is the only way to build a nest egg for retirement.

Of course, if price expectations are unreasonable, the price we pay for property may also be unreasonable. For instance, during the height of the real estate boom, in many of our nation's hot housing markets home buyers and property investors were willing to pay unreasonably high prices for rental property. Investors hoped that eventually future price gains would outweigh the negative annual cash flow generated by the mismatch of low rental income and high expenses (including the mortgage).

What is an unreasonable price? A price is unreasonable when demand is so great for a property that the buyer abandons the fundamentals of the transaction to make the purchase. One way to determine when prices are unreasonable is to look at the ratio of home-price growth to income growth. When home prices grow too quickly relative to household incomes, homes become unaffordable. During the real estate boom, households had to stretch their incomes by using interest-only mortgage loans to keep monthly costs down in order to purchase properties at lofty prices. A better, more reliable measure of unreasonable pricing is the *mortgage debt service/income ratio*. If prices are out of line with reality, households and investors have to stretch their financial capacity to purchase the property. Their hope is that as demand for housing increases—from renters, homeowners, and investors—the equity on their homes will also increase.

The **speculative element** in real estate purchasing arises when households (mostly investors) believe that future capital gains will be high *and will be able to be realized* in a short period of time. A rise in the expectations of future short-term capital gains attracts speculators to the real estate market. This, in turn, raises the demand for home buying. The 2001–2005 real estate boom attracted thousands of speculators to the real estate markets, pushing home values even higher. Such speculative activities included property flipping, preconstruction purchases, and condo-conversion purchases. Miami, Orlando, Las Vegas, and Phoenix experienced such speculative buying.

PURCHASING COSTS

In general, if the cost of purchasing a property rises, demand will fall— and vice versa. There are four major factors that influence the cost of property ownership: mortgage rates, settlement costs, mortgage-product offerings, and tax and government subsidies.

Property is still the most interest-rate-sensitive purchase in our economy. This is because the majority of property purchases are financed with a mortgage, and so those **mortgage rates** matter. A rise in borrowing costs can make the transaction cost-prohibitive. I estimate that a 1 percent rise in mortgage rates, on average, prices about 250,000 households out of the market. Conversely, a 1 percent drop in mortgage rates can encourage an additional 250,000 households to purchase homes. Although the level of mortgage rates may differ slightly across regions of the country, by and large mortgage rates are homogeneous across the nation. If they rise by 1 percent in New York, they rise by 1 percent in California. Changes in mortgage rates directly influence the demand for housing.

That said, a 1 percent rise in mortgage rates in San Diego will impact local housing demand in San Diego quite differently than it impacts demand in Buffalo, New York. The demand for home buying in San Diego is more sensitive to interest-rate changes than the demand for home buying in Buffalo. Why? The median-priced home in San Diego is a bit over $600,000, while the median-priced home in Buffalo is a bit under $100,000. Households in San Diego are already stretching their incomes by taking out adjustable-rate mortgages (or interest-only loans) to be able to afford and qualify for homes that are vastly more expensive than similar homes in Buffalo. As a result, a 1 percent rise in mortgage rates results in a much higher per-month payment in San Diego than in Buffalo (1 percent of $600,000 is six times more than 1 percent of $100,000).

Settlement costs include title insurance, appraisal, mortgage insurance, credit-report fees, escrow fees, homeowner's insurance, and loan-origination fees. These are payable at a property closing. They assure the lender that the property transfer is in order and that the lender (the bank) can use the property as collateral if you default on the mortgage loan. Most of the time, your real estate agent or lender will recommend settlement service providers, but you can find service providers on your own as well. Either way, settlement costs can be quite substantial (1 to 4 percent of the loan balance). A rise in settlement costs, too, can inhibit home buying, especially among first-time buyers; conversely, a drop in settlement costs can motivate home buying. Settlement costs can vary across states because of different state and local requirements and pricing for settlement service providers.

A VARIED MENU OF MORTGAGE PRODUCTS

Let me mention just a few of the mortgage loans currently available on the market: thirty-year and fifteen-year fixed-rate mortgage loans; interest-only loans; cash-flow option ARMs; FHA loans; VA loans; Fannie Mae loans (Flex 97, Flex 100 ARMs, seven-year balloons, biweekly fixed-rate mortgages, Fannie 3/2, energy-efficient mortgages, MyCommunityMortgage, community renovation mortgages, smart commute initiative mortgages); Freddie Mac loan products (A-minus ARMs, cost of funds rate-capped ARM, Alt 97 fixed mortgages, Freddie 100 mortgages, streamlined purchase mortgages, five- and seven-year balloons, affordable gold mortgages, affordable 3/2 mortgages); jumbo mortgage loans; Rural Housing and Community Development Service (RHCDS) mortgage loans; low-/no-down-payment loans; buy-down mortgages; reverse mortgages . . .

Had enough? My point is that there is a long and varied menu of mortgage products offered to potential property buyers. One of the least discussed but most influential factors that affect demand for home purchases are the many ways that consumers are able to finance real estate purchases. The greater the number of available mortgage loan products, the easier it will be for households to find a mortgage loan that works for them. As lenders create and offer more and more mortgage loan products, the demand for home purchases tends to increase.

One example of this that arose during the real estate boom was the interest-only mortgage loan. These loans have lower monthly payments compared to amortizing loans, so they help households stretch their incomes to be able to afford the monthly payments on homes that they would otherwise not be able to afford. The market share of adjustable-rate mortgage loans in California in 2005 was an astonishing 70 percent, even as thirty-year, fixed-rate mortgages were near historically low levels (around 5.7 percent). More surprising was that most of the adjustable-rate mortgage loans were interest-only loans.

TAX AND GOVERNMENT BENEFITS

No other sector of the economy receives more of the attention and generosity of federal, state, and local governments than real estate. On a national level, the Department of Housing and Urban Development (HUD), the Federal Housing Administration (FHA), the Veterans Administration (VA), Fannie Mae, Freddie Mac, and the Federal Home Loan Bank System are dedicated to promoting housing and assisting low- and moderate-income and minority households. This is true on the state and local levels as well. The more government assists the housing sector, the greater the demand for home buying.

For most households, the largest deduction on their tax returns is the mortgage-interest deduction. Other important **tax benefits** include the deduction of property taxes, home-purchase deductions, and capital gains exemption from a home sale. The interest you pay on a mortgage loan of up to $1 million for your primary residence is tax-deductible on your tax return. You may also deduct the interest paid up to $100,000 on a second-home and/or home-equity loan (although the total loan amount on a primary and second home cannot exceed $1 million). Property taxes are completely deductible on all real estate owned. A home buyer may also deduct closing costs with a real estate purchase on his or her personal income tax in the year of the purchase. These items include origination fees and loan discounts, transfer taxes, recording fees, and title insurance that serve to increase the basis (the original cost of the property). Finally, there is a very generous tax exemption on the capital gains from the sale of a home. The current exclusion is $250,000 for individuals and $500,000 for married couples filing jointly. The only requirement for this capital gains exclusion is that the seller live in the home for at least two of the previous five years. The capital gains exemption plus all the other deductions provide a distinct advantage for the purchasing and selling of real estate over other assets. If and when the real estate tax rules change, so does the demand for property purchases.

Let's look at the following example to see how the capital gains exemption impacts the demand for housing. You make a $500,000 capital gain by selling your home for $700,000 after buying it for $200,000 fifteen years ago. You and your wife are now empty-nesters—your children have grown up and left home, and you no longer need the same space to live. So you want to trade down to a smaller home. You purchase a smaller home for $450,000. That leaves you with $250,000 minus your broker's commission, which for the sake of simplicity I will set at $40,000. What should you do with the remaining $210,000? One option is to invest these funds back into real estate for investment purposes—that is, property you can rent out. This is another way in which demand for real estate can be affected.

SUPPLY OF PROPERTY

When it comes to selling property, one is company and two's a crowd. Additional properties for sale in your neighborhood create a potential competitive barrier.

Housing supply depends on a number of factors, including construction costs, local growth restrictions, and homeowners' and builders' responses to demand conditions. If five of your neighbors decide to sell their homes just as you are ready to put your home on the market, now may not be the best time to add to the housing supply.

The various materials that go into the building of a residential property influence its cost and thus the number of homes that are built, as well as the price for each home.

Take, for example, lumber. The United States imports a great deal of lumber from Canada. The tariffs and quotas between the two nations may influence the price of lumber imports and the amount of lumber imported. A more restricted supply of lumber will affect both the price and the supply of homes. In recent years, the prices of steel, copper, and other materials have risen significantly, contributing to the relatively tight supply of new homes as well as home-price appreciation.

Labor costs and other nonmaterial builder costs also influence the supply of homes. If the local housing market is hot, a general contractor will have a difficult time holding down costs from subcontractors (such as electrical work, framing, and so on). In some local areas, subcontractors are busy, limiting the total number of homes that can be constructed in that area and increasing costs.

The cost of construction—or even the ability to build—is very much dependent on the local political climate and relationships that builders develop with local policy makers. Local growth restrictions rein in the number of homes available for sale by limiting their construction. For those homes that are being built, getting site permits, building permits, and so forth adds to the cost of construction. Smart-growth policies, as they are called, have become more common throughout the nation. The notion behind "smart growth" is that as our population grows, we must use land more efficiently and plan for growth. Comprehensive planning, innovative land-use techniques, well-planned infrastructure, and urban revitalization are universally recognized smart-growth strategies. On the other hand, urban growth boundaries and development regulations disrupt markets and drive up the price of housing.

Like any business, builders will increase or decrease the inventories of their products with changing market conditions. A high growth rate in housing starts (construction projects) reflects builders' response to healthy housing conditions; a slowing in the growth of housing starts reflects builders' lack of confidence in the housing markets. By tracking starts and housing permits (such information about the local markets you are interested in can be provided by your real estate agent), you can get a sense of how builders are responding to market conditions. If builders are producing too many homes, an excess inventory of properties can result and home values could soften. Conversely, if builders are not building enough homes, you may find a lean supply of homes and home values could rise.

More than 85 percent of all homes available for sale are being sold by current homeowners listing their homes with a real estate agent or selling their homes themselves. The remaining 15 percent of homes are newly constructed properties. *It is property owners, not builders, who control the majority of homes for sale in any local market.* Understanding why and when current homeowners put their properties on the market is important in determining property value.

A local area dominated by young households would have a higher frequency of home listings than a local area dominated by established households. That's because young households, on average, are more likely to eventually trade up to larger homes because they have children or relocate because of job advancement. There are many other reasons why homeowners list their home: expected price gains, an improvement in the local economy (creating a more favorable selling environment), the construction of a new highway through a particular location (motivating homeowners to move away from a transportation-dominated area), and so on.

PUTTING MEAT ON THE BONE

My intent in this chapter has been to help you gain a sense of demand and supply conditions in a local market. So far I have dealt with general concepts and explanations. Now let me put aside the academics and give you some trends and tools that will help you evaluate the magnitude of demand and supply in your local market. This is the first rung of the ladder you need to climb to achieve success in real estate. I suggest that you monitor three indicators on the demand side (population, jobs, and investor share) and two indicators on the supply side (housing starts and months' supply).

Population. I strongly suggest that you compare population-growth rates across local real estate markets. Net migration (how many additional households are moving into the local market) is a good proxy for this. This information is easily obtainable from your real estate agent. You can also go to the local economic development office of the city or county you are targeting and request the information. The higher the net migration number, the healthier are the prospects for local real estate activity.

Jobs. Positive job growth is essential for the long-term viability of a healthy real estate market. Again, this information is available from your real estate agent or the local economic development office. Every county and city in the United States makes job gains/losses information available to the public. Robust job markets are an excellent indicator of an active real estate market.

Investor share. Before committing to a property purchase, estimate how many investors are involved in the local market. Investors add some degree of risk to a local real estate market because they are the first to pull out of the market if the good times turn to bad. "Investor flight" exerts downward pressure on prices. I admit that obtaining investor-share information is difficult. If the information is not available from your real estate professional, ask him or her for their "gut feeling" about the investment share in the local market. Investor-share information is available on a national basis from the National Association of Realtors. Sometimes they may be able to provide some local share information. It does not hurt to ask.

Months' supply. It is essential that you know the inventory of properties available for sale in a particular market before committing to a purchase. Months' supply is the most reliable indicator of inventory and is easily accessible from a real estate professional.

Housing starts (new residential construction). Even if the demand for home buying is healthy, it is possible that local home builders overbuilt in the local market, creating excess housing inventories that eventually could exert downward pressure on property values. Housing starts and housing permits are good indicators of how many properties builders are planning on constructing. This information is easily obtainable from the Department of Commerce and is reported on a monthly basis in every major newspaper in the country.

Keep in mind that my overall goal in this book is to help *you* evaluate and compare local real estate markets so that you can become a smarter property buyer. You have already taken the first step—understanding demand and supply conditions in your local marketplace. But there are many other influences in local markets that we will examine next and that will help you become a smarter real estate investor.

Chapter Four

REAL ESTATE MARKETS AND DNA

Why do some local markets perform better than others? Most real estate professionals will tell you that the three most important factors influencing property values are location, location, and location. It seems logical that properties close to water or convenient to public transportation and/or good school systems tend to be more expensive than properties in areas without those amenities. But location does not tell the whole story. Home prices in the cities and areas we visited in Chapter Two were heavily influenced by the local economy, climate, and other characteristics. Just as your success in adult life draws from a mix of your abilities, characteristics, and personal experiences (e.g., education, parents, upbringing, friends), so too does a local housing market's success. Each local market has a set of attributes or characteristics that, to some degree, predetermines future performance. I call this a local market's DNA. And, as is the case with living organisms, some cities are blessed with better DNA than others.

Before modern advances in transportation and technology, cities that were built beside lakes, rivers, and oceans—and consequently had ports to ship from and receive valuable products—had a comparative advantage over inland cities in terms of attracting people. In other words, cities located on or close to water had better DNA than those not on the water. Two hundred years ago, Boston became a populous major city while Atlanta was a sleepy town because Boston was on the water and Atlanta was not.

But trains, trucks, and airplanes replaced boats as the major means of transportation and commerce. Atlanta, a city that was burned to the ground during the Civil War, was on its way to becoming a major city when the Atlantic Railroad laid tracks in the city in 1869, making it a major distribution hub for the South. Then trucks complemented trains and Atlanta took advantage by building a major interstate highway system, making Atlanta even more accessible to more people and businesses. Finally, Atlanta was the first major southern city to build an international airport when other southern cities chose not to, and thus became a major hub for air transportation. This helped draw even more people, jobs, and services to the city and its environs. The city changed its DNA. Boston, while still benefiting from its location by the waters of Massachusetts Bay and the North Atlantic, takes great advantage of the interstate rail, air, and highway systems as well. The DNA of both cities has changed.

Atlanta and Boston are good illustrations of the importance of a local market's DNA. Every local real estate market has a DNA that makes that market unique and that distinguishes it from other local markets. People are attracted to many different types of living environments. Some choose to live in a cold-weather climate, while others prefer warm weather. Similarly, some people choose to live by the water, while others prefer the woods or mountains. The point is that the more robust a city's DNA, the greater advantage it has in attracting households.

It is a local area's DNA, combined with current and future influences on local housing demand and supply, that determines a local market's real estate fate. In examining a particular real estate market, ask yourself what attributes that local market or area has. A temperate climate? A lower cost of living? Great public transportation? A robust local economy creating new jobs? Special sports or entertainment attractions?

THE ROLE OF DNA

The term *deoxyribonucleic acid* is a mouthful. That's why most of us just abbreviate it as DNA. DNA is the molecule that contains the genetic information in the nucleus of every living cell. It determines the structure, function, and behavior of each cell. Every living organism has its own DNA. It is our DNA that makes each of us unique in physical makeup and, to some extent, behavior.

Similarly, every local real estate market's DNA makes that market unique. San Francisco has great real estate DNA. It sits comfortably perched on a peninsula between the Pacific Ocean and San Francisco Bay. The weather is temperate year-round thanks to a warm, northerly ocean current. Of course, most cities are not situated on the Pacific Ocean with favorable weather. But each city has its own DNA, with its own unique features and characteristics.

Bad DNA can work against you. San Francisco has one real estate gene that could permanently damage its livability. The city sits on the San Andreas Fault, between the Pacific and North American tectonic plates, making the city susceptible to earthquakes. As the plates move, stress builds up along faults. When this stress is released, the blocks or plates move and an earthquake occurs. The city was all but destroyed by earthquake and fire on April 18, 1906. And it could happen again, something the citizens of San Francisco are keenly aware of.

Human beings are stuck with their DNA for life. But as we saw with Atlanta and Boston, real estate DNA can change over time. San Francisco, for example, boasts more than just the ocean, bay, hills, and good weather. It has grown over the last century and a half into one of the nation's most diversified cities, filled with restaurants, entertainment, tourist attractions, and a vibrant economy. From the Golden Gate Bridge to Fisherman's Wharf, from Chinatown to Lombard Street, from the San Francisco Giants to the San Francisco 49ers, from Union Square to the college town of Berkeley in the East Bay and on to Presidio Park, the city named for the Spanish mission of San Francisco de Assisi has extraordinary DNA in the eyes of most people. As a result, it is a very desirable place to live. Real estate values are among the highest in the nation.

Here are some of the characteristics that tend to attract households to a metropolitan area:

NOTABLE CHARACTERISTICS INFLUENCING REAL ESTATE DNA

Characteristics	Examples
Mountains	Rocky Mountains, CO
Water: ocean/river/lake	Myrtle Beach, SC (beach resort)
Climate	San Diego (mild)
Resources	Houston (oil)
Diversified economy	New York City
Job situation	Detroit, MI
Exciting downtown	San Francisco

Education/universities	Charlottesville, VA, University of Virginia
Hospital and medical services	Minneapolis, Sinai Cancer Hospital
Recreation/parks	Park City, UT (skiing)
Transportation systems	Denver Airport
Government	Tallahassee, FL, state capital
Professional sports teams	Philadelphia (Eagles, Flyers, and 76ers)
Culture/ethnicity	Washington, D.C., Smithsonian, Kennedy Center
Entertainment	Las Vegas (entertainment and gambling)
Affordability	Buffalo, NY
Safety	Minneapolis
X or undefined factors	Miami (international banking)

Each characteristic affects potential buyer's reactions to a city's desirability. What is attractive or unattractive about a real estate market's DNA can be seen differently by different people. We all have our own tastes and aspirations about how we want to live, and we decide which shortcomings we can tolerate. There is no one characteristic that attracts all households. But the more people who are attracted to a city, the stronger its real estate value.

Some people want to live near the ocean; others couldn't care less. My wife would like to live our future retirement waking up each morning to the panoramic view of ocean waves washing over the white sands of a beachfront property. She is not alone. There is a relatively large segment of our population that is attracted to real estate located near or at the ocean. We can apply this approach to every DNA characteristic. Some households are attracted to warm climate, some to the beauty of the mountains, some to extensive cultural opportunities, and so on.

For each local marketplace, it is the mix of DNA characteristics that determines the likelihood of people being attracted to that city or region. For example, West Palm Beach, Florida, is composed primarily of a large retiree population seeking warmer weather and the ocean, as well as younger households who provide services (merchants, health and financial service providers) to those retirees. Charlottesville, Virginia, on the other hand, is composed primarily of a young population of students, professors, and young professionals who are attracted to a town dominated by the University of Virginia (my alma mater, as it happens) and the cultural activities that go with that.

Let's look at some of the characteristics described above through the lens of potential home buyers, and different population groups, to better understand how they view the importance of those DNA traits.

DNA CHARACTERISTICS

Mountains. From the Appalachians to the Great Smokies to the Rockies, Americans seem attracted to high places with breathtaking views. Many of the people who have settled in Park City, Utah, did so not because of the annual Sundance movie festival nearby, but because of the city's renowned steep ski slopes and views of the Rocky Mountains. In recent years, the Great Smoky Mountains have become popular with Floridians who are tired of the hurricane season and desire a mountain retreat instead. Some favorite mountain locations include Asheville, North Carolina; Cashiers, North Carolina; Aspen, Colorado; Sun Valley, Idaho; Vail and Boulder, Colorado; and the like.

Water. Our fascination with water isn't surprising. A great many towns and cities are located by a lake, bay, river, or ocean, attracting people from the surrounding region. In summer, people flock to beaches to swim and sunbathe. But Americans crave the water in the winter as well. Weather is less of a factor when a real estate market is situated close to the water, as it is in Chicago. Property values in the high-rise condominiums on Lake Shore Drive along Lake Michigan are some of the most highly priced in the city, despite the wind and cold. The closer a property is to a body of water, the higher the value of the real estate.

A 2005 study conducted by Florida International University and based on a popularity survey ranks the top ten best beaches in the United States:

1. Fort Desoto Park's North Beach, St. Petersburg, FL
2. Ocracoke Island, Outer Banks, NC
3. Hanalei Bay, Kauai, HI
4. Caladesi Island State Park, Clearwater, FL
5. Fleming Beach, Maui, HI
6. Coast Guard Beach, Cape Cod, MA
7. Coronado Beach, San Diego, CA
8. Cape Florida State Park, Key Biscayne, FL
9. Main Beach, East Hampton, NY
10. Hamoa Beach, Maui, HI

Rankings by Dr. Stephen Leatherman, Professor and Director, International Hurricane Center, Florida International University

Climate. If you had a choice, would you rather live in Naples, Florida, or Duluth, Minnesota? If you are like most people, you would likely choose Florida over Duluth. Nothing against Duluth, but far more people—and real estate purchasers—prefer the warm weather of southern Florida over the harsh winters in Duluth.

Resources. In the early days of our nation, a location's natural resources determined the size and success of a city: oil, gold, coal, iron, mineral springs, and so on. Texas got rich from oil. Pittsburgh got rich from making steel. The huge steel factories in Pittsburgh provided many jobs and spurred the local economy. The same is true today. But as we have seen, real estate DNA changes over time. The "resources" in Pittsburgh changed in recent decades, as, for example, more and more materials were made from aluminum and plastic and steel production surged overseas. The steel industry is no longer the driving force it once was in Pittsburgh. Other industries have taken its place.

Diversified economy. Like living organisms, a local market needs some inherent favorable DNA in order to build a robust and diversified economy. Local markets that have achieved such DNA create a gravity that continues to attract households into the future. Diversified city economies are found in New York City, San Francisco, and Chicago and are a huge plus. New York is known not only for Wall Street and its financial district, but also for its garment district, diamond district, theater, media industries, corporate headquarters, advertising agencies, and its hundreds of exceptional restaurants. San Francisco boasts a strong financial district, Chinatown, Fisherman's Wharf, top retail shopping, great restaurants, and proximity to wine country. Chicago has a strong financial district, the Magnificent Mile (great downtown retail shopping), and, of course, one of the greatest ballparks in the nation, Wrigley Field. Every major city that has experienced or is experiencing population growth can make similar claims, because a diversified local economy helps them to continue to grow. It is one of the major keys to a long-term successful real estate market.

Job situation. A healthy diversified local economy usually provides a favorable backdrop for job creation. But sometimes a single event can boost an area. A large company relocating to a town or city can create a significant number of jobs, bringing a number of new households to the region looking for job opportunities.

Education/Universities. Some towns grow up around universities. A college or university can be a genuine spur to the local economy. My alma mater, the University of Virginia, located in Charlottesville, is a good example. The university is a focal point for Charlottesville, and the student and faculty population supports the local economy via jobs and spending, while the school's research facilities attract other businesses to the city. And the cultural, sports, and other activities generated by the university and the surrounding community create an attractive ambience to those living in the area. There are hundreds of examples of universities positively influencing local economies and real estate markets: Penn State in State College, Pennsylvania; Princeton, located in Princeton, New Jersey; the University of North Carolina in Chapel Hill; the University of California in Berkeley; the University of Michigan in Ann Arbor; and so on. Even a small college in a relatively small town can exert a significant influence on the surrounding area. Coastal Carolina University, located in Conway, South Carolina, is a prime example of this.

There are times when a university, however, is dwarfed by the city in which it is located, limiting its influence. George Mason University, which is a relatively large school, is an example. GMU is located in populous Fairfax County, Virginia. There are more than one million households in Fairfax County, and a school of about 30,000 students has only a modest impact on the Fairfax County local market. New York University in New York City is another example.

Government. A state capital, however small or large, adds to local real estate values as well as local economic activity. State capitals provide jobs to government employees and government contracts to businesses that deal with the state government. From Tallahassee, Florida, to Albany, New York, to Sacramento, California, state government operations create job opportunities, attract business, and exert upward pressure on property values.

Professional sports. Ask the people who live in Green Bay, Wisconsin, about the importance of having a professional sports team. Any city fortunate enough to house a professional sports team from the National Football League, Major League Baseball, or the National Basketball Association has a special DNA characteristic that can influence real estate values. I'll go into more detail on the influence of sports—professional and otherwise—on real estate values in Chapter Six.

Hospital and medical services. While this is one of those DNA characteristics that will probably not attract many *new* households, if a city lacks adequate medical services it most certainly will lose households. Some metropolitan areas are known for their hospitals, but they tend not to have a meaningful impact on local economic and real estate growth.

The one exception might be local markets with large elderly/retirement populations: The availability of quality health and medical services is very important to elderly and retirement households. Successful retirement destinations, such as Phoenix and Scottsdale, Arizona, and West Palm Beach, Florida, offer these services at a high level.

Recreation/Parks. Skiing, water sports, beach, mountains—a town that has plentiful recreation facilities and parks has a significant plus in terms of positively influencing real estate values.

Transportation systems. The quality of a major transportation system can make or break a local real estate market. Decades ago, railroad stations helped to determine the success of a local economy and real estate market. Today, it is the airline industry that takes center stage. Becoming a hub for a major airline has elevated a number of metropolitan areas to a higher economic status. As noted earlier, when Delta Airlines located its headquarters and training operations in Atlanta, the southern city's population grew, its economy revived, and its real estate market blossomed. While Chicago has been a major transportation hub since the heyday of rail travel, United Airlines elevated Chicago to prominence as an air transport hub. Today, O'Hare Airport—the old Orchard Field—is one of the busiest airports in the world. The easy access to Chicago it provides has encouraged business and continues to attract households to Chicago and its suburbs.

Conversely, the inability to build an airport that attracts major airlines will most likely limit the ability of a metropolitan area to grow. Richmond, Virginia, is a prime example. Its city government was not willing to invest the money to attract major airlines to become a hub. Corporations pay attention to hubs. An airline hub facilitates company travel plans, attracting companies to locate their headquarters or regional offices there, or to use the local market to hold meetings with staff and clients from different locations around the nation.

Of course, airports are by no means the only form of transportation that can positively affect a local real estate market. Woodbridge, New Jersey, is an example of a town where a number of major highways cross— Route 18, the Garden State Parkway, the New Jersey Turnpike, and Route 9—making it convenient for traveling.

Culture/Ethnicity. To many people, having access to cultural events is enormously appealing. Theater, dance, music, art, and dining out are all part of American culture. Washington, D.C., boasts the Kennedy Center for the Performing Arts and the Smithsonian Institution (which is, actually, a group of museums). Baltimore developed the Inner Harbor, the Aquarium, and Little Italy. Cleveland has the Institute of Music, the Rock and Roll Hall of Fame, the Cleveland Orchestra, and a renowned museum of art. New York City has it all. But from a local market perspective, culture is also influenced by ethnicity. An Italian neighborhood will attract more Italians to the area. A neighborhood with a significant Asian population will attract more Asian households. The cultural tone of any city, town, or neighborhood is justifiably part of its DNA.

Entertainment. Las Vegas has gambling, and New York has Broadway and the theater. But if you are looking for up-and-coming local economies and real estate markets, identify those cities that are trying to build up their theater and entertainment facilities, from theme parks to casinos. Such towns are attractive to home buyers because they attract businesses and are more fun to live in.

Downtown (the core of the city). Bright lights, theater, retail stores, restaurants—all are components of a healthy downtown sector. But there is a magic to a bustling downtown that is difficult to describe. Baltimore discovered some of this magic in recent decades. For many years, Baltimore had been an older, stagnant city. But then local government made a commitment to reinvigorating the downtown area by the harbor. The Rouse Company was commissioned to rebuild the Inner Harbor (it had done a revitalization of Boston's old Quincy Market to great success). What a job it did. Baltimore now has a beautiful harbor, shops, hotels, an aquarium, and state-of-the-art professional baseball *and* football stadiums close by. Both Baltimore natives and tourists are attracted to this newly revived area. The city of Baltimore "is back," and it is because of the revival of the core part of the city. Many cities followed Baltimore's lead—Cleveland, Washington, D.C. (with the Verizon Center), and San Antonio (River Walk), to name a few.

Affordability. Unfortunately, affordability and the cost of living in a particular market can be a two-edged sword. The median home price is a good proxy for affordability. Local markets, like Buffalo, New York, that register the lowest median home prices are therefore the most affordable, and affordability can play the most important role in a household's location decision. If you were deciding which of two local markets to live in and both possessed the characteristics you were looking for (near the water, ample entertainment, and a great transportation system, for example), affordability might be the deciding factor. But high affordability may be a sign that a city has difficulty in attracting new residents. If a metropolitan area is unable to attract new residents due to lack of jobs, home values will probably fall, improving affordability conditions.

Safety. Living in a safe neighborhood is likely close to the top of anyone's list of desirable DNA characteristics. Our sense of the safeness of a city or neighborhood, whether conscious or unconscious, has an important if intangible impact on its desirability.

X factor. Some cities have what I call an X factor—some quality that may not be obvious or tangible. Miami has such an X factor: a unique international flavor due to its proximity to Latin America. New York City (Manhattan) has the X factor because of its sheer size and population, all jammed onto a small island. Los Angeles has it because of Hollywood and, to a lesser extent, its ocean location. And Washington, D.C., has it because it is the nation's capital, where power brokers jockey for position. Cleveland tried to create an X factor—by serving as home to the Rock and Roll Hall of Fame—but failed. For a time the newly built Jacobs Field and the success of the Cleveland Indians baseball team gave it a bit of an X factor. Today, Cleveland now has LeBron James—a great young professional basketball player who has captured national interest, giving Cleveland, once again, at least a small X factor.

DIFFERENT STROKES FOR DIFFERENT FOLKS

Real estate DNA, of course, is in the eye of the beholder. Some people love living near the water, while others prefer the magic of a dynamic city. Let's look at some of the more important population groups to gain a better understanding of their DNA preferences.

Young households. This includes people in their twenties and thirties in the early stages of their careers, possibly looking to start a family. They are primarily attracted to a diversified economy with lots of job opportunities as well as entertainment. Not surprisingly, some of our more diversified cities, such as New York, San Francisco, and Chicago, are magnets for such households. These cities have job opportunities in a wide variety of industries and offer outstanding entertainment, shopping, and quality transportation systems, not to mention a plethora of professional sports teams. Of course, plenty of other young households are attracted to smaller markets. The biggest single key is a region that offers employment opportunities.

Aging boomers. The largest population group in the history of the United States—baby boomers—is aging. That has created havoc across a significant number of local real estate markets. What DNA characteristics do the boomers seek? The answers have meant a real estate bonanza for some local markets and promise to impact many other local markets in the future. Boomers will be seeking second homes and retirement homes, particularly in ocean resort areas, boosting property demand on both coasts. And they will be downsizing their primary residences, likely boosting demand for condominiums throughout the country. Warm weather, water, mountains, and entertainment are all characteristics that will be desired by aging boomers in the next decade or two. Florida, Arizona, and Nevada will continue to be the focus of many boomer households, but there will be plenty of secondary destinations that are more affordable for boomers. Real estate in key areas in the Carolinas, Georgia, Washington, Oregon, and New Mexico are but a few.

Retirees. Retirees are living longer due to improved health care technology and as we nationally trend toward healthier living. That has elevated their impact on local real estate markets. Like aging boomers, they are focused on warmer climate and access to recreational activities like tennis and golf. But more important to retirees is access to hospital and medical services. At present, both Arizona and Florida have an abundance of facilities to serve their needs.

Immigrants. Record immigration during the 1970s, 1980s, and 1990s has elevated the influence immigrants have had on local real estate markets. Immigrants tend to live close to other immigrants from the same country of origin, so culture becomes an important characteristic for them. Most of the nation's large cities have established immigrant populations and thus continue to attract new immigrant households. Of course, job opportunities are critical, as well, to immigrants trying to establish their families in America.

Low- and moderate-income households. Affordability is perhaps the dominating characteristic among low-income households. Local markets like Cincinnati, Houston, Dallas, and Salt Lake City have far more affordable neighborhoods compared with San Diego, Washington, D.C., or Boston. As a result, these markets may rise in value over time. It is not just low- and moderate-income households that are seeking affordable housing. Some markets have become superheated, such as San Francisco, Los Angeles, and San Diego, where a number of households are moving to more affordable cities and states to live, such as Las Vegas, Reno, and Phoenix.

Vacation/Resort households. Households looking for vacation homes focus on a very different mix of characteristics than do households purchasing a primary residence. Education, job growth, and transportation are no longer as important. A beautiful setting, warmer climate (near lakes and oceans or in the mountains), and recreation/parks rise to the top of the list for vacation-home buyers.

ARE SOME CHARACTERISTICS BETTER THAN OTHERS?

Is it possible to explain why some metros are more successful than others because of their DNA makeup? And is it possible that some DNA characteristics are more influential than others? For example, are metropolitan areas with professional sports teams more successful than metropolitan areas without professional teams if everything else is the same? Is a diversified economy a more important DNA characteristic (as my "economist gut" would tell me)? Is a quality transportation system more important than culture or education to households? Is entertainment crucial? The answers to these questions would help city governments with their long-term planning goals. But it would also help *all* real estate buyers in making more intelligent decisions about future real estate purchases.

There have been attempts to evaluate cities by their DNA characteristics. *Cities Ranked and Rated* by Peter Sander and Bert Sperling (John Wiley & Sons, 2004) is one recent attempt. Sander and Sperling examined hundreds of characteristics for each city and grouped them into nine categories, including jobs, economy, cost of living, climate, education, arts and culture, and an intangible characteristic (what I refer to as our X factor). But their data is subjective and difficult to verify. Nontheless, they did come to some general conclusions that are consistent with what I call DNA analysis.

Their research found that real estate in college towns does especially well, and that the presence of higher education spills over to raise the levels of all education and health care facilities. State capitals tend to do well, relative to surrounding cities, because they are clean, exhibit stable economic growth, and usually have a strong cultural presence.

LOCAL MARKET RANKINGS

If you are looking for an edge in comparing local real estate markets by DNA characteristics, one easy way to do it is to look at the popular lists of the best places to live. They range from ranking by crime rates to quality of education to cost of living by city, metropolitan area, or state. These lists can be found almost anywhere—magazines, newspapers, academic studies, local government handouts, marketing promotions. Here are a few of the sources you can go to: *Realtor Magazine,* published by the National Association of Realtors; *Money* magazine, which just published "Best Places to Live: 2006"; *Forbes* magazine and Forbes.com, which regularly publishes "best places of careers and businesses and to live" lists; *Kiplinger's* magazine, which recently published "50 Smart Places to Live," and so on. For the easiest and fastest search for ranking lists, conduct a search (Google) on the Internet and literally hundreds of sites will be displayed presenting city/metro rankings of some kind.

Don't rely solely on these lists to judge a market's potential. Most lists give you just a small piece of the real estate puzzle. Do not pass on a local real estate market just because that particular market ranks lower on someone's list than a nearby city. Everyone values real estate characteristics differently. There are hundreds of lists to choose from. To save you time, I'll review a handful of them.

I rank lists by those I call most useful, those I call somewhat useful, and those I call entertaining (i.e., not so useful). Finally, there are composite rankings available for cities, assigning specific weights to a number of characteristics, weighted by importance. I will include some of these lists at the end of this section.

MOST USEFUL RANKINGS

To qualify as "most useful," the information about the metropolitan area should be relevant to the current and future viability of real estate and the local economy. Ranking metros by their cost of living (affordability) is very useful information and fits most people's selection criteria quite nicely. I also think most of us are interested in whether a particular region or city has a high or low crime rate. Quality-of-education and job-creation rankings are also useful characteristics to compare. Here is just a brief list of what I consider the most useful characteristics to compare across metropolitan areas and regions:

- Cost of living
- Safety
- Education
- Transportation
- Job creation
- Income growth
- Best places for business
- Arts and culture
- Affordability
- Climate
- Affordable housing
- Entertainment

For example, if you are interested in purchasing property in St. Louis, Missouri, it would be foolish to ignore the fact that the Gateway to the West is ranked the fourth most dangerous city in America, according to Morgan Quitno Press. This information should not by itself deter you from purchasing real estate in St. Louis. There are many beautiful and safe neighborhoods in and around St. Louis. But it does suggest that this aspect of St. Louis is likely to hold prices down in the future relative to a city that does not suffer from this handicap. It should spur you to ask follow-up questions of your real estate professional about the safety of the neighborhoods you are targeting.

THE 5 MOST DANGEROUS CITIES IN AMERICA

1. Camden, NJ
2. Detroit, MI
3. Atlanta, GA
4. St. Louis, MO
5. Gary, IN

Source: Morgan Quitno Press, November 2004

SOMEWHAT USEFUL RANKINGS

Somewhat useful ranking lists are just that—somewhat useful information for you to consider in your overall real estate purchase decision. A list that ranks cities by those with the lowest health-care costs is interesting but may not be a deciding factor in your purchase decision. Low health-care costs likely have little influence over current and future real estate values. I also include a "resort" category in this list, because while rankings of top resorts are very subjective, they can be helpful in determining future real estate values. The following are what I consider to be "somewhat useful" ranking lists:

- Shortest daily commute
- Most leisure amenities
- Lowest health-care costs
- Best air and water quality
- Most days of sunshine
- Population density
- Top resorts

TOP RESORTS

Ocean Isle Beach, NC	Santa Fe, NM
Bend, OR	Wisconsin Dells, WI
Mammoth, CA	Poconos, PA
Fort Myers, FL	Park City, UT
Gatlinburg, TN	South Padre Island, TX

Source: EscapeHomes.com editors' picks as of May 2006

ENTERTAINING (NOT-VERY-USEFUL) RANKINGS

Lists that rank locations by interesting but obscure characteristics are not very useful in making a real estate decision. But they can contain fun and entertaining information. Knowing America's top twenty-four cities in terms of obesity certainly is not going to influence your decision to purchase property, but curiosity may entice you to review the list (it makes for great party conversation). Some of my favorite lists are metro rankings on the best romantic beaches and the sweatiest (in terms of humidity) cities.

- Cities with the best skylines (largest number of high-rise buildings)
- Best sports cities

- Obesity
- Sweatiest city rankings
- Cities with the most sunshine
- Best beaches for walking
- Best wild beaches
- Best beaches with nightlife
- The top heartburn (highest incidence) cities

AMERICA'S TOP 24 HEARTBURN CITIES*

1. Charlotte, NC	13. Milwaukee, WI
2. Jacksonville, FL	14. Pittsburgh, PA
3. Roanoke, VA	15. Boston, MA
4. Louisville, KY	16. Raleigh, NC
5. Denver, CO	17. Baltimore, MD
6. Spokane, WA	18. Albany, NY
7. Miami, FL	19. Salt Lake City, UT
8. Tampa-St. Petersburg, FL	20. Columbus, OH
9. Atlanta, GA	21. Cincinnati, OH
10. Grand Rapids, MI	22. Omaha, NE
11. Orlando, FL	23. Des Moines, IA
12. Minneapolis-St. Paul, MN	24. Peoria, IL

*The National Home Buyers Association has ranked the twenty-four cities most impacted by heartburn using the "Burn Factor Index," which is based on several points of data, including high per-household spending on acid controllers/antacids [according to barcode scanner data tracked by Information Resources Incorporated (IRI)], multiple "quality of life" aspects of how heartburn affects sufferers, and respondent-cited consumption of various heartburn products.

COMPOSITE RANKINGS

There are numerous attempts to measure the attractiveness, performance, and livability of cities. Attractiveness and performance rankings are usually based on evaluating scores of city characteristics such as job market, quality of transportation and education systems, and climate. Livability rankings and quality-of-life rankings are more difficult to measure because the term "quality" is so subjective. Nevertheless, there are several well-known composite rankings worth mentioning.

Places Rated Almanac, by David Savageau (Macmillan Publishing Company, published annually since 1981), provides lots of information on performance and attractiveness and ranks cities across the nation. *Cities Ranked and Rated* by Peter Sander and Bert Sperling (cited above) provides information and evaluations on more than 400 metros across the United States and Canada. Then there are the attempts at quality-of-life and livability rankings. SustainLane City Rankings provides a detailed report card on city quality of life, combined with indicators of sustainability programs, policies, and performance; these rankings look at clean air, water, local foods, climate change, environmental toxins, and city revitalizations employing green building techniques. For the serious real estate purchaser, I recommend reading these books or books like them. Their objective is focused not on future real estate values but on the livability of specific area locations. Here are some of the major categories that all of these composite rankings share.

- Cost of living
- Climate
- Quality of life (subjective)
- Quality of transportation and education
- Fastest-growing cities
- Job market
- Air and water quality
- Health-care costs
- Daily commute time
- Leisure amenities
- Housing costs
- Recreational facilities
- Environmental factors

CITIES RANKED AND RATED: THE TOP 50

1. Charlottesville, VA	18. Colorado Springs, CO
2. Santa Fe, NM	19. Nassau-Suffolk, NY
3. San Luis Obispo-Atascadero-Paso Robles, CA	20. Pueblo, CO
4. Santa Barbara-Santa Maria-Lompoc, CA	21. Eugene-Springfield, OR
5. Honolulu, HI	22. Austin-San Marcos, TX
6. Ann Arbor, MI	23. Lafayette, IN
7. Atlanta, GA	24. Minneapolis-St. Paul, MN-WI
8. Asheville, NC	25. Dover, DE
9. Reno, NV	26. Washington, DC-MD-VA-WV
10. Corvallis, OR	27. Fayetteville-Springdale-Rogers, AR
11. Roanoke, VA	28. Pittsburgh, PA
12. Portland-Vancouver, OR-WA	29. Bloomington, IN
13. Raleigh-Durham-Chapel Hill, NC	30. Stamford-Norwalk, CT
14. Bryan-College Station, TX	31. State College, PA
15. Lynchburg, VA	32. Abilene, TX
16. Olympia, WA	33. Champaign-Urbana, IL
17. Norfolk-Virginia Beach-Newport News, VA-NC	34. Athens, GA

35. Wichita, KS	43. Sarasota-Bradenton, FL
36. Fort Worth-Arlington, TX	44. Bremerton, WA
37. Madison, WI	45. Albuquerque, NM
38. Bellingham, WA	46. Harrisburg-Lebanon-Carlisle, PA
39. Las Cruces, NM	47. Evansville-Henderson, IN-KY
40. New York, NY	48. Tampa-St. Petersburg-Clearwater, FL
41. Dayton-Springfield, OH	49. Punta Gorda, FL
42. Bloomington-Normal, IL	50. Columbia, SC

CHARACTERISTICS INFLUENCING A TOWN/NEIGHBORHOOD'S DNA

So far we have been focused only on the DNA characteristics of metropolitan areas. DNA comparisons across metros are useful when making decisions on where to purchase or invest in real estate. But for most of us, the decision is not what metropolitan area to live in, but rather what town or neighborhood to live in within a metropolitan area. Here are some of the characteristics that I believe tend to attract households to a town and/or neighborhood. The only way to gather this information is to ask a Realtor or to conduct a site visit to each location and neighborhood yourself.

Movie theaters. Moviegoing has been an American pastime for many years. Millions of us make a night of it by going to the movies numerous times throughout the year. Close proximity to a multiplex movie theater is usually an attraction that a neighborhood or town can boast.

Local restaurants. There is nothing more enticing than a high-quality neighborhood restaurant where neighbors can socialize.

Starbucks. Many of us are hooked on Starbucks latte and other drinks and covet a Starbucks close to the neighborhood. And Starbucks isn't going to locate in a neighborhood that doesn't have enough customers to buy its upscale lattes.

Supermarkets. The convenience factor is crucial for grocery shopping, and having a close-by supermarket is a must for many households.

Large hardware stores. America's preoccupation with fixing up our own homes dictates that we live near a large hardware store like Lowe's or Home Depot.

Fitness centers. America's latest craze is fitness, and the convenience of driving quickly before or after work to a fitness center, like Gold's Gym or Lifetime Fitness, has become a priority among households. Again, these centers tend to open in areas that their research indicates will be able to afford gym memberships.

Bus stops, train stops, or commuter pickups. Commuters living in towns that are relatively far from where they work (probably in the city) put a premium on accessible transportation, making bus stops, train stops, and commuter pickup locations an important factor when selecting a location to live.

Fire/police stations. Most of us want to live in a safe, crime-free location. Knowing that there are a firehouse and a police station nearby is important.

Recreation centers. A place to play basketball or baseball, swim, and engage in other recreational activities is important to young households (and sometimes even older households).

Golf courses. Tiger Woods entered the professional golf scene in 1996, and the popularity of golf for everyday people rose geometrically in the decade that followed. For some households, living near or actually on a golf course is a priority. On the other hand, there are signs that golf's rising star is beginning to fade. In some areas of the country, there is an oversupply of golf courses, and they are not making money. Some of these courses are now being plowed to make way for residential and commercial developments.

Country clubs. For those households that can afford club membership, neighborhood proximity is a plus.

Places of worship. For many households, proximity to churches, temples, or mosques is important.

Gated communities. Neighborhood safety is important to all of us, and a gated community may be favored over nongated communities by some households.

Chapter Five

THE POWER OF INFLUENCE

Any home builder will tell you that the construction business is driven by local factors. Just try to get a county government or a local board of supervisors to approve a site permit and/or a building permit. Working with local governments can be time-consuming, lengthy, and costly. As a matter of survival, many local builders get involved with their communities, building relationships and trust with local officials. But as you might guess, it doesn't stop there. Once the property is built, local influence on a property's value only intensifies. It is no longer just the local government or construction costs that influence price and sales activity. Its value is now subject to all factors affecting demand and supply. There are the traditional factors, such as population growth, job gains, and mortgage rates, discussed in Chapter Three. Then there are what I call nontraditional factors. Those are the focus of this chapter. Nontraditional factors can range from the revitalization of a downtown to the building of a large supermarket within walking distance of your neighborhood. The common thread among these nontraditional factors is their power to influence real estate values and activity.

Let's go back in time. It is 1969. You live in the Washington, D.C., metropolitan area. One morning, you pick up the *Washington Post* and read that the District of Columbia government just approved funds for the construction of one of the largest public-works projects ever built in America—the Washington Metro (subway) system. You learn that the plan is to build a 103-mile rapid transit system that will serve Washington,

D.C., and the surrounding areas of Maryland and Virginia. The first segment of the new transit system is projected to open for operation sometime in 1976.

Your first impression is relief—traffic will be lessened on the way into the downtown area via the major highways, making your commute quicker and more comfortable. You even contemplate the possibility of becoming a commuter, taking the Metro train and not having to deal with driving at all. But the notion that the new expansive transit system would influence property values in the D.C. metropolitan area probably does not enter your mind.

Of course, now it is after the fact. It is obvious that the construction of the D.C. Metro system had a significant impact on property values all across the D.C. metropolitan area. A new paradigm was created in 1976 in the D.C. metropolitan area: Property values increased for the neighborhoods close (within walking distance) to the designated Metro stops relative to other neighborhoods. Furthermore, these "Metro neighborhoods" spurred construction of new residential and business properties, raising the overall quality of life in those locations compared with other, *non-*Metro neighborhoods.

A great example of what happened occurred in the Ballston area of Arlington, Virginia, when the Metro system was built. Ballston was a sleepy neighborhood about twelve miles outside of Washington, D.C., before it was selected as a Metro stop in the transit system. Today Ballston is a flourishing neighborhood experiencing a robust local economy with bustling construction activity and high-priced, high-rise office buildings and condominiums. It also has those "altered" DNA characteristics that local residents want in their neighborhoods: a good educational system, a wide variety of restaurants, shopping, and other activity facilities (movie theaters, health clubs, etc.).

The real estate effects of the D.C. Metro system are a prime example of what I mean by the power of influence. A political decision by the local government affected (influenced) the relative distribution of all real estate prices in the D.C. metropolitan area. Some neighborhoods and their homeowners profited from the Metro train decisions by being in the right place at the right time or by investing in real estate by the proposed Metro stops in anticipation of the construction of the Metro system. And some neighborhoods and homeowners were left out in the cold.

As you will see, many such nontraditional factors affect local real estate activity by changing a local market's DNA—by adding or subtracting a positive characteristic. But nontraditional factors can also negatively influence demand for home buying. For example, if you were thinking of purchasing a second home on Kiawah Island, South Carolina, and heard that the local government was considering doubling the property tax rate, you might think twice about purchasing property there.

WHAT DO I MEAN BY INFLUENCE?

For our purposes, I define *influence* as an event or a change in activity that affects or alters real estate activity and/or values. For example, local housing supply and local politics are two of the many local influences on the value of your home. On the most local of levels, let's say you list your home for sale. Your real estate agent tells you that two neighbors on your street are also listing their homes for sale. To be competitive, you (reluctantly) list your home at a sales price a bit less than you had originally planned. Or let's say your neighborhood is redistricted into the best school system in the county, so the value of your home has just jumped significantly. On a broader scale, if a local government works with major developers to revitalize your town's downtown, property values in the city will almost assuredly rise over time.

Influences on local market conditions can originate from outside or from within your local area. They can be local, national, or even global. The Iraq War effort is as global an influence as they come, and its impact on property values is widespread. War begets uncertainty. That uncertainty in turn can cause financial risk avoidance, driving investors to a safer haven or more tangible assets like real estate instead of intangible assets such as stocks (thus contributing to the real estate boom). War also means more government borrowing in order to fund military expenditures. Increased government borrowing eventually exerts upward pressure on mortgage rates (i.e., rates go up over time), which can reduce home buying down the road. The local influence of war can be seen when large defense companies win government contracts that will generate jobs in the areas of the country they are located in. All of these influences affect the price of property.

The same can be said for national, regional/state, city, neighborhood, and street influences as well. For example, on a national basis, influences on the direction of mortgage rates, such as the Federal Reserve or the size of the federal budget deficit, indirectly affect home values. Regionally or on a state level, a hurricane such as Katrina can have a devastating impact on home values. For individual cities, the ability of the local economy to create jobs and/or attract households from other areas of the nation can directly impact home values in that metropolitan area. High crime rates in a particular community or neighborhood can negatively impact property values. And as any homeowner will testify, the condition of your neighbors' homes on your street can influence the price of your own home.

There are literally dozens of influences on local real estate activity. For the rest of this chapter, I am going to look at some of the nontraditional influences. I put these nontraditional influences into five categories:

- Neighborhood influences
- Household influences
- Business influences
- Social/cultural influences
- Political influences

NEIGHBORHOOD INFLUENCES

There is nothing more inspiring than driving through a neighborhood on a street lined with sturdy oak and pine trees fronting beautifully landscaped homes. The homeowners who live on such a street probably have the funds (and commitment) to keep their homes in very good condition. You may drive through such a neighborhood yourself with a sense of envy and a desire to someday live in such beautiful surroundings. Homes in well-to-do neighborhoods usually enjoy more consistent demand compared to homes in neighborhoods that are not as affluent or as well kept up. It's depressing driving on a street with run-down houses, collapsing porches, and accumulating debris. Property values usually lag behind in a neighborhood where the houses are not well maintained.

My point is that a neighborhood's condition strongly influences the individual property within it. In looking at a neighborhood's condition, keep an eye on overall home appearance (e.g., landscaping, condition of streets), available parking, amount of automobile traffic during peak and off-peak hours, and quality of snow removal/garbage service, to name a few things. Here are some other influences to research or be on the lookout for:

- Relative attractiveness of the neighborhood with regard to land-scaping, property condition, and security.
- Published decisions made by the neighborhood association concerning upkeep.
- A change in the policy or support of the police and fire department with regard to the neighborhood.
- Any change in traffic patterns and available parking due to new road construction. This can have a significant impact on a neighborhood, as increased traffic on a neighborhood street can drive prices down, just as the creation of a cul-de-sac can increase property values.
- Any new residential construction activity that could help or hinder future home values.

HOUSEHOLD INFLUENCES

Changes in population can highly influence local market activity. But it is important to know who is purchasing the properties in a city or neighborhood as well as how many are buying. The composition and type of households living in the neighborhood, city, or metro are what I consider the *nontraditional component* of population measures. Are younger households moving into the neighborhood? Are there more young households than older households? What is the median household income in the neighborhood?

Let me give you an example of what I mean. When I was a boy, I grew up in Long Beach, New York, a town of about 30,000 people. The somewhat hackneyed phrase about living on "the other side of the tracks" was literally true of Long Beach during the 1950s and through the 1970s. There was a railroad station and railroad tracks smack in the middle of the town. The median income for households on the east side of the tracks was significantly higher than that for those on the immediate west side of the tracks. Property values on the east side rose throughout those thirty years, while property values on the other side were relatively flat. Knowing the "train tracks" issue kept people from purchasing homes near the railroad station—even on the east side. Only when the town made a concerted effort to revitalize the railroad station and that section of town did property values rise for all Long Beach households.

The lesson here is that it is a good idea to compare the median household incomes from one town to another. A local market with a higher median income probably will rise in value over the long run with regard to property values. Getting this information is not terribly difficult. Each local government publishes the median local income for its town or city. If you have trouble finding this information, just ask your Realtor.

The age of households in a town or city also influences home values over the long term. A lower median age in a town may suggest a preponderance of families with children. That may bode well for future trade-up real estate activity—that is, those households with children will trade up from a smaller home to a larger one. Young towns that are active with growing families tend to do well with regard to home sales and steadily rising home values. On the other hand, a higher median age in a town may be associated with a higher median income, indicating a more stable local marketplace with greater job security and eventually rising home values. My advice is to gather information on median age and median income at the same time. Median age information may be more difficult than median income information to gather. Again, the local town or city government should provide such information and your local Realtor should be able to provide it. But if you are unable to gather data on median age, look at the town's school system and ask whether there has been a rise or decline in the student population during the past five years and what they expect the student population to be in the future. New construction of schools is usually a reliable indicator of a growing population of young households with children. Just as in the Long Beach example, some neighborhoods within the town will likely perform better over time due to disparities in household age and income.

Here is what I look for with regard to household composition in local markets:

- A younger household market with trade-up potential
- An older household market with relatively high and stable income
- Local markets with growing median household income
- Few low-income/older households

Household information by metropolitan area, county, or even zip code is available and accessible to everyone. Just go to the Internet and Google "population and demographics," and you will find a plethora of sites that offer this information, such as American Factfinder, MCDC Demographic Profiles, Sourcebook of Zip Code Demographics, and Zip Code Statistics (Census Bureau). Yahoo Real Estate and its Real Estate Neighborhood Profiles are user-friendly sites offering great information on households in local markets. Here is what Yahoo offers if you were considering moving to Fairfax Station, Virginia—the 22039 zip code:

YAHOO REAL ESTATE
Neighborhood Profiles

	Fairfax Station, VA 22039	National Average
Population of Fairfax Station	18,929	11,535
Median Age	36.5 years	37.47 years
Median Household Income	$152,790	$42,350.95
Percentage of Single Households	23%	41.53%
Percentage of Married Households	77%	58.46%
Percentage Families (households with children)	46.4%	24.32%
Average Household Size	3.27 people	2.57 people
Percentage College or Better	68.7%	20.14%
Percentage White Collar	83.4%	47.14%

The table above makes it clear that Fairfax Station, Virginia, is a high-income and relatively young household town, making it an attractive real estate location for the long term. Over 46 percent of its households have children, compared with a 24 percent national average. Fairfax Station's median income of almost $153,000 is far greater than the $42,350 national average.

What we have determined so far is that Fairfax Station's household composition is attractive with regard to future property values compared with the nation's average household composition. However, it may be more useful to compare Fairfax Station with other towns in the area. For example, a neighboring town, Centerville, Virginia, could be a viable alternative. According to Centerville's profile, its median income of $29,224 is substantially less than the nation's as well as Fairfax Station's median income. More revealing is that Centerville's median age is only 30.1 years, versus 36.5 years for Fairfax Station. Only 15.2 percent of its households have children, versus a 46.4 percent composition for Fairfax Station. That does not bode well for a potential trade-up market.

CENTERVILLE NEIGHBORHOOD PROFILE

Location: Centerville, VA 24060

DEMOGRAPHICS

	Centerville, VA 24060	National Average
Population of Centerville	48,779	11,535
Median Age	30.1 years	37.47 years
Median Household Income	$29,224	$42,350.95
Percentage of Single Households	66%	41.53%
Percentage of Married Households	34%	58.46%
Percentage Families (households with children)	15.2%	24.32%
Average Household Size	2.31 people	2.57 people
Percentage College or Better	55.9%	20.14%
Percentage White Collar	64.9%	47.14%

BUSINESS INFLUENCES

Businesses create jobs, and job creation is the biggest single key to a healthy local real estate market (job creation is a traditional influence). But this is not the only influence business has on local markets. The *location* of businesses, particularly retail establishments, can significantly influence property values, as well. For instance, I purchased a one-bedroom condominium in a less-than-stellar neighborhood in Washington, D.C., that was going through a transition. I justified my investment based on the likelihood (my local Realtor told me) that a Giant supermarket (one of the large grocery franchises in the D.C. area) was slated to open within two years in the local strip shopping center two blocks from the condominium building. Lo and behold, two years later construction of a Giant supermarket was under way. According to all the real estate agents in that area, demand for property within a one-half-mile radius of the supermarket had increased markedly. This may sound too simple, but sometimes the simple rules apply. All property owners desire the convenience of grocery shopping, and we are willing to pay a premium for it, particularly in a city.

Businesses also influence consumer confidence. Consumer confidence could be rising for the nation as a whole, but *local* consumer confidence can plummet in a small town when its largest employer files for bankruptcy.

I mentioned earlier the influence of a national or international event on local markets. Let's take another example of the impact of the Iraq War on local real estate markets. During the height of the Iraq War (2005–2006), not surprisingly, local markets with relatively high concentrations of defense/military-related business activities fared better than local markets with low concentrations of defense/military-related business activities. I cannot emphasize enough the importance of examining the business health of any local market you are targeting before committing to buying in it. Here is what to look for:

- Are there plans for a large supermarket, like Publix, Whole Foods, Stop & Shop, Giant, or Safeway, or a new department store to anchor a local shopping area near a local neighborhood? Such companies do extensive research before investing in a new store in an area. Piggybacking onto that research is an easy way to identify neighborhoods that warrant a closer look.
- Are there plans to open a new Home Depot or Lowe's or Wal-Mart or other large hardware or home-improvement store in or near your local market? See my comment above regarding such stores. These "home stores" generate a great deal of activity and could help attract households to the area.
- Are there plans for a new major shopping mall in the area?
- Are there any major corporations planning on locating a headquarters or regional offices in the local market?
- How many start-up companies are planning on conducting business in the local market?
- Are there plans on the drawing board concerning retail shopping, restaurants, a movie complex, and so on?
- Are there any stores that are *closing* in the area, indicating a flagging of the local economy?

The above information may not always be readily available, but it is accessible. For plans for a new Home Depot or a new supermarket or retail shopping, I would pressure your real estate agent to provide you with as much new-business intelligence as possible. You can also get a feel for the trend in new businesses by gathering new business start-up information. The U.S. Census Bureau's Zip Code Business Patterns provides this data for every zip code in the United States. Just go to their Web site at censtats.census.gov. Here is what they provide for Fairfax Station, Virginia:

U.S. CENSUS BUREAU'S ZIP CODE BUSINESS PATTERNS
Fairfax Station, Virginia: 22039 for 2004

Industry Code Description	Total Establishments
Forestry, Fishing, Hunting, Agriculture	1
Construction	47
Manufacturing	1
Wholesale Trade	13
Retail Trade	28
Transportation & Warehousing	3
Information Services	9
Finance & Insurance	14
Real Estate, Rental & Leasing	31
Professional, Scientific & Technology	135
Management of Companies	1
Administrative Support, Waste Management	25
Education	7
Healthcare and Social Assistance	17
Arts, Entertainment & Recreation	3
Accommodation & Food Services	11
Other	25
Unclassified Establishments	1
Total	**372**

To gain a feel for the growth in business establishments for your area, just compare yearly changes. Knowing these kinds of influences will make you a far more savvy real estate investor.

SOCIAL, CULTURAL, AND EDUCATIONAL INFLUENCES

A city or town with a lot of social and cultural activities attracts potential home buyers and visitors. It adds to the DNA of a local market. So you need to be on the lookout for tangible changes in the social/cultural environment of a neighborhood or city. Is the community building a new country club or a new neighborhood pool club? Are there more cultural outlets (theaters, restaurants) being built? Or are some closing down?

In Arlington, Virginia, the Shirlington neighborhood is situated just a few miles west of the Pentagon, just off one of the major highways in the area—I-395. For years the area housed primarily very small retail, industrial, and warehouse space. It fell on hard times in the early 1980s, but then the area began to be revitalized, with a new movie theater complex, about a dozen restaurants, and new headquarters for the Washington, D.C., area's public television station. Recently, it has undergone yet another change, with the building of new residential condominiums and a new public library branch. It will shortly be home to a major professional theater company. These cultural amenities have driven the demand for home buying in the area—and property values in the area have increased and should continue to do so.

Let me give you another example. From the 1950s through the 1970s, a large Jewish population helped to support demand for southern Florida real estate (particularly Miami). But the Jewish population began settling north of Fort Lauderdale in the 1980s and beyond, slowing real estate activity in Miami and its neighboring towns. Ordinarily, if you see people leaving an area, you think *This local market is fading; people don't want to live here anymore.* But by the 1990s, relatively wealthy Cubans and other Latin Americans had migrated to the Miami area, helping to support property values. As a result, the Miami real estate market survived and flourished.

Here are some clues to use in judging whether a local market is likely to become in greater or lesser demand:

- A change in the reputation and quality of the local school system (e.g., our local high school was ranked as one of the top twenty high schools in the nation by *Newsweek* a few years ago, a major factor in increases in property demand in our community)
- Plans to build, or close, country clubs, pool clubs, tennis clubs, and so on
- Plans for new cultural or other entertainment venues—theaters and restaurants, for example
- Changes in ethnic population groups locating in the local market

Where can you find all of this social, cultural, and educational information? Drive through the area you are interested in; get a sense of the culture and social aspects of the local market. Observe the theaters, restaurants, retail outlets, and so forth. Ask your Realtor about local plans to build country clubs and about the quality of the local school system. You can go to several Web sites to gather additional information about the local school system: NeighborhoodScout.com and Psk12.com (public school ranking) provide information on public elementary, middle, and high schools for every town and city. Morgan Quitno Press also publishes annual city/metro rankings on the quality of education. The U.S. Census Bureau and the American Community Survey provide the most credible data on the percentage of educated households in each town, city, or state. And if such school rankings are not available for a particular neighborhood or town, there are statistics that will help you to judge the quality of a community's education system, from student/teacher ratios to average tax dollars spent per pupil to the number of National Merit Scholars to high school graduation rates and the percentage of students going on to college.

POLITICAL INFLUENCES

Most casual real estate investors do not appreciate the influence of local politics on property values. But I can tell you, the professional investor assuredly does. There is nothing more political than the laws, regulations, and taxes levied on local real estate. From developing land and obtaining site and building permits, to zoning restrictions, local real estate taxes, and local real estate purchase (subsidized) programs, local politics plays a critical role in local real estate. As we've seen, local political decisions on other local market activities like revitalizing the downtown and attracting new businesses are major influences on real estate activity as well.

When my hometown, Long Beach, New York, began deteriorating during the late 1970s and into the 1980s, the town did little to prevent its demise. Property values stayed relatively flat throughout this period. I remember coming back to visit and feeling ashamed of what was happening. When I was growing up there, Long Beach had been a popular beach town—a barrier island in the Atlantic Ocean, attracting thousands of visitors every summer. It had high-quality real estate DNA. But Long Beach had not fully exploited that DNA. Then, in the late 1980s, local government officials decided to revitalize the city's downtown. They hired an old high school friend of mine who had become an architect to draw up the blueprints. Local authorities provided tax incentives for development and to encourage businesses to relocate. The result: years later, a revitalized Long Beach, boasting new shopping facilities, new multifamily developments, and improved landscaping throughout the downtown. My hometown regained its dignity. Vacationing households once again coveted Long Beach in the summer, bringing added revenue to the town's economy. More important, more households desired to live in Long Beach year-round, causing property values to rise throughout the town (even around the railroad tracks).

There are countless examples of local governments making decisions and raising funds to revitalize their towns and cities.

Conversely, you need to be on the lookout for a good intention gone bad. Local governments are not perfect. In the summer of 2006, I gave a speech to a business group in West Palm Beach, Florida. The venue was across from a relatively new downtown convention center. I looked around and saw only one hotel within walking distance. So I asked the obvious question: Without hotels, how can your convention center be successful? I was told that it had taken about eight years for local businesses to convince the local government to vote for and raise funds for the construction of a convention center downtown. After winning the vote, all of the government's focus was on building the convention center. The city ignored the need to build an infrastructure to serve the convention center. Their lack of foresight would come back to haunt them. With only one hotel within walking distance, the convention center gets only local usage. But the success of any convention center is dependent on bringing in conferences and meetings *from outside the town*. Without that base, revenue from hotels, restaurants, tourist sites, and entertainment venues will be limited. My hosts in West Palm Beach told me that by 2010 they expect another hotel to be built close by. If they are right, that should help to open up the convention center to outside organizations and businesses.

The list of political factors that can influence local real estate activity is long and varied. Here are just some of the more important political factors to look for:

- The local government has raised (or lowered), or has plans to raise or lower, local property taxes.
- The local government has raised (or lowered) other real estate taxes, such as transfer taxes.
- Closing costs for financing property have increased or decreased vis-à-vis other communities due to changes in government rules, guidelines, and restrictions.
- Changes in investment property rules favor investors or renters over homeowners.
- Zoning restriction changes affect both residential and commercial building activity.
- Changes in neighborhood restrictions/covenants affect property values.

- Local government housing programs subsidize real estate building and the purchase of property.
- Local government plans to revitalize select areas of the city.
- School-funding decisions lead to an improved school system.
- Transportation-funding decisions lead to an improved transportation system.
- Local governments step up efforts to attract businesses to move to the area.

Chapter Six

WHAT BUD SELIG AND OPRAH HAVE TO DO WITH REAL ESTATE

In the summer of 1997, a nine-year-old boy in our neighborhood named Tommy Sullivan set up a lemonade stand on the weekends, selling a small cup of lemonade with a chocolate-chip cookie for 25 cents. Driving out of the neighborhood one Saturday morning, I stopped my car, rolled down my window, and gave Tommy a quarter in exchange for a cup of lemonade and a chocolate-chip cookie. They tasted awful. It was clear to me that someone in his family—either his mother or father—must have been on a serious diet, because there was no sugar in either the lemonade or the cookie. When my car was out of Tommy's sight, I found a place to throw them out.

Despite that first experience, every Saturday morning I stuck to my routine of driving out of the neighborhood, stopping my car, rolling down my window, and throwing Tommy a quarter. Only, from that point on I passed on the lemonade and cookie. Then deep into the summer, sometime in August, as I followed my routine—stopping my car, rolling down my window, and throwing Tommy a quarter—I heard Tommy yell as I started to drive off: "Mr. Lereah, please come back!" I backed up and rolled down my window and said, "Tommy, I know what you are going to ask. Why am I giving you a quarter and not taking the food?" To my surprise, Tommy said, "No, Mr. Lereah, I just wanted to tell you that I raised the price to 50 cents!"

The lesson here is that there are conventional and unconventional ways of doing or thinking about things. Tommy turned conventional wisdom on its head that day. He raised the price—a donation in my case, even though I got nothing in exchange other than the feeling of goodwill. At various points in history, conventional wisdom held that the world was flat; that Democrats would always rule Congress; that with the unlimited money they have to spend, the New York Yankees would win the World Series every year. Well, conventional wisdom is frequently wrong.

The same is true in the real estate market. Conventional wisdom said that if mortgage rates go up, home sales would go down. And if the economy was experiencing a recession, home sales would drop. The housing market in the past ten years has belied both these adages. Thirty-year mortgage rates rose by over 2 percentage points from 1998 to 2000, but home sales were strong. And the recession of 2001 turned out to be the beginning of five consecutive record years of home sales. My point? There must be more to real estate markets than meets the eye. That is what this chapter is about—the unidentified forces that impact the market. This is not to say that I can explain all unconventional behavior. There are factors and forces out there that might not be easily observable and yet may have an acute impact on real estate sales. But it may take some thinking outside the box to identify these forces.

Let's say you live in the fictional town of Davidson, Idaho. Davidson has always been a sleepy but pleasant town with a hardworking, middle-class population. Property values and property appreciation have been modest. One day, CBS decides to produce a television show in this Idaho town. The show becomes a hit—everyone is talking about it. The increased exposure most assuredly would raise this town's popularity. A town that most people in the country never knew existed is now on everyone's radar. People come to visit, explore, and vacation in the surrounding area. That helps Davidson's local economy, which results in new jobs. Some of those visitors return as residents, filling those new jobs. And all that activity spurs home building and home buying. Existing property values increase.

Let's say Oprah Winfrey decides to devote one of her shows to her favorite towns and Davidson, Idaho, is high on her list. Not only are you filled with pride in your hometown, but now you are part of a community that Oprah has validated as unique and worthy. And it is likely that some of her viewers will follow Oprah's lead. Property values over time would likely rise due to Oprah's interest.

These are what I call unconventional influences—influences that have no direct link to real estate activity but nevertheless impact local activity in a meaningful manner. Because of their indirect nature, you need to learn to identify what is an unconventional factor that will cause real estate values to rise, and what is not. Imagine if you could anticipate the next city to be awarded a Major League Baseball franchise by Bud Selig, the commissioner of baseball (or in a smaller town, a minor league team). The arrival of a Major League Baseball team virtually guarantees increased revenue and interest for the city, creating a very favorable real estate environment.

There are many factors that influence real estate activity that are not traditional. Most of these factors in some fashion affect property values and sales. Let's go over some of them.

SPORTS INFLUENCES

Like it or not, Americans love sports. Professional sports and college athletics can generate substantial revenue for a local economy, energizing real estate activity as well as generating interest in and pride for the local town or city.

The most recent expansion in Major League Baseball was the Washington Nationals in 2005. Approximately 2.7 million fans attended the Washington Nationals games in their first year, generating hundreds of millions in revenue for the city. The added revenue improved the D.C. business environment and created jobs. It is impossible to directly quantify baseball's influence on D.C. property values, but it has clearly had an impact. An improved local economy has always had a positive influence on property values eventually. In a local market, when more jobs are created than homes built, property prices tend to rise.

While a stadium already existed in Washington, RFK Stadium, in which the Nationals will play their first couple of seasons, there are plans to build a $500 million stadium in another area of the city. This will have an enormous impact on that neighborhood's local economy, jobs, commercial activity, retail, and other businesses. And it will eventually push property values upward. Of course, if city taxes are raised to fund construction, Washington taxpayers are indirectly subsidizing those neighborhood homeowners whose property values will rise due to the new stadium. But our intent here is to predict relative property values, not fairness.

Similarly, any midsized metropolitan area that boasts an NFL team is boosted significantly by the team's presence. Just look at what the Packers did for the town of Green Bay, Wisconsin. The NFL effect may not be as significant in large metropolitan areas. The Los Angeles Rams left Los

Angeles over a decade ago, and the team's departure appears to have had no discernible impact on the local L.A. economy or the area's real estate. But midsize cities such as Cincinnati, Pittsburgh, Kansas City, and Denver all enjoy the benefits that an NFL team brings.

In smaller and midsize cities, college football can have a similar impact. Universities steeped in football tradition, such as Notre Dame, the University of Texas, the University of Oklahoma, Ohio State, and Penn State, have had a strong impact on the local economies and real estate markets in South Bend, Indiana; Austin, Texas; Norman, Oklahoma; Columbus, Ohio; and University Park, Pennsylvania.

So it pays to be mindful of the sports impact. I live in the Washington, D.C., area (on the Virginia side). For many years, the Washington Bullets (now the Wizards) played outside of the District of Columbia in Largo, Maryland. Then, a decade ago, Abe Pollin, the owner of the team, built a new arena—the MCI Center (now the Verizon Center)—in downtown D.C. The arena has dramatically transformed that downtown area. Restaurants and retail shops are now plentiful, as are the people to fill them.

Traveling on business to St. Paul, Minnesota, in 2005, I stayed at a hotel right across from a large hockey arena. I asked my hosts (who were local Realtors and mortgage lenders) what impact the NHL hockey team had on the area. Did the arena fill regularly? Without the arena, they insisted, St. Paul would slowly have become dwarfed by its bigger brother, Minneapolis, which had both professional baseball and football teams. It was critical that St. Paul own the professional hockey franchise to keep the town vibrant. The strategy seems to be working.

Of course, most towns and small cities do not have professional sports teams. But in many cases, the sports impact is just as great. It may be an annual tennis tournament, a golf tournament, or a minor league baseball or basketball team that exerts a meaningful influence on the local economy and real estate markets. The lesson here is that there are many sports-related activities and actions that create great real estate investment opportunities.

TECHNOLOGY INFLUENCES

Advances in technology and the increasing role it plays in people's lifestyles are changing the way we work. Let me run through an example—BlackBerrys and laptops.

With e-mail, the Internet, an address book, a calendar, a notepad, and a phone, among many other functions, the typical BlackBerry/laptop combination has become a mobile office for many business travelers. More than twenty years ago, the desktop computer provided people with the capacity to work from home rather than the office. Now people have the capacity to work on the road—in autos, trains, airplanes, ships, and, of course, their hotels. They can work on vacation, during weekends, while traveling to visit family, on holidays, and so on.

What are the implications for the real estate markets? Before mobile technology, businesses that required a great deal of travel by its employees had incentives to locate near large airport hubs that facilitated travel in many directions. Mobile technology has altered the incentives a bit. Businesses and employees are no longer as dependent on major airport hubs. With the ability to carry your office with you, many businesses and workers are willing to live in what they believe to be more livable communities that may not necessarily be located near a major transportation hub. Mobile technology has essentially reduced the opportunity costs of business travel. Because more businesses and employees locate in more diverse communities farther from major airport hubs, employees' airport time may increase by an hour or two to get to where they need to go, but they can continue to work on the way, and with the growth of technology, need to travel less often.

Advances in mobile technology are clear victories for smaller communities that are less accessible to big cities, airports, or other major transportation hubs. This helps to explain in part the rise of smaller metropolitan areas such as Raleigh/Durham, North Carolina; Richmond, Virginia; Reno, Nevada; and the like. So don't assume lack of access to a sizable airport today is the drawback to real estate growth that it would have been in the past.

MEDIA INFLUENCES

As I discussed in the previous chapter, magazines from time to time put out lists ranking metropolitan areas in such categories as crime, education, cost of living, and so on. Just as a town or region near you at the top of the crime list may scare potential buyers away, the reverse is also true. An extremely safe neighborhood is a draw, a plus in assessing future real estate value. The same is true of any number of "attractors" and "detractors." It does not hurt Jupiter Beach, Florida, that the most popular golfer in the world, Tiger Woods, decided to take up residence there in 2005. On the other hand, a media story about a nearby nuclear power plant or toxic waste site may inhibit demand in a particular neighborhood, keeping property values at bay, or the media reporting on a robbery or murder in a neighborhood you are contemplating moving to might make you think twice.

GOVERNMENT INFLUENCES

The government has tremendous influence over our economy and over real estate markets. Perhaps the single most influential government official in terms of the real estate market is the chairman of the Federal Reserve, Ben Bernanke. The chairman chairs the Federal Open Market Committee, which decides the direction of interest rates. Monitoring the Fed's actions will help you to understand what their current position is in the marketplace. Sometimes the Fed raises interest rates (which eventually raises mortgage rates) to combat inflationary pressures. And sometimes the Fed lowers interest rates to energize a slumping economy, which can lower mortgage rates. Either way, Fed policy and behavior are important influences on current and future real estate values.

The Treasury Secretary and Congress, too, play key roles in terms of real estate values, as they determine the deductibility of mortgage interest and property taxes. The Secretary of HUD can influence the quantity and quality of housing-subsidy programs—to help home buyers (increasing demand) or to help home builders (increasing housing supply). Governors, mayors, state legislators, and city councils can also affect taxes, subsidies, and the real estate market. They can have an influence in encouraging larger companies to relocate to their state or city, offering rebates and tax breaks, or underwriting necessary infrastructures such as roads and sewers. Keeping up with local, state, and federal incentives can help you gauge the attractiveness of the real estate market in your area.

SOCIAL INFLUENCES

Did you know that home prices in Delray Beach, Florida, were highly correlated (that is, moved up and down) with the number of restaurants offering early-bird specials? An early-bird special is a discount dinner for seniors eating in the early evening, usually between the hours of 5 and 6 P.M. This sounds like a stretch—and it is. Who would think some seniors/retirees select a place to live based on the number of restaurants offering early-bird specials? I happen to know some: My parents are seniors living in Delray Beach, and like many of their friends, they seek out restaurants offering early-bird specials close by.

Social influences are abundant in local markets. In some markets, religion plays a major role in deciding whether or not to live there. Amish people choose to live in Lancaster County (in Pennsylvania). As lovely a place as it is, Lynchburg, Virginia, as the home of Jerry Falwell and his Liberty University, might be seen as a somewhat awkward home for a Jewish household to settle in. Similarly, it would be equally awkward for a Christian household to move into a Hasidic (Jewish) community in New York City. Of course, there can be a downside to this. A local market that is heavily influenced by a particular sect or religion may limit the potential pool of property buyers, placing the market at a competitive disadvantage compared with other local property markets.

The impact of ethnic groups on local property markets is similar. Many metropolitan areas across the nation boast a Chinatown or Little Italy community—San Francisco, New York City, Baltimore, and Washington, D.C., to name a few. But these communities limit the potential pool of buyers, thereby limiting the rise in property values over time. One could argue that because of the ethnicity, these communities have a more stable and steady demand for home buying because people with similar ethnic backgrounds are attracted to live there. In some cases, that is true. But in general, these areas are held back compared to other neighborhoods when it comes to property values.

Another social factor to keep in mind is the NIMBY effect—the "not in my backyard" effect—on property values. For example, in many areas, multifamily rental, low-cost, or affordable housing projects are rejected by existing residents (and their local county governments). They understand the need for such housing supply to attract new households to their communities (thereby increasing the demand for housing as well as property values). And most civic-minded people are in favor of providing affordable housing options to public servants (such as police and teachers) who serve their neighborhoods. But the NIMBY effect says in essence that homeowners don't want such projects built across the street from their own homes. And when they are, property values often decline.

OTHER INFLUENCES

The list of influences—conventional and unconventional—on the real estate markets is never-ending. But there is one category of influences that, because of their sheer scale, I want to address in the next chapter. They are called megatrends. These are factors or trends that affect real estate activity and values over the long term. Their impact is lasting and can have a significant impact on property values for years to come.

Chapter Seven

BABY BOOMERS AND OTHER MEGATRENDS

Imagine if Orville and Wilbur Wright had relied only on their common sense instead of their imagination. What would our nation's cities—and real estate markets—look like if there had been no airplane? Would Las Vegas, Phoenix, and Charlotte, North Carolina, be the major metropolitan areas that they are today? I doubt it.

What if the elevator had never been invented? Better yet, what if Henry Bessemer had never invented the process for mass-producing steel inexpensively, essential to the development of skyscrapers? Without elevators and inexpensive steel, New York City would not be the Big Apple. In fact, the island of Manhattan would be quite different today. Without tall buildings, Manhattan could not possibly house 1.57 million residents (according to the 2000 U.S. Census) on what essentially amounts to twenty-three square miles of land. Manhattan is the most densely populated city in the nation, boasting 66,940 people per square mile. It is difficult to imagine Manhattan without the Empire State Building, the Chrysler Building, Wall Street, Trump Tower, and—until that fateful day of September 11, 2001—the World Trade Center.

Although the inventions of the airplane, elevator, and inexpensive steel may not be uppermost in your mind when purchasing a property, if you think about them now it is obvious how much a local real estate market is dependent upon them. Flying made it possible for people to move more efficiently around the country. Elevators and steel made the building of modern cities a reality. Such *megatrends* are widespread and have huge impact on both economic and real estate activity as well as changing people's lives. An invention, a war, a population shift, and a change in weather patterns all qualify as megatrends. Megatrends can structurally change a local market's DNA. They can also directly influence both the demand for and supply of property.

Here are some of the most notable innovations that have resulted in megatrends with regard to travel and communication throughout history:

- Wheel
- Horse
- Boat
- Telegraph
- Telephone
- Train
- Automobile
- Airplane
- Computer
- Internet
- Cell phone
- BlackBerrys and other multifunctional communication devices

The invention of the wheel permitted households to travel, as well as allowing the transport of heavy loads, facilitating construction of buildings and homes. You can imagine how the early property markets in ancient times were impacted by the wheel. The domestication of horses for transportation, as well as more recent technological inventions such as trains, automobiles, and airplanes, have all impacted a location's DNA. The ability to move more easily or relocate one's residence has attracted households to areas other than the one in which we are born. This, too, has a major impact on a local real estate market.

Communications technology, too, has had significant impact on real estate markets. The telegraph and telephone facilitated the breakup of extended families living together in the same neighborhood. With advanced communication, friends and family could reside in faraway places and still be able to communicate with one another frequently. Today's most advanced communication tools—computers, the Internet, cell phones, and BlackBerrys—dominate household and business communication. This dominance has changed our lifestyles, the way we interact, the way we work, and the way we live.

Advances in communication have provided many households with opportunities to work from their homes. Because of that technology, households can live where they want to—in areas with more favorable weather, closer to the water, in more rural rather than urban surroundings—instead of having to live where they work. It has provided opportunities for people to run their own start-up businesses, offering flexibility on location.

Identifying and understanding megatrends that affect real estate activity is the final piece of the real estate puzzle. Megatrends are long-term developments or movements in the nation that eventually impact local real estate activity. This chapter should give you a clearer picture of a local real estate market's current and future outlook, helping you become a smarter buyer.

A LONG-TERM PERSPECTIVE

Imagine that you are 10,000 feet in the air, looking down to identify large new movements in our nation's activities. Are there new technologies that may eventually alter household or business behavior? Are population patterns shifting? Have weather patterns changed the way people live? What will our nation look like in, say, 2050? These compelling questions have equally compelling answers. When I look out at America's landscape, I see a number of forces or trends developing that could significantly impact the way we live and thus impact future real estate activity. These forces are like the proverbial snowball rolling downhill, gathering snow as it goes. Eventually, it can become a significant factor in our thinking.

Many trends affect real estate activity today and will do so in the future. I will cover a few of them here. But I recommend that you read other books and research dedicated to megatrends and the future in order to get a more complete analysis. For our purposes, I will limit the discussion to what I believe are the top six megatrends affecting household lifestyles and the real estate industry.

- The baby boomer generation
- The aging of America
- The changing face of America
- Nanotechnology

- Terrorism
- Global warming

THE BABY BOOMER GENERATION

Imagine taking 10 million American men in the prime years of their lives and sending them overseas to spend four long years to fight a war. Then imagine these same men returning to the United States and their home communities, populated by a large number of impatient single young women. The result? About 78 million baby boomers!

The baby boom generation is defined as those people born between the years 1946 and 1964. The most interesting and relevant fact about boomers is that they tend to do things *together* in a big way. When the boomer generation decided that golf was not just for older gentlemen wearing plaid pants and green blazers, golf became big business. Millions of boomers spent millions of dollars on titanium golf clubs, hoping to hit the ball farther and straighter. When baby boomers found that "over-the-air" reception on three television channels was too fuzzy, cable television was born—first as a means of generating a clearer picture, then eventually to provide a wider variety of programming. Remember when all we needed on our feet was a good pair of sneakers? As baby boomers began to age and put on that middle-age spread, health-related activities became more popular—and so did the shoes for each of those activities. Now there are shoes for running, shoes for walking, shoes for the squash court, and cross-training shoes for the gym.

Everything boomers do as a group has a significant impact on the economy, the financial markets, and, of course, the real estate markets. Yes, there are plenty of other population groups aside from boomers—retirees, the baby bust, immigrants, and echo boomers. Focusing on the life-cycle trends for *all* of these population groups will help you better understand trends in real estate values. But baby boomers are the largest single generational group in history, and they possess the greatest wealth. It is the boomer generation that qualifies as a megatrend and thus is the focus of our attention.

You no doubt saw the impact of the baby boom on the housing market in the 1990s. During that decade, boomers entered their peak earning years, and home sales exploded. There are 78 million boomers, and they fueled the purchase of larger homes (trade-up buying), second homes (vacation and/or investment), and condominiums (downsizing). They are still driving the demand for all types of homes. Following the footprints of the boomers will help identify the active real estate markets over the next ten years. Let's take a look at some of those footprints.

Boomers will soon become empty-nesters and/or be retiring. As a consequence, cash-rich boomers are purchasing more second homes. Empty-nester boomers—those whose children have left home—are downsizing and buying smaller homes, including condominiums. Retiree boomers are moving to retirement locations. It is no coincidence that over the past ten years, property values climbed substantially in resort and retirement locations such as Florida, Arizona, and Nevada, during the same period when sales and prices of condominiums soared.

There is a great geographical and financial transition taking place in America. Millions of boomers are physically relocating. Perhaps more important, they are transferring large amounts of wealth from the Northeastern and Midwestern regions of the United States to the Southern and Western regions of the country. A large amount of this wealth is being invested in real estate. Follow the boomers' footprints and you will find rising and healthy property values.

Here are some observations that I have picked up about boomers over the past several years. (These observations are based in part on the 2006 survey of baby boomers conducted by the National Association of Realtors and Harris Interactive.) Some of this information is fact, some anecdotal, but it all can be used as a guide about boomers and their tastes and lifestyles, providing information about the type of real estate they own and desire.

- In 2011, the first wave of America's 78 million boomers will turn sixty-five.
- Boomers are far more ethnically diverse than are prior generations.
- Less than 75 percent of boomers are white, while nearly 90 percent of Americans born before 1946 are white.
- Boomers are more highly educated than are their predecessor generations: 27 percent of boomers have college degrees, compared with 12 percent of today's older Americans. More than 60 percent of boomers have high school diplomas, compared with only 44 percent of older groups.

- Boomers are less interested than older groups in politics, government, international news, religion, and business.
- Boomers are more interested in consumer information, sports, and technology than are preceding generations.
- Boomers, as a group, view their old age or retirement years as a time of lifestyle transition rather than as a termination of employment.
- Many boomers intend to keep working after retirement but not in their primary occupations. Eight of ten boomers said they will continue to work during their retirement years.
- Boomers may not be prepared for retirement; they will have a difficult time balancing the financial needs of retirement on traditional Social Security, pensions, and savings.
- Studies show that boomers are not saving enough to finance the lifestyle they envision in retirement.
- Some boomers are experiencing the sandwich-generation phenomenon—middle-aged people struggling to raise children and take care of their aging parents at the same time.
- As boomers age, a greater number of people will want to do community service and volunteer work.

So what will be the boomer impact on relative property values and activity across the nation for, say, the next ten years in America? The answer is: a great deal. Boomers have already made a dramatic impact on property values and sales during the 1990s and the first half of the first decade of the twenty-first century. Because there are so many boomers, everything they do as a group is highly influential. Today's boomers are divided into several subgroups: trade-up boomers, empty-nester boomers, retiring boomers, and vacation-property boomers. Because there are so many households in each of these groups, each group's behavior will substantially impact future real estate activity.

TRADE-UP BOOMERS

Trade-up boomers are in their peak income years. Most of them are already homeowners and have experienced substantial equity gains on their primary residences. Thus, they have the financial wherewithal to trade up to larger homes. Boomer trade-up buying promises to exert upward pressure on larger and higher-priced homes over the next five years—that is, the prices and values of these homes are likely to increase. But those property values will not rise as much in some of the already high-cost markets, such as San Diego and Los Angeles. It is important to note that beginning in 2011 some retiring boomers will be selling their homes, exerting offsetting downward pressure on property values.

VACATION-PROPERTY BOOMERS

Boomers have the greatest appetite for purchasing vacation/resort properties. Almost 13 percent of all home purchases in 2005 were vacation-home purchases, and boomers were a major force behind that second-home-buying activity. Cash-rich boomers are expected to continue to purchase high-end properties in popular resort destinations. Moderate-income boomers are expected to avoid overpriced and expensive resort locations and purchase modest vacation properties in locations closer to their primary residences.

EMPTY-NESTER BOOMERS

There is an increasing number of boomer households with children having left home that are looking to downsize their primary residence. The need for smaller properties rather than the boomer "McMansions" is readily apparent. Condominiums and townhomes are filling this need.

RETIREE BOOMERS

With every year there is an increasing percentage of boomers close to retirement age. The first boomers will reach the official retirement age of sixty-five in 2011. However, there are a number of boomers between the ages of fifty-five and sixty who have already taken early retirement. They are already exerting upward pressure on retirement-home values. Look for retiring boomers to dominate the home-buying marketplace during the next ten to fifteen years.

BOOMERS AND GEOGRAPHY

The forces I see are these: Cash-rich boomers from the Northeast who have substantial equity gains from their primary residence are likely to purchase retirement homes in the southern Florida and Arizona markets. They are the boomers who can still afford to purchase in those markets that are becoming unaffordable to most other households. Boomers from the Midwest who do not have as much primary-residence equity (because they did not experience the real estate boom) will be forced to look outside of southern Florida or purchase a retirement home close to their primary residence. If they go outside of Florida, there are a number of likely destinations. First, they will seek destinations in other warm-weather states: northern Florida, Georgia, North and South Carolina, Tennessee, Nevada, and New Mexico. We find that these boomers are becoming increasingly attracted to the Great Smoky Mountains in Tennessee, Georgia, and the Carolinas. Boomers from California are leaving the nation's highest-cost state and heading to nearby low-tax states such as Arizona, Nevada, and Washington.

BOOMERS MAY HAVE THE LAST SAY

As much as the baby boomer generation drove home sales and home values upward in many locations across the nation during the past two decades, it may also leave the housing markets with a thud. Aging boomers could cause a big housing slump in home prices. Remember, the first of 78 million boomers become eligible for Social Security in 2008, turning sixty-two. Most of them are homeowners—and many of them will presumably want to sell their homes and downsize or move to a retirement location, extracting some cash for retirement in the process. Theoretically, that implies a glut of houses for sale, particularly in the Northeast and Midwest regions of the nation, which would surely mitigate an upturn in prices and could drive them ever lower.

The trillion-dollar question is who would purchase the boomer homes? There will be many homes for sale at once, and fewer buyers. The generation after the boomers was called the bust generation, and for good reason—there were only 40 million of them. There are just not enough busters to purchase all of the boomer homes. There was record immigration in the 1970s and 1980s because of the boomer-bust void. But immigrant families take longer before they can fully participate in the home-buying marketplace. The result from these dynamics is downward pressure on relatively high-priced homes (the boomer homes for sale) and upward pressure on lower-priced homes (homes that boomers and other population groups will want to purchase). Economists agree that the retirement of the baby boom generation will influence housing prices, but they differ over how powerful the effect will be. What is clear is that baby boomers affect real estate values—driving them up when they are purchasing homes by trading up or acquiring second homes and down when they are selling homes into retirement. If you happen to be a boomer, my advice is that you make sure that you are not among the last boomers to sell your home and retire—if you do, it will certainly be at a lower price than your friends will get if they sell before you.

THE AGING OF AMERICA

The human life span has been a fascination of ours since the beginning of our species. During the past several centuries, due to improved health habits, medical advancements, and better nutrition, life expectancy has trended up. But human longevity has taken a leap forward during the past several decades and promises to continue to improve markedly due to technology advances such as organ transplants, nanotechnology (see next section), and laser surgery.

What you may not realize is that human longevity has a direct impact on real estate activity. The longer a person lives, the longer that person needs to have a place to live. If 1,000 retired homeowners live five years longer due to new medical technology, then those 1,000 people are living in homes that are not available to others for purchase. That reduces the inventory of homes available for sale. And as people live longer, the over-sixty-five-year-old group—seniors—increases in size as well. This group promises to influence the types of residential homes, retirement homes, vacation homes, and investment properties that will be in demand over the next several decades.

Japan has one of the highest life expectancies in the world, 81.15 years (2005 estimate). The United States life expectancy is 77.7 years (2005 estimate).* The Census Bureau predicts that life expectancy in the United States will be in the mid-eighties by the year 2050. It also predicts that America will have 5.3 million people aged over 100 in 2100. Here are some interesting statistics on longevity in the United States:

---

* These estimates and most of the longevity data that follow are taken from two studies: "The Future of Old-Age Longevity: Competitive Pricing of Mortality Contingent Claims," by Charles Mullin and Tomas Philipson, issued by the National Bureau of Economic Research, Inc., 1997; and "How Long Will Older Americans Live?" by William Harms, *The University of Chicago Chronicle*, 1997.

- In the late 1700s, in the United States, life expectancy was 23 years.
- Life expectancy in the United States in 1900 was 47.3 years.
- Life expectancy in the United States in 1950 was 68.2 years.
- Life expectancy in the United States in 2005 was 77.7 years.
- According to a 2003 General Electric study, an individual who reaches age 65 has a life expectancy of age 85.
- By 2030, 20 percent of the American population will be 65 years old or older; the size of our 65-and-over population is expected to double over the next 30 years.
- The fastest-growing population segment is people over 85.

Most households enter retirement at age sixty-five and downsize their home by purchasing a retirement home. According to the U.S. Census Bureau, the number of persons in the sixty-five-plus age group is projected to be 39.7 million in 2010 (compared to 35 million in 2000). That projection jumps to 53.7 million in 2020 and leaps to 70.3 million by 2030.

How will these people fund their retirement? They will live, on average, twenty years in retirement, a great deal longer than they expected to (according to most retirement surveys). Most will not have the available funds to generate the income to which they were accustomed when they worked. Generally, retirement funds should produce about 75 percent of your working income. Stretching a person's retirement savings to fund twenty years in retirement when you've saved enough to fund, let's say, ten to fifteen years places a heavy financial burden on you and your family. As a result, many retirees in their twilight years will be motivated to seek more affordable (less costly) housing to ease their financial burden. Affordable retirement communities will become more attractive than high-priced communities to these retirees. This may bode well for the smaller and lesser-known retirement locations in northern Florida, Oregon, New Mexico, Utah, the Carolinas, Georgia, and Alabama. It does not look as favorable for the more established and higher-priced retirement communities in southern Florida, Arizona, and Nevada.

- Immigrants who come to the United States live an average of three years longer than people born in the United States.

That statistic may raise eyebrows, but nevertheless it is true. Immigrants are less likely to eat in fast-food restaurants and smoke. Healthier diet and not smoking add to their longevity. The United States experienced record immigration in the 1970s, 1980s, and 1990s. That suggests that there will be a relatively large number of immigrant retirees during the next ten to twenty years.

The housing behavior and tastes of immigrants will be crucial to evaluating real estate markets in the coming years, as immigrants account for a disproportionate share of the retiree population as retirees age into their twilight years. Where will these older immigrants live in their final years? Some will move to the usual retirement destinations. But others are expected to cling to their ethnic culture and families, motivating them to retire near their primary residence to be close to their children. This promises to provide a healthy demand for smaller retirement homes/condos in metropolitan areas that house large shares of immigrant groups. The Los Angeles and the Miami metro areas both come to mind, as their populations experience a sizable immigration growth.

- In 1990, women accounted for 60 percent of the population age sixty-five or older; by 1996, that share had declined to 59 percent. This trend is expected to continue throughout this century.

Women have been blessed with better longevity compared to men as long as statistics have been kept. This is due to a variety of factors: Men die in more accidents than do women, men smoke more than women, and men are more often killed in homicides than are women. But the trend is reversing. The number of men over sixty-five years old is likely to increase over the next few decades. The increasing number of men in the seniors' housing market could affect what type of retirement homes are developed and purchased. Men have decidedly different tastes than women. They will likely seek different amenities than women in their senior years. One example is the explosion in golf course communities over the past ten years.

The Internet has had a dramatic impact on the real estate markets, providing some households with the freedom to locate wherever they want to rather than having to live close to where they work. This same freedom has now been bequeathed upon retirees and seniors, thanks to their ability to communicate by e-mail. Retirees and seniors m be more inclined to select locations that they *prefer* rather than those that are convenient for their children to stop by. Again, this suggests that we need to pay extra attention to the housing tastes and needs of the retiree and senior population groups.

• Retirees and seniors favor locations with easy access to quality medical facilities.

As longevity lengthens, more and more seniors will need acute health care. Geriatric medical care is crucial to aging seniors, and they will seek locations that offer these services. Local real estate markets that will be attractive to them are those that offer accessible, quality geriatric medical care. Phoenix, West Palm Beach, and Palm Springs, for example, already possess a more than adequate amount of senior medical services.

• More retirees will want to work beyond traditional retirement age.

We know from surveys (e.g., the 2006 National Association of Realtors Boomer Survey) that aging baby boomers want to work well beyond the traditional retirement age of sixty-five. They may take a different job from the one they had before retirement, or in a different location. But they want to work and earn income to supplement their retirement accounts (which may be insufficient if they live longer than they anticipated). Some of these households will postpone their retirement and their move to permanent retirement locations.

A good indicator of which states are likely to become popular retirement destinations is the growth rates of the sixty-five-plus population group during the past ten years. According to the U.S. Census Bureau, Nevada posted the highest percent increase in the sixty-five-plus population group from 1990 to 2000. Alaska was second, followed by Arizona, New Mexico, and Hawaii. Florida did not make the list, but that is somewhat misleading, since Florida has the largest concentration of sixty-five-plus people. It's simply not growing as fast.

PERCENT INCREASE IN 65+ POPULATION FROM 1990 TO 2000

State	% Increase
Nevada	71.5
Alaska	59.6
Arizona	39.5
New Mexico	30.1
Hawaii	28.5
Utah	26.9
Colorado	26.3
Delaware	26.0
U.S. Average	12.0

Source: U.S. Census Bureau

THE CHANGING FACE OF AMERICA

Over a century ago, the United States was described as a "melting pot" because so many different ethnic groups (primarily from Europe, and primarily white) immigrated to our shores, learned our language, found jobs, and became U.S. citizens. A century later, record immigration again has engulfed the United States, but with a different twist. These new immigrants are primarily from different racial and ethnic groups than their melting-pot predecessors. Today's America is changing its face, and the changing face of America has enormous implications for the way we live and work.

The faces of America are primarily white, Hispanic, African-American, Asian, and American Indian. In 1970, minority groups comprised just 16 percent of the population. By 1998, the share of minorities had increased to 27 percent. By 2004, it rose to 32 percent. The Bureau of the Census projects that these groups will account for almost half of the U.S. population by 2050. The rapid ascent of minority groups is based on continued immigration and higher fertility rates among these minority groups relative to non-Hispanic whites.

Record immigration is the primary reason for the dramatic growth in our minority population. The increase in immigration by decade is revealing:

IMMIGRATION TO THE UNITED STATES BY DECADE

	Number of Immigrants
1950–60	2,500,000
1960–70	3,300,000
1970–80	4,400,000
1980–90	7,300,000
1990–2000	9,300,000
2000–2004	5,300,000 (est)

Source: Immigration and Naturalization Service

The United States experienced record immigration in the 1970s, 1980s, and 1990s, and the first decade of the twenty-first century is likely to post another immigration record. In 2003, the contribution from immigrants to the U.S. population gain was 45 percent. What does this mean for our nation's real estate markets?

To begin with, the changing face of America differs across and within regions of the country. It is important to pay attention to the *geographical distribution* of racial/ethnic groups. According to 1995 Census Bureau projections, the West region has the highest concentration of minorities (36 percent), followed by the South region (30 percent), the Northeast (23 percent), and the Midwest region (15 percent). A cursory glance shows that African-Americans are most likely to live in the South and Northeast, while Asians and Hispanics are most likely to live in the West. Digging deeper, racial composition differs among cities, suburbs, and rural locations. Hispanics, African-Americans, and Asians are more likely than whites to live in central cities.

Moreover, the top immigration destinations—states that attract minorities—are California, New York, Texas, Florida, Illinois, New Jersey, and Georgia. But the list is quite different if we look only at population gain where more than half of a state's gain comes from immigrants. That list is led by California, Connecticut, Washington, D.C., Illinois, Iowa, Kansas, and Massachusetts.

TOP IMMIGRATION DESTINATIONS BY STATE (2003)

State	Number of Immigrants
California	288,051
New York	136,185
Texas	135,010
Florida	107,303
Illinois	66,911
New Jersey	59,067
Georgia	38,914
U.S. Total	1,290,000

Source: Immigration and Naturalization Service and U.S. Census Bureau

STATES WITH MORE THAN HALF OF POPULATION GAIN COMING FROM IMMIGRANTS (2003)

California	Michigan
Connecticut	New Jersey
Washington, D.C.	New York
Illinois	North Dakota
Iowa	Ohio
Kansas	Pennsylvania
Massachusetts	West Virginia

Source: U.S. Census

As our nation's face changes over the next several decades, real estate markets, too, will feel the impact. The Hispanic and Asian population groups will continue to have the greatest impact on our real estate markets. Their growth rates dwarf those of African-Americans and whites. The increased immigration of Asians and Hispanics over the past several decades is largely the result of changes in immigration policy. The 1965 Immigration Act ended the system of national-origin quotas that had previously restricted immigration from non-European countries. The Immigration Reform and Control Act of 1986 also contributed to the increase in the documented Asian and Hispanic populations by legalizing a large number of undocumented immigrants. The number of Hispanics in the United States more than doubled between 1980 and 2000, accounting for 40 percent of the growth in the country's population during that period. And by 2003, the U.S. Census Bureau designated Hispanics as the nation's largest minority group, an amazing event given that in 1980 the Hispanic population was only slightly more than half the size of the African-American population.

MINORITY SHARES OF U.S. POPULATION

Group	1990	2000	Change	% Change
U.S. Population	248,709,873	281,421,906	32,712,033	13.2
Hispanic	22,354,059	35,305,818	12,951,759	57.9
African-American	29,216,293	33,947,837	4,731,544	16.2
Asian	6,968,359	10,476,678	3,508,319	50.3
American Indian	1,793,773	2,068,883	275,110	15.3
White	188,128,296	194,552,774	6,424,478	3.4

Source: Estimates by Rogellio Saenz, Russell Sage Foundation, and Population Reference Bureau based on U.S. Census Bureau 1990 population statistics.

As you can see, while the U.S. population grew by 13.2 percent during the 1990-to-2000 period, the Hispanic and Asian population groups registered remarkable 57.9 and 50.3 percent growth rates, respectively.

POPULATION PERCENTAGES IN 2000 VERSUS PROJECTED PERCENTAGES IN 2050

Population Group	2000 Share of Population (%)	2050 Share of Population (%)
White	68	51
Hispanic	13	24
African-American	12	12
Asian	4	8
Other	3	5

One key to successful real estate purchasing is to follow the footsteps of the immigrant population groups. It is well known that immigrant homeownership rates rise over time—the longer they reside in America, the more likely they are to purchase homes. For the first five years, their impact on housing activity is minimal; only 15 percent own homes. But if you follow the foreign-born population over a long period of time, home-ownership rates rise considerably. For example, immigrants who came to America in the 1970s now have a 69 percent homeownership rate—virtually equal to the national homeownership rate as a whole.

IMMIGRANT HOMEOWNERSHIP RATE OVER TIME

Number of Years Residing in U.S.	Homeownership Rate (%)
5 or less	15
6–10	27
11–15	36
16–20	47
21–25	58
26–30	60
31–35	69
36–40	72
More than 40	79

Source: U.S. Census

Immigrants, and particularly Latinos, will also partially determine which local business will be successful, the type of restaurants that will be patronized, the potential number of school-age children, the quality of education, and the type and number of religious institutions located in that local market.

NANOTECHNOLOGY

The word *nanotechnology* comes from the Greek prefix *nano* and was defined and coined by Tokyo Science University professor Norio Taniguchi in 1974. As a measure, a nanometer is one-billionth of a meter, about the diameter of ten atoms placed side by side. To put the size of a nanometer in proper context, consider that a human hair is approximately 70,000 to 80,000 nanometers thick. Nanotechnology is about building things *one atom at a time*, and in doing so constructing devices with unprecedented capabilities.

The potential for nanotechnology applications and products is inspiring, to say the least. Most scientists hope that its applications will eventually cure cancer and replace fossil fuels, two of today's greatest challenges. Yet these achievements may be dwarfed by what may lie ahead. Some scientists envision an army of nano medical robots that will be able to cure most known diseases and meaningfully extend human life. The consensus among nano scientists is that nanotechnology will likely become the core technology underlying twenty-first-century medicine. Some nanotechnology-manufactured products exist today; they range from tennis rackets and golf balls to foot warmers and skin-care products.

With such a bold prediction, how could we exclude nanotechnology from our list of the great megatrends affecting real estate activity? Although there is an awkward gap between nanotechnology and real estate activity, it's hard to deny the enormous impact nanotechnology will have on our lives in the future.

The potential of nanotechnology's reach is best summed up by Dr. Ralph Merkle, Distinguished Professor of Computing at Georgia Tech College of Computing.

> *Nanotechonology will let us economically arrange atoms in most of the ways permitted by physical law. Computers will be orders of magnitude more powerful, materials will be remarkably light and strong, medical technology will be able to heal and cure in cases that today would be abandoned as completely hopeless, the environment will be restored—in short, many of the material dreams of humanity can be fulfilled.**

Other nano scientists are equally enthusiastic and bold with their predictions. Steve Jurvetson, Managing Director of Draper Fisher Jurvetson, says:

> *Nanotech is the next great technology wave, the next phase of Moore's Law, and the nexus of scientific innovation that revolutionizes most*

---

* "Why Should You Care about Nanotechnology?" 2004, Georgia Tech, Atlanta, Georgia.

industries and indirectly affects the fabric of society. Historians will look back on the upcoming epoch with no less portent than the Industrial Revolution.

There is a long and varied list of potential applications of nanotechnology. Immediate uses include medicine, diagnostics, drug delivery, tissue engineering, energy applications, chemistry, consumer goods, cosmetics, foods, optics, textiles, and sports equipment. Nanotechnology's impact on property values will be indirect but strong and permanent. Here are some educated guesses as to its impact:

• It will change the way households commute to work and will influence where people live. Just like laptops and BlackBerrys, nanotechnology promises to generate a menu of products that will improve communication, increasing telecommuting and stay-at-home businesses in the years ahead.

• The greatest impact on real estate markets is where the nanotechnology businesses locate, exerting direct influences on relative property values.

• It will positively impact the creation of jobs, household migration, and local economic activity, all of which will influence local real estate activity.

TERRORISM

It is unfortunate that in today's world, terrorism is one of the six megatrends that have the potential to impact lifestyles, the economy, and real estate activity in the years ahead. The term *terrorism* comes from the Latin verb *terrere*—to cause to tremble. Terrorists use or threaten to use violence in order to create fear and disruption to achieve specific political, religious, ideological, or personal ends. The targets of terrorist attacks typically are not the individuals who are killed, injured, or taken hostage, but rather the societies to which these individuals belong.

According to the U.S. State Department, between 1985 and 2003 there were more than 4,300 deaths attributed to terrorism. Many of these deaths resulted from the September 11, 2001, attacks (about

3,000) and from suicide bombings in Chechnya, Iraq, India, and Israel (state terrorism is not included in these numbers). Notable terrorist acts include the 1985 Air India jet; Pan Am Flight 103 over Scotland in 1988; the 1993 Mumbai (formerly Bombay) bombings; the 1995 Oklahoma City bombing; the 1996 Centennial Olympic Park bombing in Atlanta; the 1998 Omagh bombing in Northern Ireland; the 2000 USS *Cole* bombing; the 2001 attack on the Indian Parliament; the September 11, 2001, attacks in New York and Washington, D.C.; the 2002 Passover massacre in Netanya, Israel; the 2002 Bali bombing; the 2004 Madrid attacks; the 2005 subway bombings in London; and the second Bali bombing in 2005.

In the wake of September 11, 2001, economic activity came to a virtual halt. Stoppages in airline travel, financial services, local businesses, and so on inflicted substantial damage to our nation's economic output.

How does the threat of terrorism influence future property values and real estate activity? I believe the effects are plentiful and long-lasting. The four major effects of terrorism on real estate activity are:

- Shaken consumer confidence
- Negative industry and regional impact
- A move to real estate from the stock market, as properties become a safe financial haven
- A move to safe real estate markets

SHAKEN CONSUMER CONFIDENCE

Consumer confidence was shattered within hours of the 9/11 attacks. The immediate impact on real estate markets on that day and the ensuing days was a halt in most real estate brokerage activity. Potential home buyers appeared not to have the energy or desire to shop for a home. Some sellers chose to take their homes off the market. On or about the fourth day, real estate activity on behalf of both buyers and sellers started to recover some momentum, but it remained below pre–September 11 levels. According to surveys conducted by the National Association of Realtors, housing activity throughout the nation plummeted 50 to 70 percent the week of the attack. Nationally, activity was still down 10 percent during the second week. But in the areas most directly affected—New York

City and Washington, D.C.—real estate business was down over 20 percent. By the third week, national sales and listing volume rebounded to almost 90 percent of pre–September 11 levels. Regional markets like Atlanta, Chicago, Las Vegas, Orlando, New York City, and Seattle were hard hit by large corporate layoffs due to the attacks.

The threat of a terrorist act places consumers in a state of high anxiety. Durable goods and large financial purchases like homes are hit hardest under this environment. Unfortunately, the fear of terrorism is now permanently ingrained in our consciousness.

INDUSTRY AND REGIONAL IMPACT

A number of industries can be crippled or partially damaged by terrorist attacks. They include the air transport, aircraft and parts, and tourism and travel industries.

- Northeast: The financial services and securities industries could be severely harmed in the event of new terrorist attacks on or around New York City. Connecticut's economy would also suffer, as the insurance industry is negatively impacted due to larger-than-expected payouts from disaster/terrorist insurance.
- Midwest: The aircraft industry could be hit particularly hard. There are aircraft and parts companies located in Kansas, Ohio, Iowa, Nebraska, Minnesota, Wisconsin, and Illinois.
- South: The airline industry—Atlanta, home of Delta Airlines—would be hard hit. Fort Worth, Texas, houses AMR Corporation; Miami houses both American Airlines and United Airlines. In addition, a slowdown in travel would hit the tourism and travel industry hard. This would hurt Orlando, Florida, and other tourist meccas (amusement and recreational services, hotels, motels, and restaurants).
- West: The airline industry centers again would be hard hit. Denver, Colorado, is a hub for United Airlines; Honolulu is a hub for Hawaiian Airlines and Aloha Airlines; Phoenix, Arizona, is a hub for America West; San Francisco is a hub for United Airlines and American Airlines; and Seattle is a hub for Alaska Air. Much of the aircraft and parts industry is based in Los Angeles and Seattle. And the tourism centers, such as Las Vegas, Southern and Northern California, and Honolulu, would be severely impacted.

PROPERTIES BECOME A SAFE FINANCIAL HAVEN

The threat of terrorism, in an awkward way, can have a positive influence on real estate activity. Two months after the 9/11 attacks, households and investors turned to property as a safe haven for their financial assets. The uncertainty and threats of terrorism created an increased desire among people to put their money into something tangible—something they could feel and touch. Something similar happened in the 1960s, 1970s, and 1980s, when investors across the globe turned to gold as a safe haven for funds when an international crisis arose. Property assumes this role when we are haunted by terrorism. Billions of dollars flowed out of the equities markets and into real estate between 2001 and 2005. With the real estate boom cooling in 2006, the flow of funds has ebbed. But our renewed interest in the real estate markets has not gone away. Real estate has become a viable alternative investment to stocks and bonds, particularly in times of uncertainty.

A MOVE TO SAFE REAL ESTATE MARKETS

Which local property markets are viewed as safe places to live, and which markets are viewed as unsafe markets? Some households refuse to live in a high-rise building in a large metro, like New York City or Chicago. They still see images of the collapse of the twin towers of the World Trade Center. Major cities with large, dense populations, with subway systems, large tunnels, or bridges are ideal targets for a terrorist attack. Some households will inevitably shy away from living in such locations.

IF THERE IS ANOTHER ATTACK ON U.S. SOIL?

From an economic perspective, the impact of additional attacks will go much further than the actual destruction of buildings. The tragic event that took place on September 11, 2001, has changed the world forever. Not many actions can equal a major terrorist attack on our soil. Pearl Harbor is the only comparable example. But very little economic data (and no housing data) were available in 1941 that would allow us to measure the economic impact from that calamity.

America may be entering a new era with a new set of priorities. A prolonged war against terrorism may change our way of life politically, socially, and economically. Americans have lived comfortably off the peace dividend (created by the fall of the Soviet Union in 1990) for the past fifteen years. Defense spending has fallen over 40 percent as a percentage of GDP since 1990. That trend is expected to be reversed over the next ten years.

As America enters a new political and economic environment, so will local real estate markets. In the event of another terrorist act, our resources will be redirected even more to military operations, as well as rebuilding critical industries such as the airline and insurance industries. Free trade could become a thing of the past. Immigration restrictions could tighten an already tight U.S. labor market, particularly affecting the West (California), the Southwest (Texas), and the Northeast (New York).

GLOBAL WARMING

When Hurricane Katrina devastated New Orleans and other areas of the Gulf Coast, former Vice President Al Gore and others took that opportunity to attribute the unusual weather patterns to global warming. This has become a hotly contested debate within the United States.

Global warming refers to the observed increase in the average temperature of the earth's atmosphere and oceans. The earth's average atmospheric temperature rose 1.1 (±0.4) degrees Fahrenheit in the twentieth century, significantly higher than in past centuries. And based on estimates by NASA's Goddard Institute for Space Studies, 2005 was the warmest year on record since reliable instrumental measurements became available in the late 1800s. The debate among scientists is how much of that temperature change is due to human activities. Most scientists believe that increased amounts of carbon dioxide and other greenhouse gases are the primary causes of global warming. Greenhouse gases released by the burning of fossil fuels, the cutting down of rain forests, and the clearing of land and agriculture are all human-induced.

As we are discovering, a significant increase in global temperatures can play havoc with the earth's atmosphere and weather patterns. Glaciers melt, sea levels rise, and the pattern and magnitude of precipitation change, leading to severe weather changes such as heat waves, droughts, hurricanes, tsunamis, tornados, and flooding. It is difficult to attribute extreme weather patterns to global warming alone, and the relationship between global warming and an increasing number of hurricanes actually is being debated. But scientists do observe less ice at the polar ice caps, extreme weather changes, and rising sea levels.

According to some major weather forecasters, the United States has entered into the hurricane phase of its weather cycle. We can expect a heavy dose of hurricanes over the fifteen-year period that began at the turn of this century. The last such hurricane cycle occurred back in the 1950s and 1960s. The impact has been enormous on local real estate markets—as we can see in Louisiana and particularly New Orleans. Severe prolonged weather patterns can have a long-term impact on relative real estate values. Here are four major ways the real estate markets would be affected:

- More households avoid severe-weather-prone areas
- The reduced availability and rising costs of property insurance
- Demand for severe-weather-resistant housing
- Increasing aversion to locations on the water

MORE HOUSEHOLDS AVOID SEVERE-WEATHER-PRONE AREAS

So far, there has been a rational response to weather-affected real estate areas—some households moved away, some are contemplating moving, others are stubbornly staying on. Hurricane Katrina is the most vivid example of these responses. Katrina inflicted devastation on a large portion of the Gulf Coast, including Louisiana, Mississippi, and Alabama. New Orleans experienced severe flooding, wiping out a good portion of the city and surrounding suburbs. Some experts predict that portions of New Orleans have been destroyed forever. Approximately half of New Orleans's 400,000 population was forced to leave and/or abandon the city. Most have not yet returned. According to most economists and city planners, it may take well over a decade for New Orleans to return to normalcy. And normalcy might well mean a city downsized to a 200,000 to 300,000 population. Many New Orleans households have migrated to Baton Rouge and other cities to the north.

During the past decade, many cities and local real estate markets have been hammered by severe-weather patterns. Sanibel Island, Marco Island, and Naples, Florida, all within 100 miles of one another, have experienced a minor exodus of risk-averse households. According to real estate professionals serving these locations, some seniors who have been living (retired) in these locations for at least a decade are moving out of Florida completely. Many are taking up residence in the Great Smoky Mountains in Georgia, Tennessee, and western North Carolina. This risk-averse behavior is not unexpected. Seniors, if they can afford it, have a lower tolerance level for a deteriorating quality of living.

This is one example of the impact of hurricanes and severe weather on local real estate. Younger households, too, are thinking twice about moving to such locations. This could affect vacation-home purchases and retirement-property purchases.

REDUCED AVAILABILITY AND RISING COSTS OF PROPERTY INSURANCE

According to a 2002 United Nations Environmental Program study, the increasing frequency of severe climatic events, coupled with social trends, could cost the U.S. economy almost $150 billion a year over the next ten years. These costs, through increased costs of insurance and disaster relief, burden customers, taxpayers, and industry alike. In the aftermath of a large number of severe hurricanes (e.g., Katrina, Wilma, Rita) since this study was published, the revised annual costs are far greater. The United Nations Environmental Program recently announced that severe weather around the world made 2005 the costliest year on record.

With weather-related insurance costs rising, insurance coverage availability and the rising costs of insurance coverage are becoming an increasing problem throughout the East Coast of the United States, particularly in Florida. Lack of hurricane and/or disaster insurance creates huge uncertainty in purchasing real estate, reducing demand for properties on or near the ocean in those hurricane-prone markets. Unless the federal government (or state government) intervenes and creates a backstop disaster-insurance fund, the lack of disaster-insurance coverage as well as rising costs of insurance coverage will plague U.S. coastal areas for some time to come.

DEMAND FOR SEVERE-WEATHER-RESISTANT PROPERTIES

One result of this decade's severe weather has been an increased need for single-family detached residences, high-rise condominiums, and multifamily buildings that are built to withstand extreme weather such as hurricanes. Local markets that satisfy these new demands will attract more households (home sales) than locations that are slow to adapt to these changing construction needs.

AVERSION TO WATER LOCATIONS

There is a growing movement among some households to move away from water locations. These households still covet the ocean but are uncomfortable with living right on it. Look for some intra-metro migration—households moving within their own metropolitan area or local real estate market, from oceanfront or ocean-view properties to properties that are several miles away from the water. This trend provides risk-averse households with the best of both worlds—they continue to derive the benefits of the ocean and beach, while calming their fears of experiencing a direct hit from hurricanes. I expect these intra-metro trends to increase if our severe-weather patterns continue.

LIVING IN A MEGA WORLD

So what is the "takeaway" from this chapter en megatrends? First, such megatrends should always be in the back of your mind when contemplating one of the largest financial transactions in your life—purchasing real estate. Knowing what the megatrends portend in terms of real estate activity can help you make a smart long-term decision.

The lesson here is to make a real estate decision not just for the near term, but for the long term. Unlike stocks and bonds, real estate is not a liquid asset—it is a long-term investment. When you purchase property to live in, you are usually in it for the long run. Most households live in properties for five years or longer. You may find yourself bringing up your children there and sending them off to college before contemplating selling your home. If you are *investing* in a property, the usual time horizon is five years, and sometimes it is ten. With stocks, you could purchase IBM shares today and sell within the next month if you wished.

The megatrends identified in this chapter are certainly not complete. These are just some megatrends that I believe are important and will impact local real estate activity for years to come. The impact of the baby boomers on everything from retail sales to fashion to real estate activity has been enormous during past decades and promises to be equally dramatic during the next two decades. Similarly, the aging and changing face of America is having a profound impact on society—on the way we live, speak, and behave. Who could deny that such social trends will influence local real estate markets in the future? The last three megatrends—nanotechnology, terrorism, and global warming—at first glance appear to have only a thin connection to real estate activity, but they may have such a profound impact on the way we will live that their influence over the real estate markets is inescapable.

Chapter Eight

BACK TO FUNDAMENTALS

The real estate boom during the first five years of the twenty-first century—and the media stories reporting on it—distorted people's view of property values. Newspapers, magazines, television, even the real estate press—in some cases unknowingly—painted a *national* picture of real estate. Even the phrase "real estate boom" conjures up images of property values surging everywhere across America. Many investors and households rode the real estate boom's wave during those five years. And they thought that no matter what property they purchased or where it was located, a rising tide would lift all boats.

Conversely, headlines such as "Will the boom go bust?" suggested that most metropolitan areas were vulnerable to home-price declines. When all properties in all markets did not register double-digit or record-breaking price increases, property buyers were surprised. And when some of the hot real estate markets cooled and home-price appreciation slowed, stalled, or fell, some investors were caught with their financial pants down, holding high-priced properties they no longer wanted and had problems selling. Why? They ignored market fundamentals and emphasized market momentum. They evaluated their property purchases without a full examination, ignoring individual markets' DNA and local and outside influences. Some speculated, hoping they could flip their properties within one year at a profit. Some home buyers who marginally qualified for a mortgage loan stretched their incomes by taking interest-only mortgage loans that permitted them to purchase higher-priced homes. For example, a $250,000 thirty-year, fixed-rate mortgage loan at 6 percent requires a $1,499 monthly mortgage payment, while a $350,000 interest-only mortgage loan at 5 percent requires a $1,458 monthly mortgage payment. In the latter case, the interest-only loan stretched a household's ability to obtain a 40 percent larger mortgage loan.

Some investors, too, leaned heavily on some nontraditional mortgage loans, such as interest-only and option adjustable-rate mortgage loans. These loans have a negative amortization feature in order to minimize the already negative cash flows on high-priced investment properties. Those investors were purchasing rental property based not on investment fundamentals but on unreasonable expectations that property prices would continue to rise at double-digit rates. For example, it was not uncommon for an investor to use a ten-year, interest-only loan to finance a rental-property purchase in the $200,000 to $400,000 range and still experience a $700 to $1,200 *negative* monthly cash flow. Those were the investors who got caught when the hot real estate boom cooled. All of these trends fed the demand for property buying, pushing prices to even higher levels than they would have if home buyers and investors had stuck to the fundamentals.

Again, all real estate is unique. We all have different tastes on where we want to live and what property to live in. But everyone's goal is to pay a "fair" price for the property. You certainly don't want to overpay. So, no matter what your tastes, you need to pay attention to basic supply-and-demand principles when considering the property you want to purchase. In other words, you need to stick to the fundamentals.

WHAT DOES "FUNDAMENTAL" MEAN?

It is important to look at real estate purchasing in two ways: purchasing a primary residence and purchasing a property for investment. The fundamentals are the same for both—you need to pay a fair market price based on market data on supply-and-demand conditions as well as the characteristics (DNA) of the community where the property is located. But the reasons for buying and the methods by which you purchase a primary residence and invest in a rental property differ markedly. I will examine both. But first, let's define what we mean by fundamentals.

To help you better understand the fundamentals for the real estate market, let me draw a parallel from the equities market. In the stock market, the stock price reflects the anticipated future earnings stream of the company. Estimates of future earnings are based on a number of factors as well as company and market information. A company's performance measures, such as quality of management, income statement and balance sheet, asset composition, and strength of competition, are reviewed daily by investors. A proxy for whether a stock price is in line with fundamentals is the price/earnings ratio, or *P/E ratio*. When the P/E ratio is historically high—when the stock price has overstepped a company's earnings—the stock is said to be overpriced. When the P/E ratio is historically low, the stock is said to be underpriced. This is fundamental investing. Of course, there is also speculation in stocks—based on rumors, hunches, and so forth. And charting—following the upswings and downswings of the stock price—plays a role in the pricing of stocks as well. But most of the time, investors lean heavily on company and market fundamentals when investing in equities.

In real estate, price reflects supply-and-demand conditions. Thus, future property prices reflect future supply/demand conditions. Based on a local market's DNA and influences and trends affecting demand and supply for property, the price of a property is established. But there is one significant difference between valuing real estate and valuing stocks— affordability. Affordability is not an issue with stocks. Most stock purchases are cash transactions. Conversely, a real estate transaction is usually a leveraged purchase involving financing. The buyer's debt service (the costs associated with the loan) and affordability of the property come into play when valuing property. So the equivalent P/E ratio for property would be price growth/household income growth *or* mortgage debt service/ household income. Both give some measure of affordability and/or the ability of a purchaser to service the loan. The price growth/income growth ratio is readily observable in most markets, and it is simple—but it is misleading. Nonetheless, it is a good first glance to see if home prices in a specific market are getting out of line and becoming unaffordable.

But the more appropriate measure is mortgage debt service *as a percentage of household income*. Why do I say that? Most households finance the purchase of a home. As a result, their ability to purchase property depends not on their income level but on whether they can afford the monthly mortgage payments. Historically, the mortgage debt service/ income ratio hovered between 18 and 22 percent. This range seems to be associated with relatively normal demand and supply conditions in real estate. A ratio well above this range reflects affordability problems, suggesting that homes may be overvalued. A ratio well below this range suggests that homes might be undervalued. So I use the debt service/income ratio as the real estate market's P/E ratio.

From a personal perspective, you need to first decide whether your household income and expenses can manage the estimated monthly payments on a property purchase. In other words, determine how much home you can afford before applying market fundamentals to the list price. This is what makes real estate so different from stocks. You need to pass the "affordability test" first because financing is involved. If you fail this test, you need to look at lower-priced properties. Aside from the mortgage debt service/income ratio, there are other ratios to examine that lenders look at before granting a mortgage loan: your debt (all kinds of debt)/income ratio and the housing expense/income ratio. Lenders usually require a debt/income ratio of 36 percent or less, while they require the housing expense/income ratio to be 28 percent or less.

Assuming you can afford the payments for a property in the price range you have selected, market fundamentals take over. First, ask your real estate professional to provide you with a comparative market analysis, or CMA. That will help you determine what a fair price for the property is in your area. Your real estate agent will focus on searching the multiple listings and other property lists, comparing your targeted home to comparable properties and their prices. Second, assess current market conditions, including factors affecting demand, supply, and DNA.

THREE SIMPLE FUNDAMENTAL STEPS

Here are the steps I suggest you follow to ensure that you are sticking to the fundamentals when purchasing real estate:

1. TAKE THE AFFORDABILITY TEST

   a. *Mortgage debt service/income ratio less than 23 percent.* This is the P/E ratio for real estate. If real estate transactions in the Washington, D.C., metro area were generating a mortgage debt service/income ratio of 25, and historically in the D.C. metro this ratio hovered in the

18–22 range, you should check all the fundamentals associated with the metro area to justify a higher real estate P/E of 25.

b. *Debt/income ratio less than 36 percent.* Assuming that you have the required down payment on the mortgage loan in question, lenders next look at your debt-to-income ratio. The debt-to-income ratio compares the sum of monthly debt obligations (including the prospective mortgage) to monthly gross income. Lenders look for debt payments of 36 percent or less of gross income. (Note, however, that most of the low-down-payment mortgage loans and other flexible mortgage products involve somewhat less stringent credit guidelines.)

c. *Housing expense/income ratio less than 28 percent.* Lenders also measure a household's ability to meet its mortgage payments by comparing the sum of monthly housing expenses to monthly gross income. Generally, lenders look for this ratio to be 28 percent or less. Monthly housing expenses include mortgage payment, property taxes, private mortgage insurance, hazard insurance, and homeowner's fees.

d. *Credit score.* Your lender will request your credit score from one of three credit bureaus (Equifax, Experian, and TransUnion). A credit score is a number that indicates how likely a borrower is to repay future debts. You should know your credit score before purchasing a home. The credit bureaus generate credit scores based on consumer credit data, including debt and payment history on credit cards, student loans, consumer loans, automobile loans, tax liens, judgments and bankruptcies, and previous collections and inquiries for new credit. The most common credit score system, called FICO, assigns scores that range from 300 to 950. The higher your credit score, the lower is the assumed risk that you will fail to repay a loan.

e. *Home affordability calculator.* Aside from looking at the simple ratios presented above, you should calculate how much home you can afford. There are many home affordability calculators available on housing Web sites. I recommend using one of them. For example, go to Realtor.com and use its Home Affordability Calculator. The calculator covers every item associated with the purchase of a home, including your gross income, monthly debt payments, funds available for home purchase, the mortgage rate, closing costs, minimum down payment, property tax rate, hazard insurance, private mortgage insurance, housing-expense-to-income ratio, and the debt-to-income ratio.

2. PERFORM A COMPARATIVE MARKET ANALYSIS

Some real estate companies offer what is called a comparative market analysis, which will help you determine a fair price for the property.

a. *Have your real estate company put together a package of "comparables" for your review.* Comparables (colloquially called "comps") are properties that are similar in size, characteristics, and condition to the property that you want to purchase. Some comps will have been sold within the past six months to a year, and some are currently listed on the market. Comps will help you determine a listing price *range* for the property.

b. Make sure the CMA includes the following information on the "subject property" (the one you want to buy) and three to ten additional properties:

~ Street address

~ Square footage

~ Number of bedrooms, number of baths, number of total rooms

~ Age

~ Listing price and sold price if closed

c. Here is an example of a CMA that you can expect to receive:

The property that is being compared is 1250 Oregon Street, which is the "subject property."

	Address	Bedrooms	Baths	Square Ft.	Garage	List Price	Sold Price	DATE
COMPARABLE MARKET ANALYSIS								
S	1250 Oregon	4	2	1804	Y	$153,500		
1	1255 Oregon	4	2	1788	N	$147,500	$145,000	1/18/06
2	1146 Oregon	4	2	1896	Y	$152,900	$152,000	2/15/06
3	744 Lincoln	4	2 1/2	1912	N	$149,950	$149,950	11/21/05
4	912 Jeffers	4	2	1692	N	$145,000	$142,750	9/12/05
5	6000 Fulton	4	2	1692	N	$154,000	$152,000	2/1/06

Average List Price: **$149,870** Average Sold Price: **$148,340** Average Sq. Ft.: **1796**
Average Sold per Sq. Ft.: **$82.59**

3. ASSESS CURRENT MARKET CONDITIONS

This final step is the most difficult for people to do—studying current demand and supply conditions of the local marketplace. This can seem intimidating. It requires a little work, a little thinking—you need to "feed yourself" rather than have someone else (a real estate professional) spoon-feed you. But if you want to become a smart real estate investor—or even just make a smart decision about purchasing your own primary residence—this step is mandatory. I will make it as simple as I can for you.

   a. *Have your real estate professional provide you with as much local market information as possible.* OK—get a spoonful from your real estate agent. Your real estate agent knows better than anyone about current market conditions. Have your agent provide you with a subjective view of current DNA and market conditions. Do not be afraid to ask as many questions as you can think of about the characteristics of the local market and the current influences on demand/supply conditions. I suggest questions on the following topics:

     i. The health of the local market

     ii. Education and transportation systems

     iii. Culture and social ambience

     iv. Local politics

     v. Population growth

     vi. Job situation

     vii. Demographics—what type of households (e.g., income, age) live in the local market

     viii. Business environment

     ix. Retail shopping

     x. Sports/recreation activities

     xi. Home-sales activity

     xii. Home-building activity

     xiii. The number of homes available for sale (the inventory of homes in the area that are for sale) and how long they have been on the market

   b. *Monitor market conditions.* Now you are on your own. You need to do just a little homework by studying local market conditions. A smart real estate investor does not just rely on third-party views. You need to form your own opinions about the local marketplace. As you already know, there are many factors that influence the current and future price of a home—local economic conditions, population information, and housing information, to name a few. Gather as much information as you can about the local real estate marketplace. To keep it simple, I strongly suggest that you gather information about the following local measures (some of these reports can be provided by your real estate agent and/or lender):

  i. *Existing and new home sales.* Your local real estate agent should be able to provide you with some local home sales data—maybe by metro, county, or zip code. If not, you can get some of this information from your local real estate association.* All metros have their own local associations. For example, if you were living in Fairfax, Virginia, you would call the Northern Virginia Association of Realtors, NVAR. The volume and growth in existing home sales is a good indicator of activity and health of a local marketplace. If home sales are on a downtrend, it could indicate that the market may be transitioning to a buyer's market, giving you a better negotiating position against a seller. Conversely, if home sales are robust, the opposite may be true.

 ii. *Local home prices.* Metropolitan-area home prices are reported quarterly by the National Association of Realtors. However, your local real estate agent should be able to provide you with some local price data, maybe by county or zip code. Compare the current home-price appreciation for a local market to its historical average. For example, if you are looking to purchase a property in Phoenix, Arizona, and the current price appreciation is 13 percent, compared with a ten-year appreciation average of 6 percent, it would be prudent of you to assume that future appreciation will more likely fall in the 5 to 7 percent range rather than the higher 10 to 15 percent range.

iii. *Local housing inventories/months' supply.* Real estate agents should also be able to provide you with the months' supply of homes in the local marketplace. The months' supply measures the number of months it would take to exhaust the current supply of homes in your local marketplace at the current sales pace. Again, it is useful to compare the current months' supply to the historical average (usually between five and seven months). Anything less than a local market's historical average is considered a lean inventory, while anything greater is considered an

---

*If you have the time and inclination, you can also track the individual properties that are being sold. Home sales are a matter of public record, and in most cities and towns, home sales are published in the local newspaper. The information includes who sold the home, to whom it was sold, and what the sale price was.

excess supply of homes. If your local market is experiencing a lean supply of homes available for sale, it is likely a seller's market, making it more difficult for buyers to effectively negotiate on price. If your local market is showing an excess supply of homes, it is likely a buyer's market, making it easier for buyers to negotiate on price.

iv. *Days-on-market*. This is perhaps the most important short-term housing measure. Days-on-market measures how long the property that you are considering for purchase has been on the market. The longer a home is on the market, the stronger the negotiating position of a potential buyer. The shorter a home is on the market, the stronger the negotiating position of the seller in the transaction. But be very careful with these numbers. Some properties could have been on the market for five months, then taken *off* the market, and then brought back one month later as a new listing. This is very deceiving to potential buyers. Ask your real estate agent about the "listing" history of each property—is this the first time this property has been listed? Also, try to get from your real estate company the historical average length of days-on-market to put the current days-on-market in perspective.

v. *Local housing starts/permits*. Virtually every metropolitan area provides housing starts/permits information. High growth in local housing starts/permits reflects a healthy local housing economy, while low growth in housing starts/permits may reflect some weakening.

vi. *Job growth*. It is important that you obtain information about the local economy when you are considering purchasing property. My favorite economic indicator for a local market is job growth. Positive job growth is essential for the long-term viability of a healthy real estate market. You are always looking for positive job gains in a local area that you are considering for investment. If the area is losing jobs, you need to find out why. If the job loss is an aberration (due to a one-time company layoff), then the area may still be attractive. But you need to ask the right questions. Every country and city in the United States makes local job data available to the public. The local county office should provide you with job, income, and other economic data about its local markets.

vii. *Net migration.* As we have discovered, obtaining information about local population and demographic trends is very important in purchasing property. If I had to select one report from the many population reports that are available, I would choose the migration report. Local migration reports are available by metro area from the National Association of Realtors, but also from the U.S. Census Bureau. These reports will tell you how many people are migrating into the metro area versus how many people are leaving the metro area. Obviously, you are looking for local markets that, on net, are growing via population growth. Positive net migration into the market is a plus for future real estate activity.

HOW TO BUY RENTAL PROPERTY

Investing in rental property requires a strategy quite different from the one employed in purchasing a home. The acquisition of a rental property is a business decision, and it has to be made in a businesslike way. Let's say you've identified a property that *could* be a good investment. Now you need to estimate the property's current value, project its future value, and make a realistic assessment of how much rental income you can expect to get from the property versus anticipated expenses in order to arrive at the property's profit potential. You want to get expert advice about the benefits of depreciation and tax write-offs. Your calculations must be based on how long you plan to own the property and what it will take to manage the property over that period of time. Your calculations should also reflect whether you think you can personally manage the property or will need to hire a professional manager to do the job. All of these factors contribute to what I believe is sound, fundamental real estate investing.

BIDDING ON AN INVESTMENT PROPERTY

You will probably not make money the first year of owning a rental property—more of your cash will go out than comes in. (Cash that comes out of *your* pocket is *negative* cash flow.) It is rare to find a property that is priced low enough so that your rental income more than covers your mortgage and operating expenses (assuming a 20 percent down payment or less). But what makes rental property such an attractive investment is that your rental income will grow over time while your mortgage payments are fixed (unless you have a one-year adjustable-rate mortgage) and your other costs, such as property taxes, generally increase at a slow rate. Moreover, buying a rental property (similar to your primary residence) will give you a tax break, so you will reap significant tax savings, increasing the real return on your investment. If you fall under the AMT (alternative minimum tax) structure, you may relinquish some or all of those tax benefits. Check with your tax advisor.

When bidding on a rental property, approach it quite differently from the way you approached bidding on your residence. Remember, you aren't looking for cash income from the place in which you live; but you are in a rental-property investment. Let's examine how you do a potential income/cash flow analysis.

A one-bedroom condo in downtown Washington, D.C., is being offered for an asking price of $195,000. Your investment strategy is to put 20 percent down and finance the remaining balance with a thirty-year, 7 percent mortgage loan. How much do you bid for the condo? Do you bid the asking price? Do you underbid or overbid? Of course, the price you eventually pay has a great deal to do with market conditions (is the market tight or sluggish?). But to make an intelligent, informed, and fundamental investment decision, you need to run the before-tax cash-flow calculations, then estimate the tax benefits from rental-property ownership.

BEFORE-TAX CASH FLOWS

Calculate and compare the before-tax annual and monthly cash flows of the condo over a range of bid prices. As you begin the bidding, have a firm idea of how much you can afford to pay out to "carry" the property. For example, you may be willing to pay up to $300 per month to own the rental property. So the maximum price you can bid will be a price that generates a negative monthly cash flow of $300. Prices lower than the maximum will generate lower negative cash flows, which improves your investment position.

In effect, the negative $300 cash flow represents what you are willing to pay for the privilege of owning the property, knowing that in the near future rental income will eventually grow and that negative cash flow will turn into positive cash flow. Of course, the big payoff is the price appreciation and principal accumulation on the property, which eventually creates substantial wealth gains.

To calculate before-tax cash flows, let's assume that you bid the asking price, $195,000, for the condo. Your real estate agent tells you that the rental unit can command $1,400 per month in rent, generating $16,200 in annual rental income (yes, it's relatively expensive to live in our nation's capital!). Now, net out the expenses to finance, operate, and manage the property. With 20 percent down, you will obtain a thirty-year $156,000 mortgage loan paying 7 percent interest. You will pay $12,454 in annual mortgage payments. Property taxes are estimated at $1,723 for the year (assuming the D.C. tax rate per $100 = .96 and property assessment of $179,525). Hazard insurance (protection from fire, wind, flood, etc.) costs $200 per year, and the condo fees are assumed to run $300 per month or $3,600 for the year. Finally, you need to put $2,000 (assume about 1 percent of the bid price) aside in a reserve for repairs and maintenance (R & M) of the property. Adding the mortgage payment, property tax, insurance, condo dues (these dues are paid to the condominium association, which pays for repairs, maintenance, and improvements to the shared property, including the building and any amenities—e.g., a pool, landscaping, or insurance), and repair/maintenance totals $19,977 in expenses. Netting expenses from rental revenues results in a negative annual cash flow of $3,177 and a negative monthly cash flow of $265.

CASH FLOW BEFORE TAX

Bid price	$200,000	$195,000	$190,000	$185,000
Rental Income	$16,800	$16,800	$16,800	$16,800
Expenses				
Mortgage Payment	$12,774	$12,454	$12,135	$11,815
Property Tax	$1,723	$1,723	$1,723	$1,723
Hazard Insurance	$200	$200	$200	$200
Condo Dues	$3,600	$3,600	$3,600	$3,600
R & M Reserve	$2,000	$2,000	$2,000	$2,000
Total Expenses	**$20,297**	**$19,977**	**$19,658**	**$19,338**
Annual Cash Flow	**($3,497)**	**($3,177)**	**($2,858)**	**($2,538)**
Monthly Cash Flow	($291)	($265)	($238)	($211)

The asking price of $195,000 is pretty close to what you are willing to bid, given that the $265 monthly cash outlay is a bit below your $300-per-month limit. You are now able to bid the seller's asking price. But before you do, let's run some other cash-flow scenarios around the $195,000 asking price to establish a range of prices that may be acceptable to you in case market conditions dictate that you bid something other than the asking price.

Let's run the cash flows for $200,000, $190,000, and $185,000. At $200,000, the monthly cash flow rises to $291; at $190,000, the cash flow drops to $238; and at $185,000, the cash flow drops further to $211. You are now presented with the following choices:

YOUR FINANCIAL LIMIT: $300 PER MONTH

Bid Price	Monthly Negative Cash Flow	Annual Negative Cash Flow
$200,000	$291	$3,497
$195,000	$265	$3,177
$190,000	$238	$2,858
$185,000	$211	$2,538

If market conditions are sluggish, you and your real estate agent may decide to underbid by offering $185,000 or $190,000, bringing your monthly costs closer to $200. On the other hand, if conditions are tight and your real estate agent anticipates multiple bids on the property, you certainly can afford to pay $291 per month and raise your bid to $200,000. Whatever you end up bidding, if you use the above cash-flow analysis, you will be bidding intelligently. If the price of the property rises beyond your cash-flow limit, it's probably time to move on to another property.

Of course, you may want to put less or more than the traditional 20 percent down. If so, just plug in the new mortgage payment numbers in the above cash-flow analysis to see how sensitive the cash flows are to different loan balances. There will be times when a property's value will work with a lower down payment and a higher mortgage amount, and there will be times when you may need to allocate more funds to a down payment in order to make the cash flows work for you.

THE TAX BENEFITS OF RENTAL PROPERTY

Fortunately, there are some favorable tax consequences of owning rental properties that improve the real return on your investment. Let's assume that we purchased the condo for the asking price of $195,000. To calculate the taxable income or loss from the property, subtract all deductible expenses from the rental income. For tax purposes, there are three types of expenses: mortgage-interest expense, operating expense, and depreciation.

According to the thirty-year amortization schedule, you can deduct $11,148 in mortgage-interest expenses in the first year. Deductible operating expenses include $1,723 in property taxes, $200 paid in hazard insurance, $3,600 paid in condo fees, and $2,000 paid in repairs and maintenance. This gives you $7,523 in total deductible operating expenses. You are also permitted to deduct depreciation on the property. Because you purchased a condominium, there is no land involved, so the full cost of the condominium can be depreciated. (Land does not depreciate.) You are permitted to spread depreciation expense on the property over 27.5 years. This gives you $7,144 in depreciation expenses every year ($195,000 divided by 27.5). If you purchased a single-family property, you would have to allocate some of the cost to land, so the entire purchase price would not be depreciable. Subtracting your total deductible expenses of $25,185 ($11,148 plus $7,523 plus $7,144) from rental income of $16,800 results in an annual rental loss of $9,015.

AFTER-TAX CASH FLOW

Purchase Price	**$195,000**
Rental Income	$16,800
Deductible Expenses	
Mortgage Interest	$11,148
Operating Expenses	
Property Tax	$1,723
Hazard Insurance	$200
Condo Dues	$3,600
R & M Reserve	$2,000
Total Operating Expenses	**$7,523**
Depreciation	**$7,144**
Total Deductible Expenses	**$25,815**
Reported Loss on Property	**$9,015**

There are several ways you may use the rental loss, depending on your ownership and financial situation. If your adjusted gross income does not exceed $100,000 and you actively participate in the management of the property, the rental loss (up to $25,000) can be deducted from your other income, such as wages, interest, and dividends. In the above example, you would multiply the $9,015 rental loss by your federal income tax rate (assume it's 31 percent), resulting in $2,795 of tax savings. If your state also has an income tax, that rate multiplied by the $9,015 loss would generate additional tax savings.

For households that earn less than $100,000 in adjusted gross income, your after-tax cash flow improves significantly due to the $2,795 in tax savings. Remember, the monthly before-tax cash flow was a negative $265. By adding the $2,795 tax savings to your rental income, you are left with only a $32-per-month negative cash flow. So now this rental property is already looking like a very attractive investment! Not only are you essentially breaking even in your first year of owning this property, but your rental income eventually rises over time. (Property taxes, as noted earlier, also rise, but only slightly.) You are also building equity in the property as you pay down your mortgage. As the property appreciates in value, your return on investment begins to soar.

CASH FLOW BEFORE TAX

Bid Price	**$195,000**
Rental Income	$16,800
Expenses	
Mortgage Payment	$12,454
Property Tax	$1,723
Hazard Insurance	$200
Condo Dues	$3,600
R & M Reserve	$2,000
Total Expenses	**$19,977**
Annual Cash Flow	**($3,177)**
Monthly Cash Flow	($265)
Tax Savings	**$2,795**
After-Tax Annual Cash Flow	($382)
After-Tax Monthly Cash Flow	($32)

According to the IRS rules, households with adjusted gross incomes between $100,000 and $150,000 can deduct passive losses up to a phased-out portion of the $25,000 cap. In our example, if you had an adjusted gross income of $125,000, passive losses would be deductible up to $12,500. Therefore, the $9,615 rental loss would be fully deductible. For households whose adjusted gross incomes exceed $150,000, the taxable rental loss cannot be deducted in the current year. These households will be unable to reduce the $265 monthly negative cash flow.

Property owners are permitted to carry forward their suspended rental losses, subject to the passive activity loss limitations. Each year, rental losses can be carried forward until the property is disposed (sold). (This means you accumulate the losses rather than deducting each year's loss from your income.) In the year of disposal—that is, the year you sell the property—the cumulative suspended rental losses are subtracted from your taxable income, saving you thousands of dollars in income tax. Let's look at an example.

Suppose every year for five years you were carrying forward $10,000 in rental losses from a rental property that you own. At the beginning of year six you choose to sell the property for a $250,000 gain (selling price minus the adjusted cost basis, or original cost of property plus improvements). Your wages, dividends, and other income totaled $200,000 in year six. You are now able to take a $50,000 loss in that year ($10,000 a year for the previous five years), resulting in only $150,000 in taxable income. If your tax rate were 31 percent, you would have saved $15,500 in taxes (31 percent × $50,000). Note that you will also pay a capital gains tax on the $250,000 gain from sale of the property, which as of this writing is taxed at 15 percent (however, the depreciation component of the gain is subject to a 25 percent tax rate).

The loss carry-forward delayed the benefits of rental investing. In effect, you earned another $15,500. Spread over the five-year ownership period, this provides you with another $3,100 of tax savings per year, improving your cash-flow position—after the fact. As you accumulate more rental properties (building a portfolio of properties), the loss carry-forward becomes more effective. As you sell properties, you will be experiencing tax savings that can help blunt the negative cash flows of your other properties.

CAN FUNDAMENTALS CHANGE?

Is it possible that conventional wisdom gets turned on its head and the fundamentals of a market change? Could there be a change in market structure or some other forces that alter some fundamental concepts in real estate? The simple answer is no. I cannot recall an instance where the laws of supply and demand have been revoked in any market, let alone the real estate market. But market innovations or changes in demand and/or supply behavior can impact market outcomes, and you need to stay abreast of these changes.

Today's real estate markets and all of the activities associated with it (financing, appraisals, etc.) have evolved. They are more sophisticated, and as a result, there is more activity (more people are involved), and with it, more volatility (risk). This makes home sales and home-price movements less predictable than they were in the past. It used to be that when interest rates went up, home sales came down. When population grew, sales increased and prices rose. When a local market registered job gains, home sales rose, adding upward pressure on prices. There were few surprises in the real estate markets. Now there is an element of risk and uncertainty that did not previously exist in property markets. There are several explanations for these changes.

- *There is greater liquidity in the real estate markets today.* Greater liquidity means that there are more and more households and investors who are able to buy and sell homes. This generates more property sales and, with it, more price volatility.
- *There is more speculative investing in real estate.* Speculative investing used to be dedicated to other asset investments, like stocks and bonds. Real estate is now considered an important wealth-generating asset to include in one's financial portfolio. During the final two years of the real estate boom, there was a great deal of speculation—investors purchasing property with the intent to sell within a year at a profit. Although speculative activity has slowed with the cooling off and retrenchment of some of our (previously) boom markets, there are still households and investors who are willing to take some risks in real estate. Speculative buying adds to price volatility, because it is usually speculators who dump properties quickly when local good times turn bad.
- *Investing in real estate has become more popular.* For a variety of reasons—the September 11 terrorist attacks, the real estate boom, relatively low mortgage rates, real estate's history as a successful leveraged investment, relatively high recent returns—real estate is now viewed as a viable alternative to stocks and bonds. Over 28 percent of all real estate purchases in 2005 were investment purchases. Most of these investments were not speculative (as described above) but traditional investments. A market with a higher percentage of investors is likely to be associated with greater volatility, since investors are a less stable group of purchasers compared to households who purchase properties in which to live.
- *There is a greater variety of mortgage products.* During the past decade, Fannie Mae, Freddie Mac, HUD, and a number of large mortgage companies have created a long and varied menu of mortgage products. These products range from low-down-payment mortgage loans to adjustable-rate loans to balloon loans to interest-only loans. Each loan

satisfies a potential home buyer's need, attracting more home buyers into the marketplace, improving liquidity.

• *There is greater household mobility.* Because of changes in culture, technology, and society, there is greater household mobility today than ever before. That is, households are more likely to move to different states, metros, or local markets due to job relocation, family, climate, and so on. Greater mobility means greater movement in home sales and prices (what we call turnover rate).

• *Ownership holding periods are now much shorter.* It is true that the holding period for owning property has shortened during the past several decades. Some of this has to do with the fact that households are more sophisticated about property financing and are no longer intimidated by the buying and selling process. Some has to do with the increase in household mobility, households retiring at an early age, households downsizing at an earlier age, or households being able to afford a trade-up home or a second home. Shorter holding periods means more volume for home sales and pricing.

• *Real estate has become a safe haven for funds.* Given the uncertainty in the world today—particularly war and terrorism threats—households and investors are turning to real estate as a safe haven for their funds. This has increased the size of the real estate market with regard to the number of transactions. But these households/investors may pull their money out of property if the uncertainty subsides, raising volatility concerns.

IT'S ALL FUNDAMENTAL

Hopefully, we learn from our mistakes. The recent real estate boom was a good lesson. We paid attention to market momentum rather than market fundamentals. That does not necessarily mean that the real estate market is unhealthy. The boom could not be sustained indefinitely. It needed to cool down—and it did, more so than I had previously anticipated. But the fundamentals that generated the real estate boom have not disappeared. Mortgage rates remain in single digits and hover near historically low levels. Demographic trends remain strong. The boomers remain in the peak earning years while experiencing great wealth gains from their primary residences, providing them with the financial wherewithal to consume more property. Retirees are living longer due to advances in medicine and health care, supporting continued demand for housing. Record immigration in the 1970s, 1980s, and 1990s will continue to fuel demand. Our population, according to government estimates described on a recent front-page *USA Today* article, will grow from 300 million to 400 million by the year 2040. So after an appropriate cooling period, homeownership rates are likely to modestly rise during the first two decades of this century. And boomer children—the echo boomers—are becoming first-time home buyers, exerting upward pressure on starter homes. These are all favorable trends that bode well for future real estate activity. The real estate boom ended prematurely because we got away from the fundamentals—speculative activity and the ability to stretch credit and incomes with exotic mortgage products like interest-only loans.

Before the end of this decade, most local real estate markets will be poised to proceed with expansion. But the key to successful real estate purchasing is to identify which local markets will perform better than others. All real estate is local. It is essential that you pay attention to market fundamentals.

Chapter Nine

HOW TO PURCHASE REAL ESTATE IN LOCAL MARKETS

Identifying the right location to live in or invest in is useful only if you know *how* to purchase real estate in your local market. Whether you are a first-time buyer or someone who is trading up, the home-buying process is confusing. Follow the steps below to help guide you through what will be one of the most important decisions of your life.

Step 1: Select a Real Estate Agent
I strongly recommend talking to a real estate agent about the housing market in your local area, the process of finding a home, and the process of purchasing a home.

Step 2: Determine How Much Home You Can Afford
Working with your Realtor and/or lender, determine how much home you can afford.

The actual calculation of how much you can spend, as we examined in the previous chapter, is straightforward, but there are many factors that you first need to consider. Ask yourself:

- What is my budget for purchasing and maintaining a home (property)?
- Is there any assistance available to reduce my purchase costs (e.g., government-assistance down-payment programs)?
- What is my credit score? How will this number impact the loan amount I can obtain?

- How much loan can I afford?
- How much down payment can I make?
- How big of a mortgage can I qualify for?
- How large of a monthly mortgage payment am I willing to assume?

With these answers, you are ready to calculate how much house you can afford. In the previous chapter, I discussed some good ratio tests—the housing-expense-to-income ratio and the long-term debt-to-income ratio—that lenders usually conduct to qualify you for a mortgage loan. For a more comprehensive way to determine how much home you can afford, go to Realtor.com and use their Home Affordability Calculator.

Step 3: Determine the Type of Home and Location You Desire

Aside from everything you have learned in this book about comparing locations, it might be instructive to write down on a piece of paper what features you desire in a house as well as what features you desire in your community or neighborhood. Your real estate agent may provide you with a simple survey on desired home and community features to gain a better understanding on where your agent should begin a home search. Below is a sample survey, called a home-buying wish list, provided by the Housing and Urban Development Department, HUD, at http://www.hud.gov/utilities/intercept.cfm?/buying/wishlist.pdf.

HOME-BUYING WISH LIST

The Basics

1. What part of town (or country) do you want to live in?
   _____

2. What price range would you consider? No less than _____ but no more than _____.

3. Are schools a factor and, if so, what do you need to take into consideration (e.g., do you want a specific school system, want kids to be able to walk to school, etc.)? _____

4. Do you want an older home or a newer home (less than five years old)? _____

5. What kind of houses would you be willing to see?
   _____ one story _____ two story _____ split foyer _____ colonial
   _____ no preference

6. What style house appeals to you most?

    _____ contemporary _____ traditional _____ southwestern
    _____ colonial _____ no preference

7. How much renovation would you be willing to do?

    _____ a lot _____ a little _____ none

8. Do you have to be close to public transportation?

    _____ yes _____ no

9. Do you have any physical needs that must be met, such as wheel-chair access? _____

10. Do you have any animals that will require special facilities?

    _____ yes _____ no

11. What characteristics should the lot have?

	Must have	Would like to have
Large yard (1 acre or more)	_____	_____
Small yard (less than 1 acre)	_____	_____
Fenced yard	_____	_____
Garage	_____	_____
Carport	_____	_____
Patio/deck	_____	_____
Pool	_____	_____
Outdoor spa	_____	_____
Extra parking	_____	_____
Other buildings (barn, shed, etc.)	_____	_____
Special view	_____	_____

The Interior

12. How many bedrooms must you have? _____
    How many would you like to have? _____

13. How many bathrooms do you want? _____

14. How big would you like your house to be (sq. ft.)? no less than _____ more than _____

15. What features do you want to have in your house?

	Must have	Would like to have
Air-conditioning	_____	_____
Wall-to-wall carpet	_____	_____
Ceramic tile	_____	_____
Hardwood floors	_____	_____

Eat-in kitchen	_____	_____
Separate dining room	_____	_____
Formal dining room	_____	_____
Family room	_____	_____
Great room	_____	_____
Separate den/library	_____	_____
Fireplace	_____	_____
Workshop	_____	_____
No interior steps	_____	_____
In-law apartment	_____	_____
Spa in bathroom	_____	_____
Lots of windows (light)	_____	_____

Community Features

16. Do you want to live in an area with a community association?

_____ yes _____ no

17. What else do you want in your community?

	Must have	Would like to have
Community pool	_____	_____
Golf course	_____	_____
Basketball court	_____	_____
Tennis courts	_____	_____
Gated community/doorman	_____	_____
Clubhouse/activities	_____	_____

18. Are there any other special features or needs that you must consider when you are looking for a home? _____

HUD also offers a checklist for shopping for a home that may be useful particularly when determining the type of neighborhood and location that you desire. Here is what I think are the most important checklist items that you need to consider:

Neighborhood

Appearance/condition of nearby homes/businesses
Traffic
Noise level
Safety/security

Age mix of inhabitants
Number of children
Pet restrictions
Parking
Zoning regulations
Neighborhood restrictions/covenants
Fire protection/police
Snow removal
Garbage service

Schools
Age/condition
Reputation
Quality of teachers
Achievement test scores
Play areas
Curriculum
Class size
Busing distance

Convenience to:
Supermarket
Schools
Work
Shopping
Child care
Hospitals
Doctor/dentist
Recreation/parks
Restaurants/entertainment
Church/synagogue
Airport
Highways
Public transportation

Step 4: Shop for a Home
You are now ready to find a home. At this stage, you should be able to provide your real estate agent with the necessary search criteria for your future

home: location(s), type of home, home features, and price range. There are two steps involved in shopping: First, do some preliminary searching on your own via the Internet or driving around neighborhoods, and second, have your Realtor select a limited number of homes for you to visit. The first step is made easy by visiting Realtor.com or any major real estate brokerage site in your area such as Long & Foster or Century 21. You can simply type in your zip code, enter your search criteria (home type, home features, and price range), and view the listings. This process will enable you to narrow the field a bit so that your time with the Realtor will be used efficiently. The second step is for your Realtor to take you to physically visit the targeted homes. Listen to your agent and treat him or her as a trusted advisor. They will make money whether you purchase house A, B, or C. Let them help you find the right home that satisfies your needs.

Step 5: Obtain Real Estate Financing

If you do not know a lender to use for the financing of the home purchase, ask your Realtor to recommend two or more lenders. Visit with each lender and select the one you are most comfortable with. It is important for a first-time buyer to get preapproved for a mortgage loan. Work with your lender by providing the necessary personal financial and employment information so that you can be accepted for preapproval. Here are some steps to obtain real estate financing:

• *Qualifying for a mortgage loan.* Qualifying for a mortgage loan is like filling up your gasoline tank before going on a long trip. You might as well cancel your trip if your automobile has no gas. Similarly, if you don't qualify for financing, you simply won't be able to purchase a home. So qualifying for a mortgage loan has to be your first order of business.

Lenders need to know that you are creditworthy to obtain a mortgage loan. To accomplish this, they factor in the sources of your annual income. Any long-term debts, such as car payments or school loans, will also be taken into account. The bottom line is that you need to demonstrate that you have steady employment and that your financial situation is reasonably stable according to the above ratio tests. Your lender will request your credit score from one of three credit bureaus (Equifax, Experian, and TransUnion). A credit score is a number that indicates how likely a borrower is to repay future debts. These credit bureaus generate credit scores based on consumer credit data, including debt and payment history on credit cards, student loans, consumer loans, auto loans, etc.; tax liens, judgments, and bankruptcies; and previous collections and inquiries for new credit. The most common credit-scoring system is called FICO and the scores range from 300 to 950. The greater your credit score, the lower the risk that you will fail to repay a loan. The FICO score is based on mathematical formula, developed by Fair, Isaac Company, that uses all of the above consumer credit data to measure the probability of timely repayment. You can request your credit score at any time from the three credit bureaus to see if you make the grade. Visit the following sites: www.experian.com, www.equifax.com, www.transunion.com.

• *Review the menu of mortgage loans.* Just a couple of decades back, obtaining a mortgage loan was simple: You got a thirty-year fixed-rate mortgage. There were no other types of mortgage readily available to home buyers. While a thirty-year fixed-rate mortgage is still the most common loan, there is now a long and varied menu of mortgage loans available to most home buyers.

The three most common types of financing in real estate today are fixed-rate, adjustable-rate, and balloon financing. The type of financing you select will determine the interest rate, amortization, speed of paying off the principal balance, and the monthly payment of the loan. Some of these financing types also offer a convertible feature. Ask your lender about them.

• *Financing assistance.* There are many types of loan-assistance programs available. HUD, FHA, and VA administer national loan-assistance programs, and there are many other programs administered by housing finance administrations, state and local government agencies, housing-related associations, and private organizations. Ask both your Realtor and lender for programs that are available in your area.

• *Loan application process.* Once you decide on a lender and the type of mortgage you want, you make a formal application for financing. The loan application process can be intimidating, but if you know what to expect from your lender, you are 90 percent there. Apply for a mortgage loan by filling out an application and providing information about your employment situation, income, assets (auto, investments, etc.), and liabilities (credit card debt, auto loans, etc.). You may be asked to provide paycheck stubs, bank account statements, tax returns, proof of insurance, and other documents that verify the information you submit. The lender will check all the information you have provided. This process takes one to six weeks, depending on the type of mortgage you choose, whether you are buying a home outside your local community, and other factors. Within three days of your application, the lender must give you an estimate of your closing costs—called a good-faith estimate, GFE. The closing is the actual settlement of the loan. You will also receive a statement that shows your estimated monthly payment, the cost of finance charges, and other information about your mortgage. If everything has checked out, the lender will issue a loan commitment.

• *Settlement services.* Once you have agreed to purchase a home and have set a closing date, you will have to deal with the settlement service providers. Though you might regard all the charges and paperwork that come with the services provided by settlement service companies as the most annoying (and expensive) part of the closing, these services are invariably necessary because they assure the lender that the property transfer is in order so that the lender can use the property as collateral in case of your default. Most of the time, your Realtor and/or lender will recommend all of the settlement service providers so that you will not have to spend much time lining them up. These providers facilitate the purchase and transfer of property with regard to:

~ Title insurance
~ Appraiser
~ Private mortgage insurance
~ Home inspection
~ Credit report
~ Application fee
~ Homeowner's insurance
~ Escrow fee

• *Loan closing.* You are now at the last step in purchasing a home—the loan closing. The closing is the settlement of the property transfer. At the closing, the property is formally sold and transferred from the seller to the buyer. The closing involves the delivery of a deed, the signing of legal documents, and the disbursement of funds necessary to consummate a sale of the property. The actual closing meeting usually takes place at the settlement attorney's (sometimes the title company's) office. Your real estate agent will accompany you to the closing. Your settlement attorney will also be present and will probably run the meeting. Sometimes your lender will appear, but that is highly unlikely. On the other side of the table will be the seller, the seller's real estate agent, and, on rare occasions, an attorney representing the seller. You will sign a lot of papers and write a great many checks to settle the costs, from the escrow amount to the down payment you have agreed to with your lender. When you are done—congratulations! You are now a homeowner.

Chapter Ten

HOW TO IDENTIFY A LOCAL MARKET THAT IS RIGHT FOR YOU

In the movie *Shallow Hal,* starring Gwyneth Paltrow and Jack Black, the main character, Hal, was extremely shallow when it came to dating women—he wanted to date only physically beautiful women. But under a spell, Hal fell in love with a pleasantly plump woman. The spell convinced Hal that women looked physically beautiful even though they were not. And after the spell was broken, Hal remained in love with the pleasantly plump woman and lived happily ever after. The moral of the story: Inner beauty is more important than physical appearance. Beauty is in the eye of the beholder.

So it is for most of us in life. Skinny men fall in love with fat women; short women fall for tall men. Purchasing property is no different. Some households desire a large backyard; others would rather live in a high-rise with little maintenance. Some want to live in a small town where they know their neighbors; others prefer to live in a crowded city. There is no right or wrong choice when purchasing a home.

In identifying a property that is right for you, remember, there is no *right* property. You can apply all the fundamentals in a rational manner to ensure that you are paying a fair market price, but the property and its location are a personal and subjective decision. If you are fortunate enough to have some flexibility in where you can live, you may compare local markets and select the community that feels right for you. You may find a location that has great long-term potential—one with great DNA and a bright future, one that combines livability with value. This is, of course, the perfect scenario. Unfortunately, not many of us live in that world.

In the real world, we purchase real estate under some constraints. We may not be able to live in the local community in which we work. Most of us have financial constraints: We may not be able to afford to purchase the kind of home we would like in the neighborhood where we would like to live. Only the wealthy get to live where they want. Tiger Woods's magnificent home on Jupiter Island, Florida, probably offers a perfect or close-to-perfect DNA mix of characteristics. For the rest of us, the best we can hope for is an optimal outcome given the trade-offs we are willing to accept.

WHAT DO WE MEAN BY THE BEST LOCATION?

For a home buyer, what is best for you may mean living in a location that is entirely different from what someone else considers the best location. It might mean acquiring property that is expected to generate long-term price appreciation. How can you decide what is best for you?

First, you likely fall into one of the following categories (I could create additional categories, but let's keep it simple):

- Young households without children
- Households with children
- Mature households
- Empty-nester households
- Retiring households
- Property investors

For each of these categories, the objective is similar: Identify a local market that possesses most of the characteristics that satisfy your needs. For example, most households with children want to live in an area that offers good schools for their children and a community with other families with children. You can utilize all of the publicly available ranking lists to help you make these choices. But it will come down to personally visiting the targeted locations and inspecting a market's DNA. Although none of us can be perfectly categorized in describing our location needs and wants, the information below should provide some general guidance.

YOUNG HOUSEHOLDS WITHOUT CHILDREN

If you have a household with no children (you might be single or married), you are likely looking to buy a starter home. Best for you is an affordable environment that provides both business and social opportunities. You are likely to desire local markets with the following characteristics:

- *Affordability*. Households seeking starter homes need to purchase relatively low-priced homes.
- *Recreation/parks*. Households with no children look for adult recreational facilities, such as community centers, baseball and soccer fields, parks, organized adult athletic leagues and/or intramural activities, and the like.
- *Entertainment*. With no children, young adults look for entertainment such as meeting places for singles (restaurants/bars), professional sports events, and music (concerts), to name a few.

HOUSEHOLDS WITH CHILDREN

If you have a household with young children, your primary focus is usually on your children. "Best" in your context means an appropriate environment to bring up kids. You are likely to desire local markets with the following characteristics:

- *Quality education*. Families with children are looking for neighborhoods with good schools and are willing to spend more to live in such a neighborhood or town.
- A *low-to-medium household age*. A community that has other families with children.
- *Affordable*. Couples with young children often are in the early stages of their careers. Their median income tends to be toward the low end. Older families with children may have more disposable income, but affordability is usually a critical factor for them as well.
- *Religious organizations*. Families with children look for communities that offer convenient access to the religion of their choice, from churches to temples to mosques.
- *Recreation/Parks*. Parents look for recreational facilities, such as community centers, boating and swimming, baseball and soccer

fields, parks, organized athletic leagues and/or intramural activities, and the like.

MATURE HOUSEHOLDS

Households with older children are often approaching their peak earning years. They are often looking to trade up to a larger home and a more afflu-ent neighborhood. They tend to look for:

- *Downtown.* An appealing downtown, nearby access to shopping, movies, and restaurants. Ambience is of greater concern to mature households.
- *Entertainment.* With their children now occupying themselves with their friends and social and athletic activities, parents are looking for entertainment as well, from professional sports events to music, theater, dining out, and so on.
- *Transportation.* Mature households are less willing than younger ones to make that long commute in a car. A solid and accessible transportation system is a plus for this group.
- *Culture/Ethnicity.* Museums, plays, and concerts become increas-ingly important as households age.
- *Safety.* For most of us, the older we get, the more risk-averse we become. Safety and the desire to feel protected are coveted.

EMPTY-NESTER HOUSEHOLDS

The kids are grown and out on their own. Empty-nesters are free to enjoy themselves a bit more. While their children are still a priority in their lives, empty-nester households can focus more on their *own* needs and wants.

- *Climate.* Some empty-nesters purchase second homes in locations they want to spend time in, from rural retreats to warm-climate properties near the water to mountain ski resorts.
- *Entertainment.* Empty-nesters are increasingly interested in amus-ing themselves rather than focusing their attention on their children.
- *Safety.* These households are getting older and thus more risk-averse; they are looking for safety.

- *Downtown*. A nearby downtown with diverse shopping and amenities becomes increasingly attractive.
- *Recreation*. Empty-nesters are looking for access to golfing, skiing, tennis, and other life sports.
- *Hospital and medical services*. For older folks, having access to quality medical attention is increasingly important.

RETIRING HOUSEHOLDS

Without the need to commute daily to work, retiree households have more freedom of choice in where they can live.

- *Mountains/Water*. Ocean and lake properties and properties in the mountains are the two most popular retirement destinations.
- *Climate*. Nice weather is often key for retiring households (thus the popularity of the South, Southwest, Florida, Arizona, Nevada, and Southern California).
- *Hospital and medical services*. Good facilities and health care are a must.
- *Culture/Ethnicity*. Cultural activities such as museums, theater, and the like become ever more of a premium.
- *Entertainment*. Slower and safer entertainment, but entertainment nevertheless, such as golf, gambling, theater, and dining (especially all in the same complex), as well as local card games (gin rummy, bridge, etc.) and other social activities.

PROPERTY INVESTORS

People who look at real estate as an investment are less focused on their personal wants and needs than they are on what they think other people will be interested in.

- *Diversified Economy*. A well-rounded local economy reduces risk in investment property.
- *Culture/Ethnicity*. Local markets with high concentrations of ethnic groups usually raise the available pool of renters.
- *Affordability*. Investment properties need to be affordable to potential renters.

- *Safety.* A safe neighborhood is essential to property values going up.
- *Transportation.* Accessible transportation is a must to potential renters, who usually have more limited funds.

SORTING OUT WHAT IS RIGHT

To simplify the search process, you may want to sort metropolitan areas by some basic characteristic. This might help you trim down your list of potential target markets. For example, if the cost of living is a primary concern, you may want to sort cities and regions by affordability. Depending on your income and wealth, this could help you eliminate a significant number of areas from your list of possible local markets, whether you are looking for properties exclusively in Ohio or Texas or whether you are considering a retirement home and have the entire country to choose from. You can also sort cities by job creation, from highest job growth to lowest job growth. Such a list might provide you with a sense about which cities represent the greater opportunities for job advancement in the near future. Or you can combine several characteristics, such as affordability and job gains, and sort cities or regions by the combination of these two factors.

Here are some simple lists of U.S. cities that I have presented to the real estate industry over the years that provide a way of prioritizing locations by certain characteristics. After completing this book, you may want to compile your own lists using the data presented here, or by updating these lists as new data become available (via the Internet, Realtor.org, etc.).

HIGH-JOB-GROWTH METROPOLITAN AREAS

Washington, D.C.	Orlando, FL
Las Vegas, NV	Tampa, FL
Phoenix, AZ	Riverside, CA
Miami, FL	

MOST AFFORDABLE METROPOLITAN AREAS

Danville, IL	Fort Wayne, IN
Elmira, NY	South Bend, IN
Decatur, IL	Springfield, IL
Youngstown, OH	

AFFORDABLE METROPOLITAN AREAS WITH STRONG GROWTH (LOOKING AT AFFORDABILITY AND JOB GAINS)

Dallas-Fort Worth, TX	Orlando, FL
Charlotte, NC	Houston, TX
Atlanta, GA	Tampa-St. Petersburg, FL

CITIES WITH DIVERSIFIED ECONOMIES AND HIGH-PAYING JOBS, WHERE PRICES ARE HIGH

San Francisco
New York
Boston

METROPOLITAN AREAS WITH THE STRONGEST IN-MIGRATION TRENDS (YOUNG AND ENERGETIC CITIES)

Boise, ID	Las Vegas, NV
Sarasota, FL	Phoenix, AZ
Fort Myers, FL	Jacksonville, FL

HIGH-TECH METROPOLITAN AREAS (EDUCATED WORKFORCE, POSITIVE MIGRATION, HIGH-TECH RESURGENCE)

Seattle, WA	San Jose, CA
Austin, TX	Denver, CO
Raleigh-Durham, NC	

UP-AND-COMING METROPOLITAN AREAS (CITIES WITH HIGH IN-MIGRATION LIKELY TO BECOME ATTRACTIVE TO AGING BOOMERS)

Wilmington, NC	Pensacola, FL
Charleston, SC	Port St. Lucie, FL
Myrtle Beach, SC	Mobile, AL
Panama City, FL	Virginia Beach, VA

AFFORDABLE METROPOLITAN NEIGHBORS (CITIES WITH MEDIAN PRICES SUBSTANTIALLY LESS THAN THEIR NEIGHBORING CITY)

Riverside-San Bernardino, CA	Sacramento, CA
Baltimore, MD	Providence, RI

HIGH-GROWTH SECOND-HOME-BUYING LOCATIONS

Las Vegas, NV	Honolulu, HI
West Palm Beach, FL	Charleston, SC
Tallahassee, FL	Miami, FL
Reno, NV	Tampa, FL
Orlando, FL	Fort Lauderdale, FL

The above tables were created looking at the DNA characteristics and local economic and housing measures that make cities attractive to households. Such lists, of course, change from year to year. But they should serve as an example of how you go about sorting local markets by the characteristics you are looking for as you begin your property search in a given locale. Remember, I use metropolitan areas because the data is readily accessible. In actuality, you may be comparing towns, counties, or communities, which involves gathering information on the local housing market and local economy, which may or may not be available on the Internet. Conduct a search by Googling your county or town, looking for economic and real estate data. Most of the information should be there. But if it is not, utilize local real estate and lending companies and request that they provide you with most of this information. In the examples that follow, I will show you how to gather, with little effort, the pertinent local information that you need.

SELECTING A PLACE TO LIVE

To purchase a primary residence in the *right* local market means that you know what you want and have the necessary information to find it. There are so many ways to identify and sort locations. Use your own selection criteria—you don't need to use mine. You have your own tastes and needs and aspirations of where you want to live. I recommend that you go through a "right way" process before every property purchase. Let me take you through five simple steps that I suggest you follow to accomplish this. Then I will provide local examples to demonstrate how easy it is to follow these steps.

Step 1: Determine Who You Are
Step 2: Select Desirable Location Characteristics
Step 3: Prioritize Your Needs and Wants
Step 4: Identify Local Markets with the Characteristics You Are
Looking For
Step 5: Visit Your Top Local Markets

Step 1: Determine Who You Are
It sounds simple enough, but you would be surprised how many families make the wrong location choice because they ignored some of their basic needs. How far are you willing to commute? What is the maximum amount you are able to pay for a house? How close do you need to be to

other family members? Families need to sit down and agree on who you are and what you want.

Step 2: Select Desirable Location Characteristics

Write down the characteristics that you would like to have in a house and a neighborhood. Do you want to live on a quiet street, away from traffic? Are you willing to commute a long distance to get the amenities you desire? Or is a shorter commute—say, no more than a half hour—a quality-of-life issue for you? Do you have a large enough family that four bedrooms is a necessity, or can you live with three? There are many specifics about an area that are important in making a location decision, including the age, income, and type of households residing in that area, job opportunities, the health of the local economy, the climate, education, transportation, professional sports teams, entertainment facilities, and so on.

Step 3: Prioritize Your Needs and Wants

Rank, sort, and prioritize your list according to the different traits and characteristics. For example, if you have an empty-nester household and you are looking to purchase in a warm-climate location, your top five characteristics may be:

- Affordability
- Neighborhood entertainment
- Local retail shopping
- Recreation facilities
- Safety

Step 4: Identify Local Markets with the Characteristics You Are Looking For

Prioritizing characteristics narrows the available pool of local markets. There is an abundance of local market information about every town and/or neighborhood (e.g., zip code) that provides you with the ability to compare locations. The two location examples presented below show how this is accomplished.

Step 5: Visit Your Top Local Markets

Next, plan a trip and visit your top towns, cities, or regions. If you are an empty-nester and you picked Las Vegas, Phoenix, and Reno as possible retirement locations, take a trip to each of these cities. Make an appointment with a local Realtor to take you on a tour of the possible neighborhoods so that you can begin to see how much house you can afford for the price you are willing to pay. If three-bedroom houses cost $500,000 in the nicer neighborhoods and that is more than you had planned to spend given the smaller size of your household, look for a two-bedroom house in neighborhoods farther from the center of town that might cost less. If, however, convenience to shopping and culture is critical, you may choose to get a smaller property, but in the location that best suits your needs. This also may be the time to ask your Realtor to gather pertinent market information (household composition, income, etc.) so that you can intelligently compare the local markets under consideration.

REGION, CITY, AND TOWN COMPARISONS

Comparing metropolitan areas across the United States is instructive. It is also useful for real estate investors interested in diversifying across the nation. But it is not very useful for local home buyers and local investors. Most of us are faced with more local purchase decisions, like moving to a particular region of the nation because of a job relocation or selecting a town or neighborhood within a particular metropolitan area to trade up to a larger home. Let's look at both cases. First, I'll attempt to identify the right location in Florida for a second-home buyer. Next, I'll attempt to identify the right location in northern Virginia for a household moving to the area because of a job relocation.

Selecting a Second-Home Location in Florida

Let's say an empty-nester household desires a warm-weather location and is seeking to purchase a second home in Florida. Location selection is important because this second home may become a retirement home as he approaches retirement. There are many cities and towns in Florida that would qualify, but let's assume our empty-nester has narrowed his choices to six locations:

1. Sarasota/Bradenton
2. Naples
3. Fort Myers

4. Daytona Beach
5. Miami/Fort Lauderdale
6. Tampa/St. Petersburg

First, he should follow the five steps above to select the right market, gathering as much information for each market as he can to make valid comparisons. For simplicity, let's assume he gathers the following information, which is easily obtained from Internet sites such as Realtor.com.

	MEDIAN AGE	JOB GROWTH	MEDIAN PRICE	NET MIGRATION	CRIME RATE (PER 100,000 PEOPLE)
Sarasota/Bradenton	58.8	39,600	$350,900	22,700	608
Naples	57.2	17,500	$469,100	9,200	450
Fort Myers	56.8	39,300	$271,600	29,500	578
Daytona Beach	54.9	18,700	$210,700	11,900	626
Miami/Ft. Lauderdale	48.7	165,200	$376,200	1,000	1,021
Tampa/St. Petersburg	50.9	112,000	$231,600	58,500	786

All of these locations provide warm-weather and water-recreation activities. But our empty-nester household is concerned with home value and future appreciation as well. In this case, Tampa/St. Petersburg may offer the greatest opportunity. Tampa boasts the healthiest combination of job growth (112,000) and net migration (58,500) among the six cities. It is also the second most affordable location (Daytona is first), offering a $231,000 median home price, and a more favorable median age, 50.9, for a household that has not yet retired, than four other cities. The information above helps enormously in making a location decision. The next step is to visit Tampa and two other cities from the table above. You need to see if you can locate a safe neighborhood (given Tampa's relatively high crime rate), as well as one that has the amenities and characteristics (local DNA) that you desire.

Selecting a Town Within the Northern Virginia Area

Most home buyers compare towns and neighborhoods (zip codes) within a preferred location of a metropolitan area rather than selecting among large metropolitan areas in differing regions across the nation. For example, if you are moving to the Washington, D.C., metropolitan area because of a new job and have family in the northern Virginia area, you may focus on finding a desirable location in the northern Virginia area that is in reasonable commuting distance to your office in Washington. Let's assume you have narrowed your choice to three towns:

> Alexandria
> Arlington
> Burke

Again, follow the five steps above to select the right market for you, gathering as much pertinent information for each location as possible from an Internet search for economic and housing data on these towns. Here is my search process:

1. Google: Profiles on Virginia cities, towns.
2. The inquiry generated a Google page offering many sources to choose from.
3. Next, I clicked on: "Stats about all U.S. cities," which took me to the City-Data.com Web site.
4. Then I clicked on "Virginia" and was provided with a long list of cities and towns in Virginia.
5. Finally I clicked on "Alexandria," "Arlington," and "Burke" and received a host of economic/housing information for each town.

From the information provided for each town, I constructed the table below comparing the three towns:

	ALEXANDRIA	ARLINGTON	BURKE
Population	135,337	195,965	57,737
Median age	34.4 years	34.0 years	37.6 years
Median household income	$56,054	$63,001	$93,561
Median house value	$252,800	$262,400	$215,100
Household composition:			
White (non-Hispanic)	53.7%	60.4%	69.9%
Black	22.5%	9.3%	5.0%
Hispanic	14.7%	18.6%	7.4%
Asian	7.4%	8.7%	8.9%
Never married	39.0%	41.7%	23.8%
Now married	43.1%	43.6%	64.5%
Foreign-born	25.4%	27.8%	20.2%

Education:			
High school or higher	86.8%	87.8%	94.9%
BA degree or higher	54.3%	60.2%	59.0%
Commuting time	29.7 minutes	27.3 minutes	33.4 minutes
Unemployment rate	3.2%	2.8%	2.2%
Major businesses			
Professional, scientific, management	22.0%	na	19.6%
Public administration	14.2%	na	16.4%
Education, health & services	12.9%	na	17.7%
Number of major companies	na	19	na
City-data.com crime index	245	na	na
Number of hospitals	3	3	0
Transportation			
Proximity to airports	close	close	moderately far
Proximity to railroad	close	close	close
Significant college/university	no	Marymount	George Mason
Religious establishments	many	many	many

A cursory glance at the table above reveals some important differences among the towns. Burke is a relatively wealthy ($93,561 median household income) town, but more affordable (its median home price is lower) compared to Alexandria ($56,054) and Arlington ($63,001). Burke also is farther away from D.C. (a longer commute) and has a more homogeneous population (69.9 percent non-Hispanic white) versus Alexandria (53.7 percent) and Arlington (60.4 percent). If you are willing to live in the outer suburbs at a more affordable home price with relatively wealthy neighbors who are homogeneous non-Hispanic whites, select Burke. On the other hand, if you are looking for a more diverse community and wish to be closer to the D.C. city limits, you should contact local Realtors in both Alexandria and Arlington to visit both locations and assess the local characteristics that are important to you, such as attractiveness and charm, the number and kind of local restaurants, whether or not there are recreation centers, and the quality of the school systems.

Many of us have been taken to a neighborhood by our Realtor and have fallen in love with it (I've done this myself). But what we have not yet done is our homework. Your home is not just a place to live but a large financial investment as well. You would not purchase $300,000 worth of shares of Disney Company stock because you happened to enjoy their last movie. You would assess their management, earnings potential, financial statements, and so on. The same is true for purchasing a house in a town that you will eventually call home. So don't forget to do your *home*-work.

SELECTING A LOCATION FOR INVESTMENT

Purchasing investment property in the *right* local market means that you need to know what *other* households want. I recommend that you go through the following process before every investment property purchase:

Step 1: Determine What Type of Property Investor You Are
Step 2: Select Desirable Location Characteristics
Step 3: Prioritize Your Needs and Wants
Step 4: Identify Local Markets with the Characteristics You Are
    Looking For
Step 5: Visit Your Top Local Markets

Step 1: Determine What Type of Property Investor You Are

What is your investment horizon? Three years? Five years? Ten years? What type of return on investment are you looking for? Significant price appreciation or a positive monthly cash flow? How much risk are you willing to assume? Are you willing to manage the property yourself, or do you want to hire a property management company?

Step 2: Select Desirable Location Characteristics

Write down the characteristics that you would like to see in an investment property and a neighborhood. What type of households do you want to rent to? Are you willing to rent to college-age students, who may inflict damage to the property over time? Are you aware that low-income households may have difficulty meeting rent payments on time? Did you realize that young households with favorable job prospects may be short-term renters, eventually looking to own? If you want a location that is attractive to potential renters, look for a neighborhood convenient to grocery shopping and accessible transportation (a bus stop or train station).

Step 3: Prioritize Your Needs and Wants

Rank, sort, and prioritize your list according to the different traits and characteristics. For example, are you looking only for price appreciation? Are you looking to have a stable, long-term investment? Are you looking for an affordable investment property so you are not burdened with taking on too much mortgage debt and associated housing/upkeep costs?

Step 4: Identify Local Markets with the Characteristics
You Are Looking For

Most real estate investors are likely to purchase rental properties close to their primary residence, so you will probably be comparing locations within a metropolitan area. There is an abundance of local market information about every town and/or neighborhood (e.g., zip code) that provides you with the ability to compare locations. The two location examples presented in the section on buying a home show how this is accomplished. But you also need to ask your Realtor about the local rental market. What are rents for a one-bedroom condo versus a two-bedroom condo? How much rent growth can you assume per year in the local market?

Step 5: Visit Your Top Local Markets

Next, plan a trip and visit your top neighborhoods and towns. If you are a relatively new investor, develop a relationship with some local Realtors and lenders. They can offer you important and sometimes critical guidance throughout the investment process.

AFTER MAKING A LOCATION DECISION

When you purchase real estate, you are buying both a specific property and a neighborhood or location. Always select possible locations first. Then select specific properties. There is an important reason for choosing the right real estate package—building wealth. For most households, this is one of the most important reasons for owning real estate. Over 80 percent of all homeowners in America depend more on the value of their home (their home's equity) for retirement than stocks and bonds and other savings. This is why it is so important to learn how to build wealth in real estate. Choosing the right property in the right location will take you much of the way there. In the next chapter, I'll take everything we've discussed so far and show you how to build wealth by better understanding the local market you decide to purchase property in.

Chapter Eleven

BUILDING WEALTH

What do we do with all this information and knowledge? How do we build wealth through real estate? Let's first distinguish who you are. Each type of buyer—a first-time homebuyer, a trade-up or trade-down buyer, a vacation-home buyer, or an investor purchasing rental property—requires some variation in a wealth-building strategy, but the essentials are the same.

Step 1: Create a Local Real Estate Team

You can't do it alone. You are going to need assistance from people who know real estate and know the local marketplace. Leverage as much as you can off experienced real estate professionals. Your real estate agent is your first source of information and guidance. He or she knows the local marketplace. Do an information dump with your agent. If the agent is seasoned and competent, he or she should know some of the important local business and political activities that may impact future home prices (but you need to ask). He or she should also recommend other real estate professionals who can be part of your team, including a lender, a real estate attorney (if necessary), a home inspector, and a reputable title insurance company that can administer the closing.

Step 2: Compare Local Market DNA

You need to be able to compare local real estate markets—metropolitan areas or towns or neighborhoods—by DNA characteristics. This task takes a little work, but it is very doable. Follow the DNA characteristics list I presented in Chapter Four. Fill it in for the local markets that you are comparing. Chapter Twelve offers a discussion on how to compare locations by different characteristics. I have also included an appendix at the close of this book with a great deal of metro data on some of the more important characteristics. Use these tables as a guide in making your real estate choices.

Step 3: Take Note of Outside Influences

Write down some notes on observable influences that may affect real estate activity in the local markets you are targeting, including market indicators (e.g., mortgage rates), conventional influences like local political decisions, unconventional influences like an Oprah pronouncement on real estate, and megatrends. These notes should help shape your estimates for future property values in a particular local marketplace.

Step 4: Check Your List of Fundamentals

First, make sure you pass the affordability test (see Chapter Eight). Second, review the comparative market analysis, or CMA, with your real estate agent (also Chapter Eight). And third, assess current market conditions. This may be the most important step in the process. Such a checklist will keep you from straying from the fundamentals. I'm going to share with you a current conditions list that I used at the National Association of Realtors. You may not be able to gather all of this information, but you should attempt to find at least partial data for each of the following five categories:

- Price activity
- Affordability
- Home sales
- Mortgages
- Local measures

To illustrate the usefulness of this fundamentals checklist, let's look at three important metros during this decade's real estate boom: Las Vegas, Washington, D.C., and Miami.

FUNDAMENTALS EXERCISE: LAS VEGAS 2006 Q1

	Las Vegas	National Average	Comment
Price Activity			
Latest Appreciation (06Q1 vs. 05Q1)	9.2%	10.3%	Average
Last-Year Appreciation	15.2%	12.0%	Strong
3-Year Appreciation	90.7%	31.0%	Strong
Historical Avg. Annual Appreciation	6.6%	5.0%	Average
Affordability			
Mortgage Debt Servicing Cost/Income (06Q1)	27.1%	22.0%	High
Historical Mortgage Debt Servicing Cost	22.2%	22.0%	Neutral
Home Sales			
State Existing Home Sales (06Q1 vs. 05Q1)	−15.0%	−2.1%	Unfavorable
Single-Family Housing Permits (06Q1 vs. 05Q1)	20.0%	−0.9%	Unfavorable
Mortgages			
Share of New Loans with ARMs (06Q1)	58.0%	28.0%	Unfavorable
Share of New Loans with Loan to Value Higher than 90%	4.0%	16.0%	Favorable
Percentage of Sub-Prime Mortgages	10.6%	10.1%	Neutral
Percent of Mortgages for Second-Home Purchase	28.5%	15.3%	High
State Delinquency Rate (06Q1)	2.4%	4.0%	Favorable
Local Measures			
3-Year Job Growth	19.2%	2.4%	Favorable
Unemployment Rate (06Q1)	4.0%	4.7%	Favorable
Housing Permits to Employment (05)	4.5%	1.6%	High
Net Migration	49,200	0	Favorable

FUNDAMENTALS EXERCISE: WASHINGTON, D.C. 2006 Q1

	D.C.	National Average	Comment
Price Activity			
Latest Appreciation (06Q1 vs. 05Q1)	11.0%	10.3%	Average
Last-Year Appreciation	25.7%	12.0%	Strong
3-Year Appreciation	74.9%	31.0%	Strong
Historical Avg. Annual Appreciation	6.8%	5.0%	Average
Affordability			
Mortgage Debt Servicing Cost/Income (06Q1)	25.4%	22.0%	Neutral
Historical Mortgage Debt Servicing Cost	22.3%	22.0%	Neutral
Home Sales			
State Existing Home Sales (06Q1 vs. 05Q1)	−18.2%	−2.1%	Unfavorable
Single-Family Housing Permits (06Q1 vs. 05Q1)	−13.0%	−0.9%	Favorable
Mortgages			
Share of New Loans with ARMs (06Q1)	28.0%	28.0%	Neutral
Share of New Loans with Loan to Value Higher than 90%	9.0%	16.0%	Favorable
Percentage of Sub-Prime Mortgages	7.2%	10.1%	Favorable
Percent of Mortgages for Second-Home Purchase	9.7%	15.3%	Favorable
State Delinquency Rate (06Q1)	2.6%	4.0%	Favorable
Local Measures			
3-Year Job Growth	7.0%	2.4%	Favorable
Unemployment Rate (06Q1)	3.4%	4.7%	Favorable
Housing Permits to Employment (05)	1.2%	1.6%	Favorable
Net Migration	9,200	0	Favorable

FUNDAMENTALS EXERCISE: MIAMI 2006 Q1

	Miami	National Average	Comment
Price Activity			
Latest Appreciation (06Q1 vs. 05Q1)	11.2%	10.3%	Moderating
Last-Year Appreciation	29.2%	12.0%	Strong
3-Year Appreciation	92.7%	31.0%	Strong
Historical Avg. Annual Appreciation	7.2%	5.0%	Average
Affordability			
Mortgage Debt Servicing Cost/Income (06Q1)	30.9%	22.0%	High
Historical Mortgage Debt Servicing Cost	20.8%	22.0%	Average
Home Sales			
State Existing Home Sales (06Q1 vs. 05Q1)	−15.7%	−2.1%	Unfavorable
Single-Family Housing Permits (06Q1 vs. 05Q1)	−7.0%	−0.9%	Favorable
Mortgages			
Share of New Loans with ARMs (06Q1)	43.0%	28.0%	Unfavorable
Share of New Loans with Loan to Value Higher than 90%	10.0%	16.0%	Neutral
Percentage of Sub-Prime Mortgages	13.3%	10.1%	Unfavorable
Percent of Mortgages for Second-Home Purchase	22.5%	15.3%	Unfavorable
State Delinquency Rate (06Q1)	3.4%	4.0%	Neutral
Local Measures			
3-Year Job Growth	7.4%	2.4%	Favorable
Unemployment Rate (06Q1)	4.0%	4.7%	Favorable
Housing Permits to Employment (05)	1.8%	1.6%	Neutral
Net Migration	38,600	0	Favorable

The above tables provide a barometer of local price pressures for each metro market. All three of these markets—Miami, D.C., and Las Vegas—possess desirable upward pressure on prices for the long term due to favorable local measures. However, each metro also possesses some short-term price problems. First, all three metros experienced substantial price growth over the past three years, making it difficult to maintain robust price pressure. Second, affordability conditions deteriorated in all three metros, particularly in Las Vegas and Miami. In addition, Miami and Las Vegas possess some risk of default, as evidenced by a high percentage of risky mortgages. Finally, the long-term indicators—job growth and net migration—are very favorable for all three markets. After a cursory glance at these tables, I would conclude that Miami and Las Vegas will likely experience longer and deeper sales and price corrections in their local markets in 2006 and 2007 than will the D.C. metro market. But all three possess favorable longer-term real estate prospects.

Step 5: Develop a Property Wealth-Building Strategy

For people who own a primary residence and now want to become real estate investors, what is the best wealth-building strategy? There is no right or wrong way to invest in real estate as long as you stick to the fundamentals. But some strategies perform better than others over the longer term. Because of my position in the real estate markets, I have encountered many successful real estate investors—some are good friends of mine. Although most individual strategies are somewhat different from one another, there are some common threads that are worth knowing. Keep in mind that a strategy that is effective today may not be as effective tomorrow due to changes in market conditions. With this in mind, let's identify the common threads.

- **Determine Real Estate Investment Goals.** Is your objective to become rich by age forty? Or are you willing to wait until retirement age to cash in on your property investments? Your purchase goals depend heavily on age. Young households are just usually looking to save enough money for a down payment on a starter home, while established homeowners are hoping to trade up into their dream home. Savvy property investors should look to build a real estate portfolio that will play a major role in both their investment and retirement portfolios. To do so, first quantify your real estate goals. Do you want to own $2 million of property within seven years? Or would you rather net $10,000 per month from your real estate portfolio within seven years?

- **Establish Purchase/Investment Priorities.** If you don't already own a primary residence, that should be your first priority so you can get into the real estate game. Next, review your property-expansion plans. Are you looking for a home-improvement property, a trade-up property, a vacation property, or a rental property? Depending on your personal and financial situation, all of these options are acceptable. For purposes of this discussion, let's assume that you want to invest in real estate via rental or vacation properties to build wealth.

- **Determine Your Investment Horizon.** Stick to a lengthy investment horizon. If you are looking for short-term gains, invest in the stock market; real estate is not for you. Every successful real estate investor whom I know treats real estate as a long-run play. The minimum holding period is usually five years. The typical holding-period range is between five and ten years. A longer holding period provides an opportunity for solid appreciation. It also provides enough time for rents to rise, improving your property's cash flows.

- **Determine Your Level of Risk Taking.** First, decide on a property type—single-family or condo, vacation property or rental property. Condos usually pose less operations/management risk, since there are lower maintenance costs, while single-family detached homes pose greater risk due to the higher maintenance costs. But condos may pose greater price risk, since condo prices are a bit more volatile than single-family detached property. Vacation properties pose a great deal of risk, since you are likely to be absent from the property for long periods of time and there may be little rent to cover the expenses associated with financing and maintaining the property. Rental properties also pose a relatively high level of risk due to tenant uncertainty, maintenance costs, and so on. With regard to location, some locations are riskier than others, depending on local population and economic and housing trends. You need to decide how much risk you are willing to assume with the financing of the property as well (variable or fixed-rate loan, size of down payment, and so on).

- **Determine Your Level of Diversification.** It is common sense that you don't put all your money into one real estate investment. If it turns sour, you could lose a great deal of money. This is why I recommend that households expand their real estate investments beyond their own home. As you have learned throughout this book, geography (the local marketplace) plays an important role in determining the success or failure of real estate. Property values in some locations are falling while other locations are rising. Of course, if you could physically handle purchasing properties across the entire nation, you would be well diversified. But for most households, you should diversify a portfolio of rental properties among different locations within a metropolitan area.

- **Determine the Right Method of Financing.** I recommend that you establish some criteria for the financing of property purchases.

Leverage property for returns, not because of lack of funds. It is important to be able to afford the property you are purchasing. If you do not have enough funds for a sufficient down payment, wait until you do. Toward the end of the boom, many investors stretched their credit and incomes, placing themselves in a precarious position. Take advantage of leveraging a property purchase, but only if you can afford it. The typical down payment is about 20 percent, but some forms of financing are available that will let you purchase property for 10 percent down—or even nothing down. If you put only 10 percent down, make sure you can afford the monthly mortgage payments and other expenses associated with the property. Let me show you how leveraging works.

Assuming a typical 20 percent down payment, a $20,000 investment can buy you a $100,000 property. If the price of your property rises by 6 percent (i.e., $6,000) in the first year of ownership, the return on your $20,000, were you to sell the property, would be 30 percent ($6,000/$20,000). Most people assume that when the price of their home rises by 6 percent, they are earning a 6 percent return. But since they have invested only their down payment in the property, the return is significantly greater. Of course, there are other costs associated with real estate purchases, such as closing costs, maintenance expenses, and property taxes, that bring the final return down a bit. But these costs are relatively small compared to the value of the property. Notice that I didn't include your mortgage payments in the calculation associated with the purchase. This is because if you didn't own a home, you would be paying rent, which is approximately equal to the after-tax mortgage payment. And with investment property, the rent you receive from a tenant will help offset the mortgage payments.

Identify how much negative monthly cash flow you can afford and stick to it. Lower your down payment if you can afford the negative monthly cash flows to increase your leveraging position. I own properties with 10, 20, and 30 percent down, depending on how the price of the property affects my targeted cash flow. Your down payment (leveraging position) depends on the price you pay for the property as well as the rents you expect to receive. Identify the negative monthly cash flow you are willing and able to fund, and depending on the price, the down payment will be determined. For example, assume you need to bid $300,000 to purchase a rental condominium property that is currently generating $1,200 monthly rent. If your negative-cash-flow tolerance is $500 per month and you are excited about the value potential of this property, you will need to put down 30 percent in order for the deal to work for you. This is because with 30 percent down, your monthly mortgage payments (at a 6 percent mortgage rate) would be $1,259, offsetting the $1,200 monthly rent revenue, leaving you with property taxes and condo fees totaling $500 per month. Any down payment less than 30 percent would raise your negative cash flow. Now, if you could get $1,600 monthly rent, you could reduce your down payment to only 10 percent. Monthly mortgage payments on 10 percent down (at a 6 percent mortgage rate) would be $1,618, offsetting the $1,600 rent, leaving you with a negative $500 monthly cash flow for property taxes and condo fees.

Lock into at least a three- to five-year mortgage loan in a stable and rising rate environment. The type of financing you select will determine the interest rate, amortization, speed of paying off the principal balance, and monthly payment of the loan. In a stable or rising rate environment, I suggest you lock into at least a three- to five-year mortgage loan. Three- and five-year balloons are very popular. You can even lock into an interest-only loan as well. The point is that by locking into a mortgage rate, you permit rent payment to rise while mortgage costs are fixed, improving cash flows. Of course, if you are in a falling rate environment, variable-rate mortgages become a better choice. But can you safely predict that mortgage rates will continue to fall? As an investor, you need to have enough funds to pay for the negative cash flows generated from some properties in the early years (before rents have had a chance to rise) as well as some maintenance and property-management expenses.

- **Determine level of property management.** One decision you have to make is whether or not you will manage your property personally. If you don't want to be a hands-on manager, shop around for the lowest fee (assuming the company is reputable) that a property-management company will charge for taking on that responsibility. If you are inclined to be your own property manager, you will improve your cash flows quickly, and good luck to you. Either way you go, here are some of the responsibilities of property management: finding the right tenant, getting the lease properly executed, communicating with your tenant, arranging for maintenance and repairs, inspecting your property periodically, and handling accounting and record keeping. I use a real estate company to find a tenant and execute the lease only. I do all the rest. But many successful real estate investors retain their own property-management companies, particularly when their portfolios get too big too handle (a nice problem to have).

- **Purchase a minimum of one property per year.** This seems to be a consistent goal among many successful real estate investors that I know. The intent is to force you to build up a portfolio of properties. By the end of five years, you would have accumulated at least five properties, maybe more. If each property was valued, let's say, at $200,000 at purchase and we assume a 4 percent annual appreciation rate, you would be controlling approximately $1,118,000 of real estate properties at the end of five years. You can see how this strategy forces you to build wealth. In ten years, your portfolio would consist of at least ten properties totaling at least $2,487,000!

- **Take advantage of local information.** We end your wealth-building strategy with the most important concept—all real estate is local. Acting this out will give you an edge in your property-purchasing activities. You already know how to incorporate this step into your purchases, so this step is serving as a reminder. It may also be useful to learn how successful investors used local activities to build wealth in real estate.

TIPS FROM SUCCESSFUL INVESTORS

We can learn a great deal from other investors' accomplishments. Equally important, we can learn from their problems and failures. After learning how other successful real estate investors do it, I am going to share with you an approach that was told to me by my good friend Dale Mattison, an owner of a Long & Foster franchise in Washington, D.C., and a very successful real estate investor in his own right. His approach toward real estate investing reflects the strategies of most other successful real estate investors that I know (including myself).

He said that in all of the purchases he had made or for property that he has sold to investor clients, he looks for the following:

- Always buy in the very best area that your budget will allow.
- Be aware of the neighborhood trends and follow them to take advantage of greater-than-average upswings in value.
- Do *not* view the property as an occupant. Your tastes in living are not usually relevant to the type of investment property you may purchase.

- Look to create an equity position. Leverage or maximum financing is the old-fashioned approach to ownership and can get you in trouble when markets or rental potential shifts.
- Look for property that needs very few upgrades. Use the upgrade money to create more equity.
- Long-term growth is usually more predictable and less risky than short-term growth.
- I have tried to buy as often as possible by mapping out a savings plan toward a down payment while never depleting reserves. At the point a property gets to a positive flow situation, the profit goes either to savings for the next buy or principal reduction on the current property, or partially to both.
- My purchases have been geared to long-term hold. I look to put down at least 20 percent, again looking for the equity posture, and try to have negatives not exceed 10 percent of the overall monthly costs. That way, in approximately two years the property should be in an even or positive cash-flow position.
- I have tended to favor fixed-rate mortgages, since the hold time for the property is long term.

LOCAL INFORMATION

As an example of taking advantage of local market information, consider what Linda Rheinberger, another successful Realtor and property investor, did with one of her investments:

"Looking carefully at the Las Vegas real estate market, I realized that we had very little land left in our area. The scarcity of land had driven up prices to the point where single-story homes (especially those over a certain square footage) do not pencil, and are therefore not being produced. Our local government (Bureau of Land Management) owns most of the land in the state, and with the explosion in growth, most of the movement is towards the suburbs, or vertical [high density]."

Local Investment Strategy

I took advantage of this situation by establishing the following property-selection criteria:

- Only consider properties that are single-story and over 2,700 livable square feet.

- Only consider properties in a master-planned or gated community.
- Only consider properties that are less than five years old and less than $1 million in price.

Result

- Rheinberger found four properties meeting her investment criteria that were under $1 million.
- She bought the lowest-priced home of the offerings: a one-story home with 2,865 livable square feet, a three-car garage, a pool/spa, new appointments—including granite counters, imported tile floors, and so on—in a gated community in Summerlin for $650,000.
- She put $250,000 down and she is getting $3,000/month in rent.
- This investment is at a break-even amount each month.
- As of this writing, the property was valued at over $720,000.

As for my own local stories, I have some good ones and a bad one. My first property purchase was a good one. With the help of a local Realtor in the Washington, D.C., area, I was able to purchase a condominium unit on Wisconsin Avenue in downtown D.C. The location was perfect—convenient shopping across the street (cleaners, restaurants, and a grocery store), a bus stop at the corner, two blocks from Fannie Mae, one of the city's largest employers, and four blocks from American University. Needless to say, I have never had problems renting this property and rents continue to rise while my cash flows continue to improve.

Another success story was when I purchased property in the Fairmont neighborhood in Washington, D.C. My local Realtor provided me with some useful local information—Publix, Inc., was planning on opening a Publix supermarket in two years down the block from my property. This was all I needed to hear. On schedule, two years later, Publix opened and my property continues to thrive, with tenant interest and increased rents.

But even seasoned real estate investors make mistakes. I purchased a one-bedroom condo-conversion unit in Alexandria, Virginia, a prestigious suburb outside of D.C., at the tail end of the real estate boom in the D.C. metropolitan area with the expectation of riding a significant price rise in the property. I purchased at the asking price, which burdened me with a $400 negative monthly cash flow, even after obtaining a cash-flow adjustable-rate mortgage (which had some negative amortization). The boom cooled, and my property didn't realize the appreciation I had expected. It took longer than expected for the condo-conversion company to sell all of the units. I made two mistakes with this investment. First, I ignored the fundamentals. This was a property I should not have purchased at the relatively high purchase price. Second, I obtained an exotic, cash-flow ARM. I became irrational, thinking that I would sell the property in the short term, earning substantial equity gains and relieving me of the cash-flow ARM financing. That did not occur, and I found myself left with a financing vehicle that was subject to monthly interest-rate increases. When I came to my senses, I went back to the fundamentals. I put another 10 percent down on the property and refinanced into a five-year balloon product. I am now treating the property as a five-year investment and the cash flows are more stable. But I learned my lesson about straying from the fundamentals.

Chapter Twelve

LOCAL MARKET COMPARISONS

The Internet has increased the availability of data and information to assist households in making intelligent product choices. Comparison shopping has become easier and simpler for most products due to the Internet. Automobiles are one great example, but real estate is an even better one. You can view property listings on Internet sites, including our nation's largest, Realtor.com, showing over 4 million residential properties available for sale in America. Each property listing offers a detailed description of the property: square footage, number of bedrooms, bathrooms, lot size, school district, and so on. But the Internet has also given consumers access to information about the property's location—the local marketplace.

So where is the data on the local marketplace and is it easily accessible? As I discussed earlier, your local Realtor or lender has access to local-market data like home sales and housing inventory. The more difficult task is gathering some DNA characteristics, like crime, or some household information, like age or income. This information is available in a variety of places, including government agencies, libraries, universities, magazines, and real estate associations. The good news is that all of these organizations have posted their information on the Internet, providing you with direct and easy access. You just have to know where to look. I always begin with a search engine, like Google.com. For example, if you have safety concerns about a particular metro location that you are considering to buy and live in, Google "metro crime rankings." This will lead you to several ranking surveys of metropolitan areas by crime.

In the previous chapters, I gave you examples of how I search for this information. This chapter provides a further glimpse into this type of information. Below are a host of tables, ranking metropolitan areas across the United States by different market characteristics and household information. Each table presents the top twenty-five and bottom twenty-five metro rankings for each characteristic. I include these tables so that you can acquire a feel for the rankings and disparities among metropolitan areas. If anything, these tables should alert you to the fact that metros across the nation are very different from one another. They are all unique, displaying a mix of favorable and unfavorable characteristics. Some mixes might meet your tastes and needs, and some might not. The more information you have about a region or area, the more intelligent your purchase decision. For a complete listing of all major metros, turn to the appendix of this book.

THE OLDEST AND YOUNGEST METROS

(By Median Household Age)

Top 25 MSA	Median Age of Householder
1 Punta Gorda, FL MSA	63.8
2 Sarasota-Bradenton, FL MSA	58.8
3 Naples, FL MSA	57.2
4 Ocala, FL MSA	57.0
5 Fort Myers-Cape Coral, FL MSA	56.8
6 Fort Pierce-Port St. Lucie, FL MSA	56.7
7 Barnstable-Yarmouth, MA MSA	55.5
8 Daytona Beach, FL MSA	54.9
9 West Palm Beach-Boca Raton, FL MSA	53.8
10 Johnstown, PA MSA	53.1
11 Steubenville-Weirton, OH-WV MSA	52.5
12 Cumberland, MD-WV MSA	52.4
13 Scranton-Wilkes-Barre-Hazleton, PA MSA	52.3
14 Melbourne-Titusville-Palm Bay, FL MSA	52.3
15 Wheeling, WV-OH MSA	52.2
16 Lakeland-Winter Haven, FL MSA	51.9
17 Sharon, PA MSA	51.8
18 Yuma, AZ MSA	51.6
19 Pittsfield, MA MSA	51.4
20 Monmouth-Ocean, NJ PMSA	51.3
21 Danville, VA MSA	51.1
22 Youngstown-Warren, OH MSA	51.1
23 Altoona, PA MSA	51.0
24 Gadsden, AL MSA	51.0
25 Tampa-St. Petersburg-Clearwater, FL MSA	50.9

Bottom 25 MSA	Median Age of Householder
1 Bryan-College Station, TX MSA	35.6
2 Auburn-Opelika, AL MSA	39.6
3 Lawrence, KS MSA	39.7
4 Provo-Orem, UT MSA	40.1
5 Jacksonville, NC MSA	40.2
6 Iowa City, IA MSA	40.3
7 Athens, GA MSA	41.1
8 Bloomington, IN MSA	41.3
9 Austin-San Marcos, TX MSA	41.3
10 Gainesville, FL MSA	41.4
11 Killeen-Temple, TX MSA	41.5
12 Columbia, MO MSA	41.5
13 Clarksville-Hopkinsville, TN-KY MSA	41.7
14 Champaign-Urbana, IL MSA	41.7
15 Lafayette, IN MSA	42.2
16 Greenville, NC MSA	42.6
17 Fayetteville, NC MSA	42.7
18 Dallas, TX PMSA	42.8
19 Tallahassee, FL MSA	42.9
20 Raleigh-Durham-Chapel Hill, NC MSA	43.0
21 Anchorage, AK MSA	43.1
22 State College, PA MSA	43.1
23 Madison, WI MSA	43.3
24 Fargo-Moorhead, ND-MN MSA	43.3
25 Atlanta, GA MSA	43.3

Source: U.S. Census 2000

MSA = Metropolitan Statistical Area

MOST VIOLENT AND SAFEST METROS

Top 25 MSA	Violent Crime Rate (per 100,000 people)
1 Sumter, SC MSA	1177
2 Florence, SC MSA	1132
3 Saginaw-Bay City-Midland, MI MSA	1025
4 Miami, FL PMSA	1021
5 Memphis, TN-AR-MS MSA	1009
6 Detroit, MI PMSA	992
7 Alexandria, LA MSA	926
8 Lubbock, TX MSA	898
9 Jackson, TN MSA	890
10 Baltimore, MD PMSA	886
11 Myrtle Beach, SC MSA	875
12 Nashville, TN MSA	872
13 Steubenville-Weirton, OH-WV MSA	849
14 Albuquerque, NM MSA	843
15 Wichita Falls, TX MSA	834
16 Charleston-North Charleston, SC MSA	815
17 Little Rock-North Little Rock, AR MSA	814
18 Anchorage, AK MSA	806
19 Monroe, LA MSA	803
20 Columbia, SC MSA	803
21 Gainesville, FL MSA	788
22 Tampa-St. Petersburg-Clearwater, FL MSA	786
23 Texarkana, TX-Texarkana, AR MSA	783
24 Vineland-Millville-Bridgeton, NJ PMSA	776
25 Flint, MI PMSA	768

Bottom 25 MSA	Violent Crime Rate (per 100,000 people)
1 Bangor, ME MSA	71
2 Fargo-Moorhead, ND-MN MSA	86
3 Bismarck, ND MSA	89
4 Appleton-Oshkosh-Neenah, WI MSA	95
5 Provo-Orem, UT MSA	105
6 Sheboygan, WI MSA	107
7 Lewiston-Auburn, ME MSA	115
8 State College, PA MSA	116
9 Portland, ME MSA	123
10 Grand Forks, ND-MN MSA	142
11 Binghamton, NY MSA	142
12 Wausau, WI MSA	145
13 Eau Claire, WI MSA	149
14 La Crosse, WI-MN MSA	156
15 Glens Falls, NY MSA	160
16 Bloomington, IN MSA	168
17 Rochester, MN MSA	170
18 Mansfield, OH MSA	174
19 Owensboro, KY MSA	175
20 Corvallis, OR MSA	181
21 Lancaster, PA MSA	181
22 Elkhart-Goshen, IN MSA	184
23 Monmouth-Ocean, NJ PMSA	186
24 Williamsport, PA MSA	187
25 Cheyenne, WY MSA	190

Source : FBI 2004

MSA = Metropolitan Statistical Area

PMSA = Primary Metropolitan Statistical Area

THE MOST AND LEAST EDUCATED METROS

Top 25 MSA	% with College Degree	Bottom 25 MSA	% with College Degree
1 Boulder-Longmont, CO PMSA	52.4	1 Merced, CA MSA	11.0
2 Stamford-Norwalk, CT PMSA	49.4	2 Danville, VA MSA	11.3
3 Iowa City, IA MSA	47.6	3 Visalia-Tulare-Porterville, CA MSA	11.5
4 Corvallis, OR MSA	47.4	4 Vineland-Millville-Bridgeton, NJ PMSA	11.7
5 San Francisco, CA PMSA	43.6	5 Mansfield, OH MSA	11.8
6 Lawrence, KS MSA	42.7	6 Yuma, AZ MSA	11.8
7 Washington, DC-MD-VA-WV PMSA	41.8	7 Steubenville-Weirton, OH-WV MSA	12.1
8 Columbia, MO MSA	41.7	8 Houma, LA MSA	12.3
9 Madison, WI MSA	40.6	9 Johnstown, PA MSA	12.7
10 San Jose, CA PMSA	40.5	10 McAllen-Edinburg-Mission, TX MSA	12.9
11 Charlottesville, VA MSA	40.1	11 Yuba City, CA MSA	13.2
12 Santa Fe, NM MSA	39.9	12 Brownsville-Harlingen-San Benito, TX MSA	13.4
13 Bloomington, IN MSA	39.6	13 Gadsden, AL MSA	13.4
14 Fort Collins-Loveland, CO MSA	39.5	14 Lima, OH MSA	13.4
15 Boston, MA-NH PMSA	39.5	15 Cumberland, MD-WV MSA	13.4
16 Danbury, CT PMSA	39.4	16 Bakersfield, CA MSA	13.5
17 Raleigh-Durham-Chapel Hill, NC MSA	38.9	17 Hickory-Morganton-Lenoir, NC MSA	13.6
18 Gainesville, FL MSA	38.7	18 Ocala, FL MSA	13.7
19 Champaign-Urbana, IL MSA	38.0	19 Fort Smith, AR-OK MSA	13.8
20 Middlesex-Somerset-Hunterdon, NJ PMSA	37.4	20 Altoona, PA MSA	13.9
21 Burlington, VT MSA	37.2	21 Rocky Mount, NC MSA	13.9
22 Bryan-College Station, TX MSA	37.0	22 Laredo, TX MSA	13.9
23 Ann Arbor, MI PMSA	36.9	23 Modesto, CA MSA	14.1
24 Tallahassee, FL MSA	36.7	24 Lewiston-Auburn, ME MSA	14.4
25 Austin-San Marcos, TX MSA	36.7	25 Huntington-Ashland, WV-KY-OH MSA	14.4

Source: U.S. Census 2000

MSA = Metropolitan Statistical Area

PMSA = Primary Metropolitan Statistical Area

THE HIGHEST- AND LOWEST-INCOME METROS

Top 25 MSA	Median Household Income
1 Stamford-Norwalk, CT PMSA	76,554
2 San Jose, CA PMSA	74,335
3 Danbury, CT PMSA	70,173
4 Nassau-Suffolk, NY PMSA	68,351
5 Middlesex-Somerset-Hunterdon, NJ PMSA	66,731
6 San Francisco, CA PMSA	63,297
7 Washington, DC-MD-VA-WV PMSA	62,216
8 Nashua, NH PMSA	60,082
9 Ventura, CA PMSA	59,666
10 Bergen-Passaic, NJ PMSA	59,405
11 Oakland, CA PMSA	59,365
12 Orange County, CA PMSA	58,820
13 Lowell, MA-NH PMSA	57,152
14 Newark, NJ PMSA	56,957
15 Trenton, NJ PMSA	56,613
16 Boulder-Longmont, CO PMSA	55,861
17 Anchorage, AK MSA	55,546
18 Boston, MA-NH PMSA	55,183
19 Ann Arbor, MI PMSA	55,016
20 Monmouth-Ocean, NJ PMSA	54,865
21 Minneapolis-St. Paul, MN-WI MSA	54,304
22 Bridgeport, CT PMSA	54,027
23 Santa Cruz-Watsonville, CA PMSA	53,998
24 Lawrence, MA-NH PMSA	53,478
25 Vallejo-Fairfield-Napa, CA PMSA	53,431

Bottom 25 MSA	Median Household Income
1 McAllen-Edinburg-Mission, TX MSA	24,863
2 Brownsville-Harlingen-San Benito, TX MSA	26,155
3 Laredo, TX MSA	28,100
4 Bryan-College Station, TX MSA	29,104
5 Huntington-Ashland, WV-KY-OH MSA	29,415
6 Las Cruces, NM MSA	29,808
7 Alexandria, LA MSA	29,856
8 Wheeling, WV-OH MSA	30,335
9 Johnstown, PA MSA	30,442
10 Cumberland, MD-WV MSA	30,916
11 Auburn-Opelika, AL MSA	30,952
12 Hattiesburg, MS MSA	30,981
13 Lafayette, LA MSA	30,998
14 El Paso, TX MSA	31,051
15 Gadsden, AL MSA	31,170
16 Danville, VA MSA	31,201
17 Pine Bluff, AR MSA	31,327
18 Gainesville, FL MSA	31,426
19 Johnson City-Kingsport-Bristol, TN-VA MSA	31,596
20 Anniston, AL MSA	31,768
21 Chico-Paradise, CA MSA	31,924
22 Ocala, FL MSA	31,944
23 Steubenville-Weirton, OH-WV MSA	31,982
24 Monroe, LA MSA	32,047
25 Yuma, AZ MSA	32,182

Source: U.S. Census 2000

MSA = Metropolitan Statistical Area

PMSA = Primary Metropolitan Statistical Area

WHERE THE WEALTHY ARE LOCATED

Top 25 MSA	% of Households with at Least $200K Income
1 Stamford-Norwalk, CT PMSA	17.6
2 San Francisco, CA PMSA	7.9
3 San Jose, CA PMSA	7.8
4 Danbury, CT PMSA	7.3
5 Naples, FL MSA	5.8
6 Nassau-Suffolk, NY PMSA	5.8
7 Bergen-Passaic, NJ PMSA	5.7
8 Newark, NJ PMSA	5.6
9 Middlesex-Somerset-Hunterdon, NJ PMSA	5.3
10 Trenton, NJ PMSA	5.0
11 Orange County, CA PMSA	4.8
12 Oakland, CA PMSA	4.7
13 Boston, MA-NH PMSA	4.7
14 Washington, DC-MD-VA-WV PMSA	4.7
15 West Palm Beach-Boca Raton, FL MSA	4.6
16 Santa Cruz-Watsonville, CA PMSA	4.3
17 Bridgeport, CT PMSA	4.2
18 New York, NY PMSA	4.2
19 Boulder-Longmont, CO PMSA	4.0
20 Monmouth-Ocean, NJ PMSA	4.0
21 Ventura, CA PMSA	3.9
22 Chicago, IL PMSA	3.7
23 Santa Barbara-Santa Maria-Lompoc, CA MSA	3.7
24 Lawrence, MA-NH PMSA	3.7
25 Dallas, TX PMSA	3.6

Bottom 25 MSA	% of Households with at Least $200K Income
1 Jacksonville, NC MSA	0.6
2 Cumberland, MD-WV MSA	0.6
3 Lawton, OK MSA	0.7
4 Dover, DE MSA	0.7
5 Steubenville-Weirton, OH-WV MSA	0.8
6 Altoona, PA MSA	0.8
7 Duluth-Superior, MN-WI MSA	0.8
8 Mansfield, OH MSA	0.9
9 Las Cruces, NM MSA	0.9
10 Johnstown, PA MSA	0.9
11 Huntington-Ashland, WV-KY-OH MSA	0.9
12 Jamestown, NY MSA	0.9
13 Utica-Rome, NY MSA	0.9
14 Parkersburg-Marietta, WV-OH MSA	0.9
15 Gadsden, AL MSA	0.9
16 Terre Haute, IN MSA	0.9
17 Pine Bluff, AR MSA	0.9
18 McAllen-Edinburg-Mission, TX MSA	0.9
19 Williamsport, PA MSA	1.0
20 Clarksville-Hopkinsville, TN-KY MSA	1.0
21 Sumter, SC MSA	1.0
22 Hagerstown, MD PMSA	1.0
23 Danville, VA MSA	1.0
24 Kokomo, IN MSA	1.0
25 Grand Forks, ND-MN MSA	1.0

Source: U.S. Census 2000
MSA = Metropolitan Statistical Area
PMSA = Primary Metropolitan Statistical Area

METROS BY SENIOR POPULATION SHARE

Top 25 MSA	Percentage of Senior Population (65 and over)
1 Punta Gorda, FL MSA	34.7
2 Sarasota-Bradenton, FL MSA	28.5
3 Fort Myers-Cape Coral, FL MSA	25.4
4 Fort Pierce-Port St. Lucie, FL MSA	24.9
5 Ocala, FL MSA	24.5
6 Naples, FL MSA	24.4
7 Barnstable-Yarmouth, MA MSA	24.1
8 West Palm Beach-Boca Raton, FL MSA	23.2
9 Daytona Beach, FL MSA	22.8
10 Melbourne-Titusville-Palm Bay, FL MSA	19.9
11 Tampa-St. Petersburg-Clearwater, FL MSA	19.2
12 Johnstown, PA MSA	19.1
13 Scranton-Wilkes-Barre-Hazleton, PA MSA	18.9
14 Steubenville-Weirton, OH-WV MSA	18.5
15 Lakeland-Winter Haven, FL MSA	18.3
16 Pittsfield, MA MSA	18.3
17 Sharon, PA MSA	18.1
18 Wheeling, WV-OH MSA	17.9
19 Pittsburgh, PA MSA	17.7
20 Altoona, PA MSA	17.3
21 Cumberland, MD-WV MSA	17.2
22 Monmouth-Ocean, NJ PMSA; New York-Northern New Jersey-Long Island, NY-NJ-CT-PA CMSA	16.9
23 Danville, VA MSA	16.6
24 Yuma, AZ MSA	16.6
25 Utica-Rome, NY MSA	16.6

Bottom 25 MSA	Percentage of Senior Population (65 and over)
1 Anchorage, AK MSA	5.3
2 Jacksonville, NC MSA	6.4
3 Provo-Orem, UT MSA	6.4
4 Bryan-College Station, TX MSA	6.7
5 Austin-San Marcos, TX MSA	7.2
6 Flagstaff, AZ-UT MSA	7.4
7 Houston, TX PMSA	7.4
8 Iowa City, IA MSA	7.5
9 Atlanta, GA MSA	7.6
10 Dallas, TX PMSA	7.7
11 Laredo, TX MSA	7.7
12 Fayetteville, NC MSA	7.7
13 Boulder-Longmont, CO PMSA	7.8
14 Lawrence, KS MSA	8.0
15 Killeen-Temple, TX MSA	8.0
16 Auburn-Opelika, AL MSA	8.1
17 Salt Lake City-Ogden, UT MSA	8.3
18 Clarksville-Hopkinsville, TN-KY MSA	8.4
19 Athens, GA MSA	8.6
20 Columbia, MO MSA	8.6
21 Colorado Springs, CO MSA	8.6
22 Raleigh-Durham-Chapel Hill, NC MSA	8.6
23 Fort Worth-Arlington, TX PMSA	8.8
24 Brazoria, TX PMSA	8.8
25 Ann Arbor, MI PMSA	8.9

Source: U.S. Census 2000

MSA = Metropolitan Statistical Area

PMSA = Primary Metropolitan Statistical Area

METROS BY POPULATION DENSITY

(Highest to Lowest)

Top 25 MSA	Density (people per sq mile)
1 Jersey City, NJ PMSA	13043.6
2 New York, NY PMSA	8158.7
3 Orange County, CA PMSA	3605.6
4 Bergen-Passaic, NJ PMSA	3273.6
5 Los Angeles-Long Beach, CA PMSA	2344.2
6 Nassau-Suffolk, NY PMSA	2297.1
7 Bridgeport, CT PMSA	1754.9
8 Naples, FL MSA	1744.3
9 San Francisco, CA PMSA	1704.7
10 Boston, MA-NH PMSA	1685.1
11 Stamford-Norwalk, CT PMSA	1682.7
12 Oakland, CA PMSA	1641.5
13 Chicago, IL PMSA	1634.2
14 Trenton, NJ PMSA	1552.5
15 Honolulu, HI MSA	1460.8
16 Fort Lauderdale, FL PMSA	1346.5
17 Philadelphia, PA-NJ PMSA	1323.1
18 San Jose, CA PMSA	1303.6
19 Newark, NJ PMSA	1288.6
20 New Haven-Meriden, CT PMSA	1261.0
21 Lowell, MA-NH PMSA	1208.2
22 Miami, FL PMSA	1157.9
23 Detroit, MI PMSA	1139.8
24 Middlesex-Somerset-Hunterdon, NJ PMSA	1120.0
25 Providence-Fall River-Warwick, RI-MA MSA	1041.5

Bottom 25 MSA	Density (people per sq mile)
1 Flagstaff, AZ-UT MSA	5.4
2 Casper, WY MSA	12.5
3 Bismarck, ND MSA	26.6
4 Grand Forks, ND-MN MSA	28.6
5 Yuma, AZ MSA	29.0
6 Great Falls, MT MSA	29.8
7 Cheyenne, WY MSA	30.4
8 Rapid City, SD MSA	31.9
9 Duluth-Superior, MN-WI MSA	32.4
10 Grand Junction, CO MSA	34.9
11 Missoula, MT MSA	36.9
12 Las Vegas, NV-AZ MSA	39.7
13 Redding, CA MSA	43.1
14 Greeley, CO PMSA	45.3
15 Las Cruces, NM MSA	45.9
16 Billings, MT MSA	49.1
17 Yakima, WA MSA	51.8
18 Reno, NV MSA	53.5
19 Enid, OK MSA	54.6
20 Laredo, TX MSA	57.5
21 Pueblo, CO MSA	59.2
22 Fargo-Moorhead, ND-MN MSA	62.0
23 Medford-Ashland, OR MSA	65.1
24 Richland-Kennewick-Pasco, WA MSA	65.1
25 Pocatello, ID MSA	67.9

Source: U.S. Census 2000

MSA = Metropolitan Statistical Area

PMSA = Primary Metropolitan Statistical Area

METROS BY HIGHEST JOB GROWTH
(2002–2005)

Top 25 MSA	Three-Year Job Growth
1 Phoenix-Mesa-Scottsdale	166,000
2 Miami-Fort Lauderdale-Miami Beach	154,500
3 Riverside-San Bernardino-Ontario	152,700
4 Washington-Arlington-Alexandria	145,400
5 Las Vegas-Paradise	115,400
6 Orlando	102,000
7 Tampa-St. Petersburg-Clearwater	98,800
8 Houston-Baytown-Sugar Land	70,800
9 Atlanta-Sandy Springs-Marietta	58,000
10 San Diego-Carlsbad-San Marcos	53,900
11 Anaheim-Santa Ana	51,800
12 Sacramento-Arden-Arcade-Roseville	47,600
13 Sarasota-Bradenton-Venice	45,500
14 Los Angeles-Long Beach-Santa Ana	38,900
15 Cape Coral-Fort Myers	37,600
16 Jacksonville	35,500
17 Philadelphia-Camden-Wilmington	32,900
18 Nashville-Davidson-Murfreesboro	32,600
19 San Antonio	29,300
20 Dallas-Fort Worth-Arlington	29,100
21 Baltimore-Towson	28,200
22 Virginia Beach-Norfolk-Newport News	27,900
23 Portland-Vancouver-Beaverton	25,600
24 Richmond	24,600
25 Austin-Round Rock	24,500

Bottom 25 MSA	Three-Year Job Growth
1 San Francisco-Oakland-Fremont	–79,600
2 Detroit-Warren-Livonia	–78,400
3 New Orleans-Metairie-Kenner	–77,900
4 Boston-Cambridge-Quincy	–57,200
5 New York-Wayne-White Plains	–51,900
6 Chicago-Naperville-Joliet	–44,400
7 Cleveland-Elyria-Mentor	–38,600
8 Dayton	–14,300
9 Milwaukee-Waukesha-West Allis	–12,300
10 Rochester	–10,600
11 Pittsburgh	–8,900
12 Newark-Union	–8,100
13 Toledo	–7,900
14 Bridgeport-Stamford-Norwalk	–6,500
15 Lansing-E.Lansing	–6,200
16 Canton-Massillon	–4,900
17 Denver-Aurora	–4,700
18 Gulfport-Biloxi	–4,300
19 Binghamton	–3,800
20 Saginaw-Saginaw Township North	–3,700
21 Rockford	–3,500
22 Beaumont-Port Arthur	–3,100
23 Springfield	–2,800
24 Gary	–2,700
25 Elmira	–2,200

Source: Bureau of Labor Statistics

METROS BY PER CAPITA INCOME

Top 25 City	Per Capita Income ($ thousands)
1 Bridgeport-Stamford-Norwalk	65,813
2 San Francisco-Oakland-Fremont	51,493
3 Washington-Arlington-Alexandria	48,887
4 Boston-Cambridge-Quincy	48,133
5 Nassau-Suffolk	48,094
6 Newark-Union	48,041
7 Trenton-Ewing	46,671
8 Boulder	45,604
9 Edison	44,324
10 New York-Wayne-White Plains	44,176
11 Anaheim-Santa Ana	43,752
12 Seattle-Tacoma-Bellevue	43,508
13 Barnstable Town	43,223
14 Denver-Aurora	42,781
15 Minneapolis-St. Paul-Bloomington	42,756
16 Hartford-West Hartford-East Hartford	42,720
17 Reno-Sparks	41,204
18 Baltimore-Towson	40,560
19 Philadelphia-Camden-Wilmington	40,513
20 Sarasota-Bradenton-Venice	40,074
21 New Haven-Milford	39,975
22 San Diego-Carlsbad-San Marcos	39,673
23 Norwich-New London	39,502
24 Madison	39,132
25 Chicago-Naperville-Joliet	38,842

Bottom 25 City	Per Capita Income ($ thousands)
1 El Paso	22,811
2 Farmington	22,884
3 Mobile	24,913
4 Cumberland	24,983
5 Ocala	25,863
6 Danville	26,051
7 Yakima	26,256
8 Elmira	26,610
9 Riverside-San Bernardino-Ontario	26,929
10 Spartanburg	27,289
11 Deltona-Daytona Beach-Ormond Beach	27,293
12 Saginaw-Saginaw Township North	27,605
13 Gulfport-Biloxi	27,711
14 Pensacola-Ferry Pass-Brent	27,714
15 Glens Falls	27,787
16 Erie	27,968
17 Kankakee-Bradley	28,016
18 Binghamton	28,044
19 Youngstown-Warren-Boardman	28,068
20 Beaumont-Port Arthur	28,228
21 Springfield	28,228
22 Salem	28,261
23 Amarillo	28,334
24 Tucson	28,470
25 Dover	28,520

Source: BEA, 2004

THREE-YEAR PRICE APPRECIATION
(Top and Bottom Metros)

Top 25 MSA	% chg (2002 to 2005)	Bottom 25 MSA	% chg (2002 to 2005)
1 Riverside-San Bernardino-Ontario, CA	112.0	1 Canton-Massillon, OH	-6.2
2 Sarasota-Bradenton-Venice, FL	110.5	2 Kalamazoo-Portage, MI	2.8
3 Cape Coral-Fort Myers, FL	102.0	3 Akron, OH	4.5
4 Palm Bay-Melbourne-Titusville, FL	99.3	4 Austin-Round Rock, TX	4.7
5 Miami-Fort Lauderdale-Miami Beach, FL	92.1	5 Indianapolis, IN	6.0
6 Reno-Sparks, NV	91.0	6 South Bend-Mishawaka, IN	6.2
7 Las Vegas-Paradise, NV	90.7	7 Dayton, OH	6.3
8 Los Angeles-Long Beach-Santa Ana, CA	82.4	8 Toledo, OH	7.0
9 Sacramento-Arden-Arcade-Roseville, CA	78.8	9 Houston-Baytown-Sugar Land, TX	7.7
10 Atlantic City, NJ	78.3	10 Ft. Wayne, IN	7.8
11 Orlando, FL	78.3	11 Denver-Aurora, CO	8.3
12 Deltona-Daytona Beach-Ormond Beach, FL	77.7	12 Columbus, OH	8.3
13 Honolulu, HI	76.1	13 Louisville, KY-IN	8.5
14 Washington-Arlington-Alexandria, DC-VA-MD-WV	75.7	14 Cincinnati-Middletown, OH-KY-IN	8.8
15 Phoenix-Mesa-Scottsdale, AZ	72.0	15 Greensboro-High Point, NC	8.8
16 Baltimore-Towson, MD	71.4	16 Memphis, TN-MS-AR	9.1
17 Anaheim-Santa Ana-Irvine, CA	67.7	17 Dallas-Fort Worth-Arlington, TX	9.2
18 San Diego-Carlsbad-San Marcos, CA	65.9	18 Kennewick-Richland-Pasco, WA	9.4
19 Kingston, NY	60.8	19 Boulder, CO	9.7
20 Tucson, AZ	58.2	20 Greenville, SC	9.7
21 Dover, DE	54.3	21 Grand Rapids, MI	10.0
22 Tampa-St.Petersburg-Clearwater, FL	53.8	22 Wichita, KS	10.1
23 Glens Falls, NY	53.3	23 Decatur, IL	10.3
24 NY: Edison, NJ	52.8	24 Charleston, WV	10.4
25 Allentown-Bethlehem-Easton, PA-NJ	51.1	25 Tulsa, OK	10.8

Source: NAR, 2005

MEDIAN HOME PRICE
(Top and Bottom Metros)

Top 25 MSA	Median Price in Thousands
1 San Jose-Sunnyvale-Santa Clara, CA	744.5
2 San Francisco-Oakland-Fremont, CA	715.7
3 Anaheim-Santa Ana-Irvine, CA	691.9
4 San Diego-Carlsbad-San Marcos, CA	604.3
5 Honolulu, HI	590.0
6 Los Angeles-Long Beach-Santa Ana, CA	529.0
7 New York-Wayne-White Plains, NY-NJ	495.2
8 Bridgeport-Stamford-Norwalk, CT	482.4
9 NY: Nassau-Suffolk, NY	465.2
10 New York-Northern New Jersey-Long Island, NY-NJ-PA	445.2
11 Washington-Arlington-Alexandria, DC-VA-MD-WV	425.8
12 NY: Newark-Union, NJ-PA	416.8
13 Boston-Cambridge-Quincy, MA-NH	413.2
14 Barnstable Town, MA	398.3
15 Sacramento-Arden-Arcade-Roseville, CA	375.9
16 NY: Edison, NJ	375.5
17 Riverside-San Bernardino-Ontario, CA	374.2
18 Miami-Fort Lauderdale-Miami Beach, FL	370.1
19 Sarasota-Bradenton-Venice, FL	354.2
20 Reno-Sparks, NV	349.9
21 Boulder, CO	348.4
22 Seattle-Tacoma-Bellevue, WA	316.8
23 Las Vegas-Paradise, NV	304.7
24 Providence-New Bedford-Fall River, RI-MA	293.4
25 Worcester, MA	290.7

Bottom 25 MSA	Median Price in Thousands
1 Danville, IL	67.7
2 Elmira, NY	77.1
3 Decatur, IL	82.1
4 Youngstown-Warren-Boardman, OH-PA	85.6
5 Cumberland, MD-WV	87.4
6 Binghamton, NY	94.4
7 South Bend-Mishawaka, IN	96.6
8 Beaumont-Port Arthur, TX	98.5
9 Buffalo-Niagara Falls, NY	99.0
10 Erie, PA	100.0
11 Canton-Massillon, OH	102.2
12 Waterloo/Cedar Falls, IA	102.2
13 Ft. Wayne, IN	102.3
14 Topeka, KS	105.7
15 Springfield, IL	106.4
16 Amarillo, TX	107.1
17 Wichita, KS	108.0
18 Peoria, IL	109.3
19 Syracuse, NY	110.6
20 El Paso, TX	111.8
21 Rochester, NY	113.5
22 Oklahoma City, OK	114.7
23 Pittsburgh, PA	116.1
24 Toledo, OH	117.3
25 Davenport-Moline-Rock Island, IA-IL	117.9

Source: NAR

METROS BY AFFORDABILITY INDEX

(Most Affordable to Least)

Top 25 MSA	Housing Affordability Index
1 Danville, IL	305.8
2 Elmira, NY	291.0
3 Decatur, IL	287.1
4 Youngstown-Warren-Boardman, OH-PA	262.8
5 Ft. Wayne, IN	258.5
6 South Bend-Mishawaka, IN	257.0
7 Springfield, IL	253.1
8 Buffalo-Niagara Falls, NY	252.3
9 Waterloo/Cedar Falls, IA	246.8
10 Binghamton, NY	246.7
11 Rochester, NY	241.9
12 Topeka, KS	239.8
13 Wichita, KS	238.2
14 Cumberland, MD-WV	238.1
15 Peoria, IL	237.5
16 Canton-Massillon, OH	233.9
17 Syracuse, NY	230.6
18 Erie, PA	228.5
19 Indianapolis, IN	226.7
20 Rockford, IL	224.7
21 Appleton, WI	223.7
22 Detroit-Warren-Livonia, MI	223.3
23 Akron, OH	220.9
24 Beaumont-Port Arthur, TX	220.8
25 Toledo, OH	218.2

Bottom 25 MSA	Housing Affordability Index
1 Los Angeles-Long Beach-Santa Ana, CA	45.1
2 San Diego-Carlsbad-San Marcos, CA	45.7
3 Anaheim-Santa Ana-Irvine, CA	48.0
4 Honolulu, HI	50.4
5 New York-Wayne-White Plains, NY-NJ	51.1
6 San Francisco-Oakland-Fremont, CA	52.0
7 Miami-Fort Lauderdale-Miami Beach, FL	61.9
8 Riverside-San Bernardino-Ontario, CA	65.2
9 Sarasota-Bradenton-Venice, FL	69.2
10 Barnstable Town, MA	72.3
11 Sacramento-Arden-Arcade-Roseville, CA	74.0
12 Reno-Sparks, NV	79.9
13 Boston-Cambridge-Quincy, MA-NH	81.1
14 Bridgeport-Stamford-Norwalk, CT	82.9
15 NY: Nassau-Suffolk, NY	83.8
16 Las Vegas-Paradise, NV	85.0
17 NY: Newark-Union, NJ-PA	85.4
18 Cape Coral-Fort Myers, FL	87.5
19 Washington-Arlington-Alexandria, DC-VA-MD-WV	88.8
20 Seattle-Tacoma-Bellevue, WA	91.9
21 Tucson, AZ	95.8
22 Providence-New Bedford-Fall River, RI-MA	96.8
23 NY: Edison, NJ	97.1
24 Orlando, FL	99.2
25 Boulder, CO	103.2

Source: NAR, 2005

YOU CAN'T TAKE THE LOCAL OUT OF REAL ESTATE

Perhaps the best illustration of the importance of keeping the local in real estate is the observation that price movements are quite different across local markets and there is greater price volatility in real estate values today than ever before. Of course, if you hold on to a property over a long period of time—say, seven to ten years—it is very likely to appreciate in value. That is an empirical fact—real estate is an appreciating asset over the long run and, because of its inherent leveraging properties, generates more-than-competitive returns vis-à-vis stocks and bonds. But locally, anything can happen. We now live in a dynamic real estate world, making it likely that your property-holding period is much shorter than the seven to ten years that used to be the norm. A household is forced to sell or needs to sell a home and purchase another property in a relatively short period of time (average holding period for many households is about four to seven years) for a variety of reasons: a new job, a job transfer, a divorce, a death, a growing family, becoming an empty-nester, becoming a retiree, experiencing a financial setback, inheriting money, or having your business or career take off.

Because most households, for one reason or another, buy and sell properties within a shorter period of time than in the past, they are exposed to more short-term volatility (fluctuations) in their home value. These realities raise the importance of paying attention to the local marketplace before buying a property. As you've come to see, purchasing property is a package deal; evaluating the location can help you achieve more upside in real estate but also helps you avoid (or minimize) the downside.

And remember to stick to the fundamentals: In the beginning of an expanding market, local demand is driven by fundamentals. But as the market gains momentum, speculation is not unlikely. What the wise man does in the beginning, fools do in the end.

To many of us, real estate is not just local, but special. Growing up in Long Beach, New York, I lived about six blocks from the beach—a five-minute walk or three-minute bicycle ride. I can still smell the ocean, feel the ocean breeze, and see the rough edges of the ocean's jetties. I remember strolling down Long Beach's boardwalk, stopping to play skee-ball in the arcades, eating candy apples and cotton candy on the way back home. Our house was a modest, three-bedroom ranch home with gray shingles on a corner lot. I still remember when we built a den addition and got our first color television set. I remember walking to school every day because we lived just two blocks away. Is there any doubt that real estate holds a special place in our hearts and minds?

Econometric studies show homeownership increases pride of neighborhood. Owner-occupied homes are better landscaped, better kept, and are more regularly renovated. Children in owner-occupied homes earn higher SAT scores than those who live in rental properties. And owning a home is special from a financial perspective, with the tax and government subsidies bestowed upon real estate.

As homeowners, we tend to show off our homes to neighbors, friends, and family. I have never known anyone who showed off their shares of IBM stock. And whatever is special about real estate is special because it is *local*—it is ours.

One advantage of investing in real estate is that real estate property is tangible, something you can inspect, feel, and touch. With stocks, you need to evaluate a company's performance, financial statements, performance measures, competition, and forecast of future earnings. Yes, every property is different, but all real estate is part of the same family. Unlike stocks, you know the management team because it is you, your Realtor, and your lender. How many investors personally know the members of the senior management team of a publicly traded company and can confidently comment on their abilities to run it? And the process of identifying profitable real estate never changes—only the property changes.

Whether you are purchasing real estate for the first time or are an experienced real estate investor, if you want to be successful in building wealth in property acquisitions, just keep in mind that all real estate is local. So many changes or trends in everyday life affect the value of your home. Home-price appreciation is not evenly spread across America. A real estate expansion is not necessarily fair and equitable. Some regions, states, cities, and neighborhoods will expand, while others will lag or even fall. With this book as your guide, I hope you can better identify the best places to live and the best places to invest for you.

And hopefully, my grandpa will be smiling.

APPENDIX:
METROPOLITAN AREA TABLES

NOTE: MSA = Metropolitan Statistical Area; PMSA = Primary Metropolitan Statistical Area; CMSA = Consolidated Metropolitan Statistical Area.

METROS BY MEDIAN HOUSEHOLD AGE (CENSUS 2000)

MSA	Median Age of Householder
Punta Gorda, FL MSA	63.8
Sarasota-Bradenton, FL MSA	58.8
Naples, FL MSA	57.2
Ocala, FL MSA	57.0
Fort Myers-Cape Coral, FL MSA	56.8
Fort Pierce-Port St. Lucie, FL MSA	56.7
Barnstable-Yarmouth, MA MSA	55.5
Daytona Beach, FL MSA	54.9
West Palm Beach-Boca Raton, FL MSA	53.8
Johnstown, PA MSA	53.1
Steubenville-Weirton, OH-WV MSA	52.5
Cumberland, MD-WV MSA	52.4
Scranton-Wilkes-Barre-Hazleton, PA MSA	52.3
Melbourne-Titusville-Palm Bay, FL MSA	52.3
Wheeling, WV-OH MSA	52.2
Lakeland-Winter Haven, FL MSA	51.9
Sharon, PA MSA	51.8
Yuma, AZ MSA	51.6
Pittsfield, MA MSA	51.4
Monmouth-Ocean, NJ PMSA; New York-Northern New Jersey-Long Island, NY-NJ-CT-PA CMSA	51.3
Danville, VA MSA	51.1
Youngstown-Warren, OH MSA	51.1
Altoona, PA MSA	51.0
Gadsden, AL MSA	51.0

Tampa-St. Petersburg-Clearwater, FL MSA	50.9
Pittsburgh, PA MSA	50.9
Utica-Rome, NY MSA	50.9
Redding, CA MSA	50.7
Medford-Ashland, OR MSA	50.6
Atlantic-Cape May, NJ PMSA; Philadelphia-Wilmington-Atlantic City, PA-NJ-DE-MD CMSA	50.3
Jamestown, NY MSA	50.3
Parkersburg-Marietta, WV-OH MSA	50.2
New Bedford, MA PMSA; Boston-Worcester-Lawrence, MA-NH-ME-CT CMSA	50.2
Huntington-Ashland, WV-KY-OH MSA	50.2
Nassau-Suffolk, NY PMSA; New York-Northern New Jersey-Long Island, NY-NJ-CT-PA CMSA	50.1
Johnson City-Kingsport-Bristol, TN-VA MSA	50.1
Charleston, WV MSA	50.1
Williamsport, PA MSA	50.0
Elmira, NY MSA	49.8
Buffalo-Niagara Falls, NY MSA	49.8
Canton-Massillon, OH MSA	49.8
Allentown-Bethlehem-Easton, PA MSA	49.8
Mansfield, OH MSA	49.7
Glens Falls, NY MSA	49.7
Florence, AL MSA	49.7
Pueblo, CO MSA	49.6
Duluth-Superior, MN-WI MSA	49.6
Binghamton, NY MSA	49.6
Roanoke, VA MSA	49.5
Benton Harbor, MI MSA	49.5
Decatur, IL MSA	49.4
Bergen-Passaic, NJ PMSA; New York-Northern New Jersey-Long Island, NY-NJ-CT-PA CMSA	49.4
Vineland-Millville-Bridgeton, NJ PMSA; Philadelphia-Wilmington-Atlantic City, PA-NJ-DE-MD CMSA	49.4
Sherman-Denison, TX MSA	49.3
Pine Bluff, AR MSA	49.3
Grand Junction, CO MSA	49.3
Asheville, NC MSA	49.2
Lynchburg, VA MSA	49.2
Myrtle Beach, SC MSA	49.2
Anniston, AL MSA	49.2
San Luis Obispo-Atascadero-Paso Robles, CA MSA	49.1
Bridgeport, CT PMSA; New York-Northern New Jersey-Long Island, NY-NJ-CT-PA CMSA	49.0
Reading, PA MSA	49.0
Santa Rosa, CA PMSA; San Francisco-Oakland-San Jose, CA CMSA	49.0
Chico-Paradise, CA MSA	49.0
Kokomo, IN MSA	48.9
Saginaw-Bay City-Midland, MI MSA	48.9
Enid, OK MSA	48.9
Cleveland-Lorain-Elyria, OH PMSA; Cleveland-Akron, OH CMSA	48.9

Peoria-Pekin, IL MSA	48.8
Waterbury, CT PMSA; New York-Northern New Jersey-Long Island, NY-NJ-CT-PA CMSA	48.8
Longview-Marshall, TX MSA	48.8
Texarkana, TX-Texarkana, AR MSA	48.8
Lima, OH MSA	48.8
Hagerstown, MD PMSA; Washington-Baltimore, DC-MD-VA-WV CMSA	48.8
Honolulu, HI MSA	48.8
Erie, PA MSA	48.8
Stamford-Norwalk, CT PMSA; New York-Northern New Jersey-Long Island, NY-NJ-CT-PA CMSA	48.8
Gary, IN PMSA; Chicago-Gary-Kenosha, IL-IN-WI CMSA	48.7
Alexandria, LA MSA	48.7
Fort Lauderdale, FL PMSA; Miami-Fort Lauderdale, FL CMSA	48.7
Harrisburg-Lebanon-Carlisle, PA MSA	48.7
Chattanooga, TN-GA MSA	48.7
Davenport-Moline-Rock Island, IA-IL MSA	48.6
Beaumont-Port Arthur, TX MSA	48.6
Terre Haute, IN MSA	48.6
Tyler, TX MSA	48.6
Santa Fe, NM MSA	48.5
St. Joseph, MO MSA	48.5
Owensboro, KY MSA	48.5
Dubuque, IA MSA	48.5
Rocky Mount, NC MSA	48.5
Providence-Fall River-Warwick, RI-MA MSA	48.4
Springfield, MA MSA	48.4
Wilmington, NC MSA	48.4
Jackson, MI MSA	48.4
New Haven-Meriden, CT PMSA; New York-Northern New Jersey-Long Island, NY-NJ-CT-PA CMSA	48.4
Philadelphia, PA-NJ PMSA; Philadelphia-Wilmington-Atlantic City, PA-NJ-DE-MD CMSA	48.4
Trenton, NJ PMSA; New York-Northern New Jersey-Long Island, NY-NJ-CT-PA CMSA	48.4
Dutchess County, NY PMSA; New York-Northern New Jersey-Long Island, NY-NJ-CT-PA CMSA	48.4
Mobile, AL MSA	48.4
Albany-Schenectady-Troy, NY MSA	48.3
Topeka, KS MSA	48.3
New London-Norwich, CT-RI MSA	48.2
Brownsville-Harlingen-San Benito, TX MSA	48.2
Newark, NJ PMSA; New York-Northern New Jersey-Long Island, NY-NJ-CT-PA CMSA	48.2
Hartford, CT MSA	48.2
Waterloo-Cedar Falls, IA MSA	48.2
Evansville-Henderson, IN-KY MSA	48.1
Lancaster, PA MSA	48.1
Dayton-Springfield, OH MSA	48.1
Syracuse, NY MSA	48.0
Miami, FL PMSA; Miami-Fort Lauderdale, FL CMSA	48.0
Shreveport-Bossier City, LA MSA	48.0
Kankakee, IL PMSA; Chicago-Gary-Kenosha, IL-IN-WI CMSA	48.0
Lewiston-Auburn, ME MSA	48.0

Great Falls, MT MSA	48.0
York, PA MSA	48.0
Pensacola, FL MSA	48.0
Panama City, FL MSA	47.9
Hickory-Morganton-Lenoir, NC MSA	47.9
Decatur, AL MSA	47.9
Knoxville, TN MSA	47.9
Eugene-Springfield, OR MSA	47.9
Rochester, NY MSA	47.9
Joplin, MO MSA	47.8
Salem, OR PMSA; Portland-Salem, OR-WA CMSA	47.8
Akron, OH PMSA; Cleveland-Akron, OH CMSA	47.8
Florence, SC MSA	47.8
Springfield, IL MSA	47.8
Santa Barbara-Santa Maria-Lompoc, CA MSA	47.8
Fort Smith, AR-OK MSA	47.8
Racine, WI PMSA; Milwaukee-Racine, WI CMSA	47.8
Tucson, AZ MSA	47.8
Billings, MT MSA	47.7
Danbury, CT PMSA; New York-Northern New Jersey-Long Island, NY-NJ-CT-PA CMSA	47.7
Brockton, MA PMSA; Boston-Worcester-Lawrence, MA-NH-ME-CT CMSA	47.7
Dothan, AL MSA	47.7
Sheboygan, WI MSA	47.7
Newburgh, NY-PA PMSA; New York-Northern New Jersey-Long Island, NY-NJ-CT-PA CMSA	47.6
South Bend, IN MSA	47.6
Wausau, WI MSA	47.6
Rockford, IL MSA	47.6
Detroit, MI PMSA; Detroit-Ann Arbor-Flint, MI CMSA	47.5
St. Louis, MO-IL MSA	47.5
Ventura, CA PMSA; Los Angeles-Riverside-Orange County, CA CMSA	47.5
Baltimore, MD PMSA; Washington-Baltimore, DC-MD-VA-WV CMSA	47.4
Greenville-Spartanburg-Anderson, SC MSA	47.4
Muncie, IN MSA	47.4
Janesville-Beloit, WI MSA	47.4
Worcester, MA-CT PMSA; Boston-Worcester-Lawrence, MA-NH-ME-CT CMSA	47.4
Birmingham, AL MSA	47.3
Vallejo-Fairfield-Napa, CA PMSA; San Francisco-Oakland-San Jose, CA CMSA	47.3
Fitchburg-Leominster, MA PMSA; Boston-Worcester-Lawrence, MA-NH-ME-CT CMSA	47.3
Olympia, WA PMSA; Seattle-Tacoma-Bremerton, WA CMSA	47.3
Boston, MA-NH PMSA; Boston-Worcester-Lawrence, MA-NH-ME-CT CMSA	47.3
Santa Cruz-Watsonville, CA PMSA; San Francisco-Oakland-San Jose, CA CMSA	47.3
Sioux City, IA-NE MSA	47.2
Casper, WY MSA	47.2
New Orleans, LA MSA	47.2
Louisville, KY-IN MSA	47.2
Flint, MI PMSA; Detroit-Ann Arbor-Flint, MI CMSA	47.2
San Francisco, CA PMSA; San Francisco-Oakland-San Jose, CA CMSA	47.2
Lake Charles, LA MSA	47.2
Middlesex-Somerset-Hunterdon, NJ PMSA; New York-Northern New Jersey-Long Island, NY-NJ-CT-PA CMSA	47.2

Biloxi-Gulfport-Pascagoula, MS MSA	47.1
Corpus Christi, TX MSA	47.1
Yuba City, CA MSA	47.1
Portsmouth-Rochester, NH-ME PMSA; Boston-Worcester-Lawrence, MA-NH-ME-CT CMSA	47.1
New York, NY PMSA; New York-Northern New Jersey-Long Island, NY-NJ-CT-PA CMSA	47.1
Salinas, CA MSA	47.1
Galveston-Texas City, TX PMSA; Houston-Galveston-Brazoria, TX CMSA	47.1
Bismarck, ND MSA	47.1
Yakima, WA MSA	47.1
Portland, ME MSA	47.0
Bangor, ME MSA	47.0
Cheyenne, WY MSA	47.0
Victoria, TX MSA	47.0
Jackson, TN MSA	46.9
Spokane, WA MSA	46.9
Las Vegas, NV-AZ MSA	46.9
Bremerton, WA PMSA; Seattle-Tacoma-Bremerton, WA CMSA	46.9
San Angelo, TX MSA	46.9
Eau Claire, WI MSA	46.9
Sumter, SC MSA	46.9
Montgomery, AL MSA	46.9
Goldsboro, NC MSA	46.9
Savannah, GA MSA	46.8
Milwaukee-Waukesha, WI PMSA; Milwaukee-Racine, WI CMSA	46.8
Augusta-Aiken, GA-SC MSA	46.8
Greensboro-Winston-Salem-High Point, NC MSA	46.8
Toledo, OH MSA	46.8
Stockton-Lodi, CA MSA	46.8
Kalamazoo-Battle Creek, MI MSA	46.7
Houma, LA MSA	46.7
Albany, GA MSA	46.7
Richland-Kennewick-Pasco, WA MSA	46.6
Wichita Falls, TX MSA	46.6
Lawrence, MA-NH PMSA; Boston-Worcester-Lawrence, MA-NH-ME-CT CMSA	46.6
Monroe, LA MSA	46.6
Dover, DE MSA	46.6
Columbus, GA-AL MSA	46.6
Tulsa, OK MSA	46.5
Oakland, CA PMSA; San Francisco-Oakland-San Jose, CA CMSA	46.5
Macon, GA MSA	46.5
La Crosse, WI-MN MSA	46.5
Sacramento, CA PMSA; Sacramento-Yolo, CA CMSA	46.5
Odessa-Midland, TX MSA	46.4
Fort Wayne, IN MSA	46.4
Wilmington-Newark, DE-MD PMSA; Philadelphia-Wilmington-Atlantic City, PA-NJ-DE-MD CMSA	46.4
Bellingham, WA MSA	46.4
Modesto, CA MSA	46.4
Richmond-Petersburg, VA MSA	46.4
Reno, NV MSA	46.4

Cincinnati, OH-KY-IN PMSA; Cincinnati-Hamilton, OH-KY-IN CMSA	46.3
Cedar Rapids, IA MSA	46.3
Albuquerque, NM MSA	46.3
Fresno, CA MSA	46.3
Springfield, MO MSA	46.3
Fort Walton Beach, FL MSA	46.2
Riverside-San Bernardino, CA PMSA; Los Angeles-Riverside-Orange County, CA CMSA	46.2
Waco, TX MSA	46.2
Visalia-Tulare-Porterville, CA MSA	46.2
McAllen-Edinburg-Mission, TX MSA	46.1
Chicago, IL PMSA; Chicago-Gary-Kenosha, IL-IN-WI CMSA	46.1
Kenosha, WI PMSA; Chicago-Gary-Kenosha, IL-IN-WI CMSA	46.1
El Paso, TX MSA	46.1
Rapid City, SD MSA	46.1
Huntsville, AL MSA	46.1
Elkhart-Goshen, IN MSA	46.1
Jacksonville, FL MSA	46.1
Lafayette, LA MSA	46.0
Orange County, CA PMSA; Los Angeles-Riverside-Orange County, CA CMSA	46.0
Kansas City, MO-KS MSA	46.0
Hamilton-Middletown, OH PMSA; Cincinnati-Hamilton, OH-KY-IN CMSA	45.9
San Antonio, TX MSA	45.9
Lowell, MA-NH PMSA; Boston-Worcester-Lawrence, MA-NH-ME-CT CMSA	45.9
Bakersfield, CA MSA	45.9
Abilene, TX MSA	45.9
Oklahoma City, OK MSA	45.9
Amarillo, TX MSA	45.8
Jackson, MS MSA	45.8
Wichita, KS MSA	45.8
Orlando, FL MSA	45.8
Charleston-North Charleston, SC MSA	45.8
Little Rock-North Little Rock, AR MSA	45.8
Manchester, NH PMSA; Boston-Worcester-Lawrence, MA-NH-ME-CT CMSA	45.8
Las Cruces, NM MSA	45.7
Merced, CA MSA	45.7
Phoenix-Mesa, AZ MSA	45.7
Portland-Vancouver, OR-WA PMSA; Portland-Salem, OR-WA CMSA	45.6
Nashua, NH PMSA; Boston-Worcester-Lawrence, MA-NH-ME-CT CMSA	45.6
Appleton-Oshkosh-Neenah, WI MSA	45.5
Memphis, TN-AR-MS MSA	45.5
Jonesboro, AR MSA	45.5
Charlottesville, VA MSA	45.5
Des Moines, IA MSA	45.4
Tacoma, WA PMSA; Seattle-Tacoma-Bremerton, WA CMSA	45.3
San Diego, CA MSA	45.3
Pocatello, ID MSA	45.3
Grand Rapids-Muskegon-Holland, MI MSA	45.3
Washington, DC-MD-VA-WV PMSA; Washington-Baltimore, DC-MD-VA-WV CMSA	45.3
Lansing-East Lansing, MI MSA	45.3
Columbia, SC MSA	45.2

Omaha, NE-IA MSA	45.2
Indianapolis, IN MSA	45.1
Brazoria, TX PMSA; Houston-Galveston-Brazoria, TX CMSA	45.1
Fayetteville-Springdale-Rogers, AR MSA	45.1
Grand Forks, ND-MN MSA	45.1
Tuscaloosa, AL MSA	45.0
Seattle-Bellevue-Everett, WA PMSA; Seattle-Tacoma-Bremerton, WA CMSA	44.9
Missoula, MT MSA	44.9
San Jose, CA PMSA; San Francisco-Oakland-San Jose, CA CMSA	44.9
Norfolk-Virginia Beach-Newport News, VA-NC MSA	44.9
Los Angeles-Long Beach, CA PMSA; Los Angeles-Riverside-Orange County, CA CMSA	44.9
Baton Rouge, LA MSA	44.8
Nashville, TN MSA	44.8
Burlington, VT MSA	44.7
Green Bay, WI MSA	44.7
Flagstaff, AZ-UT MSA	44.7
Jersey City, NJ PMSA; New York-Northern New Jersey-Long Island, NY-NJ-CT-PA CMSA	44.7
Rochester, MN MSA	44.7
Greeley, CO PMSA; Denver-Boulder-Greeley, CO CMSA	44.6
Ann Arbor, MI PMSA; Detroit-Ann Arbor-Flint, MI CMSA	44.6
Charlotte-Gastonia-Rock Hill, NC-SC MSA	44.6
St. Cloud, MN MSA	44.5
Minneapolis-St. Paul, MN-WI MSA	44.5
Hattiesburg, MS MSA	44.5
Fort Collins-Loveland, CO MSA	44.3
Boise City, ID MSA	44.3
Denver, CO PMSA; Denver-Boulder-Greeley, CO CMSA	44.3
Sioux Falls, SD MSA	44.2
Lexington, KY MSA	44.2
Lawton, OK MSA	44.2
Laredo, TX MSA	44.2
Corvallis, OR MSA	44.1
Columbus, OH MSA	44.1
Colorado Springs, CO MSA	44.1
Fort Worth-Arlington, TX PMSA; Dallas-Fort Worth, TX CMSA	44.0
Salt Lake City-Ogden, UT MSA	43.9
Yolo, CA PMSA; Sacramento-Yolo, CA CMSA	43.9
Lubbock, TX MSA	43.8
Lincoln, NE MSA	43.7
Houston, TX PMSA; Houston-Galveston-Brazoria, TX CMSA	43.7
Boulder-Longmont, CO PMSA; Denver-Boulder-Greeley, CO CMSA	43.5
Bloomington-Normal, IL MSA	43.5
Atlanta, GA MSA	43.3
Fargo-Moorhead, ND-MN MSA	43.3
Madison, WI MSA	43.3
State College, PA MSA	43.1
Anchorage, AK MSA	43.1
Raleigh-Durham-Chapel Hill, NC MSA	43.0
Tallahassee, FL MSA	42.9
Dallas, TX PMSA; Dallas-Fort Worth, TX CMSA	42.8

Fayetteville, NC MSA	42.7
Greenville, NC MSA	42.6
Lafayette, IN MSA	42.2
Champaign-Urbana, IL MSA	41.7
Clarksville-Hopkinsville, TN-KY MSA	41.7
Columbia, MO MSA	41.5
Killeen-Temple, TX MSA	41.5
Gainesville, FL MSA	41.4
Austin-San Marcos, TX MSA	41.3
Bloomington, IN MSA	41.3
Athens, GA MSA	41.1
Iowa City, IA MSA	40.3
Jacksonville, NC MSA	40.2
Provo-Orem, UT MSA	40.1
Lawrence, KS MSA	39.7
Auburn-Opelika, AL MSA	39.6
Bryan-College Station, TX MSA	35.6

CRIME RATES BY METRO AS OF 2004

MSA	Violent Crime Rate (per 100,000 people)
Sumter, SC MSA	1177
Florence, SC MSA	1132
Saginaw-Bay City-Midland, MI MSA	1025
Miami, FL PMSA; Miami-Fort Lauderdale, FL CMSA	1021
Memphis, TN-AR-MS MSA	1009
Detroit, MI PMSA; Detroit-Ann Arbor-Flint, MI CMSA	992
Alexandria, LA MSA	926
Lubbock, TX MSA	898
Jackson, TN MSA	890
Baltimore, MD PMSA; Washington-Baltimore, DC-MD-VA-WV CMSA	886
Myrtle Beach, SC MSA	875
Nashville, TN MSA	872
Steubenville-Weirton, OH-WV MSA	849
Albuquerque, NM MSA	843
Wichita Falls, TX MSA	834
Charleston-North Charleston, SC MSA	815
Little Rock-North Little Rock, AR MSA	814
Anchorage, AK MSA	806
Monroe, LA MSA	803
Columbia, SC MSA	803
Gainesville, FL MSA	788
Tampa-St. Petersburg-Clearwater, FL MSA	786
Texarkana, TX-Texarkana, AR MSA	783
Vineland-Millville-Bridgeton, NJ PMSA; Philadelphia-Wilmington-Atlantic City, PA-NJ-DE-MD CMSA	776
Flint, MI PMSA; Detroit-Ann Arbor-Flint, MI CMSA	768
Los Angeles-Long Beach, CA PMSA; Los Angeles-Riverside-Orange County, CA CMSA	768
Charlotte-Gastonia-Rock Hill, NC-SC MSA	763
Tallahassee, FL MSA	763
Orlando, FL MSA	755
Jacksonville, FL MSA	731
Houston, TX PMSA; Houston-Galveston-Brazoria, TX CMSA	724
West Palm Beach-Boca Raton, FL MSA	721
Ocala, FL MSA	704
Springfield, MA MSA	695
Las Vegas, NV-AZ MSA	694
Panama City, FL MSA	690
Merced, CA MSA	688
Greenville-Spartanburg-Anderson, SC MSA	687
Lawton, OK MSA	686
Pine Bluff, AR MSA	676
New Orleans, LA MSA	673
Tulsa, OK MSA	669
Dover, DE MSA	664
Visalia-Tulare-Porterville, CA MSA	661
Lafayette, LA MSA	651
Melbourne-Titusville-Palm Bay, FL MSA	647

Rocky Mount, NC MSA	502
Washington, DC-MD-VA-WV PMSA; Washington-Baltimore, DC-MD-VA-WV CMSA	501
Salinas, CA MSA	500
Yuba City, CA MSA	500
Lima, OH MSA	500
Riverside-San Bernardino, CA PMSA; Los Angeles-Riverside-Orange County, CA CMSA	499
Lakeland-Winter Haven, FL MSA	498
Goldsboro, NC MSA	493
Philadelphia, PA-NJ PMSA; Philadelphia-Wilmington-Atlantic City, PA-NJ-DE-MD CMSA	493
San Francisco, CA PMSA; San Francisco-Oakland-San Jose, CA CMSA	493
St. Louis, MO-IL MSA	490
Trenton, NJ PMSA; New York-Northern New Jersey-Long Island, NY-NJ-CT-PA CMSA	489
Knoxville, TN MSA	487
Buffalo-Niagara Falls, NY MSA	481
Santa Rosa, CA PMSA; San Francisco-Oakland-San Jose, CA CMSA	475
Tyler, TX MSA	474
Pueblo, CO MSA	474
Charleston, WV MSA	471
Santa Cruz-Watsonville, CA PMSA; San Francisco-Oakland-San Jose, CA CMSA	471
San Diego, CA MSA	468
Brownsville-Harlingen-San Benito, TX MSA	467
Tuscaloosa, AL MSA	467
Wilmington, NC MSA	464
Victoria, TX MSA	463
Mobile, AL MSA	462
Auburn-Opelika, AL MSA	460
Omaha, NE-IA MSA	459
Clarksville-Hopkinsville, TN-KY MSA	458
Grand Rapids-Muskegon-Holland, MI MSA	457
Lincoln, NE MSA	455
Greensboro-Winston-Salem-High Point, NC MSA	453
Gadsden, AL MSA	452
Naples, FL MSA	450
Columbus, OH MSA	444
Colorado Springs, CO MSA	441
Newark, NJ PMSA; New York-Northern New Jersey-Long Island, NY-NJ-CT-PA CMSA	439
Fort Worth-Arlington, TX PMSA; Dallas-Fort Worth, TX CMSA	435
Bremerton, WA PMSA; Seattle-Tacoma-Bremerton, WA CMSA	434
Denver, CO PMSA; Denver-Boulder-Greeley, CO CMSA	434
South Bend, IN MSA	433
Richmond-Petersburg, VA MSA	432
Norfolk-Virginia Beach-Newport News, VA-NC MSA	429
Lansing-East Lansing, MI MSA	419
Jackson, MI MSA	417
San Angelo, TX MSA	417
Albany, GA MSA	416
Reading, PA MSA	413
Lawrence, KS MSA	409
Roanoke, VA MSA	407
Macon, GA MSA	406

Punta Gorda, FL MSA	403
Cumberland, MD-WV MSA	401
Huntsville, AL MSA	399
Columbus, GA-AL MSA	394
Worcester, MA-CT PMSA; Boston-Worcester-Lawrence, MA-NH-ME-CT CMSA	389
Killeen-Temple, TX MSA	382
Greeley, CO PMSA; Denver-Boulder-Greeley, CO CMSA	381
Spokane, WA MSA	381
Jackson, MS MSA	377
Lexington, KY MSA	370
Pittsburgh, PA MSA	369
Topeka, KS MSA	367
Austin-San Marcos, TX MSA	365
Barnstable-Yarmouth, MA MSA	364
Columbia, MO MSA	362
Abilene, TX MSA	362
Cincinnati, OH-KY-IN PMSA; Cincinnati-Hamilton, OH-KY-IN CMSA	361
Louisville, KY-IN MSA	360
Salt Lake City-Ogden, UT MSA	360
Providence-Fall River-Warwick, RI-MA MSA	358
Seattle-Bellevue-Everett, WA PMSA; Seattle-Tacoma-Bremerton, WA CMSA	356
Johnson City-Kingsport-Bristol, TN-VA MSA	356
Kalamazoo-Battle Creek, MI MSA	354
Chico-Paradise, CA MSA	352
Danville, VA MSA	349
Muncie, IN MSA	348
Portland-Vancouver, OR-WA PMSA; Portland-Salem, OR-WA CMSA	342
Minneapolis-St. Paul, MN-WI MSA	339
Dothan, AL MSA	337
Athens, GA MSA	336
Biloxi-Gulfport-Pascagoula, MS MSA	327
Great Falls, MT MSA	326
Salem, OR PMSA; Portland-Salem, OR-WA CMSA	325
Youngstown-Warren, OH MSA	323
Fort Walton Beach, FL MSA	322
Sioux City, IA-NE MSA	322
Ann Arbor, MI PMSA; Detroit-Ann Arbor-Flint, MI CMSA	321
Springfield, MO MSA	318
Medford-Ashland, OR MSA	317
Boise City, ID MSA	315
Dayton-Springfield, OH MSA	309
Harrisburg-Lebanon-Carlisle, PA MSA	306
San Jose, CA PMSA; San Francisco-Oakland-San Jose, CA CMSA	304
San Luis Obispo-Atascadero-Paso Robles, CA MSA	304
Johnstown, PA MSA	303
Kokomo, IN MSA	299
Dubuque, IA MSA	299
Yakima, WA MSA	299
Iowa City, IA MSA	298
Waterloo-Cedar Falls, IA MSA	295

Rochester, MN MSA	170
Bloomington, IN MSA	168
Glens Falls, NY MSA	160
La Crosse, WI-MN MSA	156
Eau Claire, WI MSA	149
Wausau, WI MSA	145
Binghamton, NY MSA	142
Grand Forks, ND-MN MSA	142
Portland, ME MSA	123
State College, PA MSA	116
Lewiston-Auburn, ME MSA	115
Sheboygan, WI MSA	107
Provo-Orem, UT MSA	105
Appleton-Oshkosh-Neenah, WI MSA	95
Bismarck, ND MSA	89
Fargo-Moorhead, ND-MN MSA	86
Bangor, ME MSA	71

SHARE OF COLLEGE DEGREES BY METRO (CENSUS 2000)

MSA	% with College Degree
Boulder-Longmont, CO PMSA; Denver-Boulder-Greeley, CO CMSA	52.4
Stamford-Norwalk, CT PMSA; New York-Northern New Jersey-Long Island, NY-NJ-CT-PA CMSA	49.4
Iowa City, IA MSA	47.6
Corvallis, OR MSA	47.4
San Francisco, CA PMSA; San Francisco-Oakland-San Jose, CA CMSA	43.6
Lawrence, KS MSA	42.7
Washington, DC-MD-VA-WV PMSA; Washington-Baltimore, DC-MD-VA-WV CMSA	41.8
Columbia, MO MSA	41.7
Madison, WI MSA	40.6
San Jose, CA PMSA; San Francisco-Oakland-San Jose, CA CMSA	40.5
Charlottesville, VA MSA	40.1
Santa Fe, NM MSA	39.9
Bloomington, IN MSA	39.6
Fort Collins-Loveland, CO MSA	39.5
Boston, MA-NH PMSA; Boston-Worcester-Lawrence, MA-NH-ME-CT CMSA	39.5
Danbury, CT PMSA; New York-Northern New Jersey-Long Island, NY-NJ-CT-PA CMSA	39.4
Raleigh-Durham-Chapel Hill, NC MSA	38.9
Gainesville, FL MSA	38.7
Champaign-Urbana, IL MSA	38.0
Middlesex-Somerset-Hunterdon, NJ PMSA; New York-Northern New Jersey-Long Island, NY-NJ-CT-PA CMSA	37.4
Burlington, VT MSA	37.2
Bryan-College Station, TX MSA	37.0
Ann Arbor, MI PMSA; Detroit-Ann Arbor-Flint, MI CMSA	36.9
Tallahassee, FL MSA	36.7
Austin-San Marcos, TX MSA	36.7
State College, PA MSA	36.3
Bloomington-Normal, IL MSA	36.2
Seattle-Bellevue-Everett, WA PMSA; Seattle-Tacoma-Bremerton, WA CMSA	35.9
Oakland, CA PMSA; San Francisco-Oakland-San Jose, CA CMSA	35.0
Rochester, MN MSA	34.7
Denver, CO PMSA; Denver-Boulder-Greeley, CO CMSA	34.2
Santa Cruz-Watsonville, CA PMSA; San Francisco-Oakland-San Jose, CA CMSA	34.2
Yolo, CA PMSA; Sacramento-Yolo, CA CMSA	34.1
Athens, GA MSA	34.1
Trenton, NJ PMSA; New York-Northern New Jersey-Long Island, NY-NJ-CT-PA CMSA	34.0
Portland, ME MSA	33.6
Barnstable-Yarmouth, MA MSA	33.5
Minneapolis-St. Paul, MN-WI MSA	33.3
Nashua, NH PMSA; Boston-Worcester-Lawrence, MA-NH-ME-CT CMSA	33.2
Missoula, MT MSA	32.8
Lincoln, NE MSA	32.6
Bergen-Passaic, NJ PMSA; New York-Northern New Jersey-Long Island, NY-NJ-CT-PA CMSA	32.5
Portsmouth-Rochester, NH-ME PMSA; Boston-Worcester-Lawrence, MA-NH-ME-CT CMSA	32.2

Atlanta, GA MSA	32.0
Colorado Springs, CO MSA	31.8
Newark, NJ PMSA; New York-Northern New Jersey-Long Island, NY-NJ-CT-PA CMSA	31.5
Provo-Orem, UT MSA	31.5
New Haven-Meriden, CT PMSA; New York-Northern New Jersey-Long Island, NY-NJ-CT-PA CMSA	31.4
Nassau-Suffolk, NY PMSA; New York-Northern New Jersey-Long Island, NY-NJ-CT-PA CMSA	31.3
Huntsville, AL MSA	30.9
Orange County, CA PMSA; Los Angeles-Riverside-Orange County, CA CMSA	30.8
Chicago, IL PMSA; Chicago-Gary-Kenosha, IL-IN-WI CMSA	30.1
Dallas, TX PMSA; Dallas-Fort Worth, TX CMSA	30.0
Olympia, WA PMSA; Seattle-Tacoma-Bremerton, WA CMSA	29.8
Hartford, CT MSA	29.8
San Diego, CA MSA	29.5
Flagstaff, AZ-UT MSA	29.5
Santa Barbara-Santa Maria-Lompoc, CA MSA	29.4
Fargo-Moorhead, ND-MN MSA	29.4
Lawrence, MA-NH PMSA; Boston-Worcester-Lawrence, MA-NH-ME-CT CMSA	29.3
Richmond-Petersburg, VA MSA	29.2
Baltimore, MD PMSA; Washington-Baltimore, DC-MD-VA-WV CMSA	29.2
Columbia, SC MSA	29.2
New York, NY PMSA; New York-Northern New Jersey-Long Island, NY-NJ-CT-PA CMSA	29.2
Columbus, OH MSA	29.1
Anchorage, AK MSA	28.9
Portland-Vancouver, OR-WA PMSA; Portland-Salem, OR-WA CMSA	28.8
Des Moines, IA MSA	28.7
Lexington, KY MSA	28.7
Santa Rosa, CA PMSA; San Francisco-Oakland-San Jose, CA CMSA	28.5
Kansas City, MO-KS MSA	28.5
Albuquerque, NM MSA	28.4
Lansing-East Lansing, MI MSA	28.4
Lafayette, IN MSA	28.2
Albany-Schenectady-Troy, NY MSA	28.2
Jackson, MS MSA	28.1
Lowell, MA-NH PMSA; Boston-Worcester-Lawrence, MA-NH-ME-CT CMSA	28.1
Springfield, IL MSA	28.1
Omaha, NE-IA MSA	28.0
Bridgeport, CT PMSA; New York-Northern New Jersey-Long Island, NY-NJ-CT-PA CMSA	27.9
Naples, FL MSA	27.9
Auburn-Opelika, AL MSA	27.9
Honolulu, HI MSA	27.9
Philadelphia, PA-NJ PMSA; Philadelphia-Wilmington-Atlantic City, PA-NJ-DE-MD CMSA	27.7
Cedar Rapids, IA MSA	27.7
West Palm Beach-Boca Raton, FL MSA	27.7
Worcester, MA-CT PMSA; Boston-Worcester-Lawrence, MA-NH-ME-CT CMSA	27.7
Dutchess County, NY PMSA; New York-Northern New Jersey-Long Island, NY-NJ-CT-PA CMSA	27.6
Wilmington-Newark, DE-MD PMSA; Philadelphia-Wilmington-Atlantic City, PA-NJ-DE-MD CMSA	27.6

Monmouth-Ocean, NJ PMSA; New York-Northern New Jersey-Long Island, NY-NJ-CT-PA CMSA	27.6
Bellingham, WA MSA	27.2
Houston, TX PMSA; Houston-Galveston-Brazoria, TX CMSA	27.2
Rochester, NY MSA	27.1
Manchester, NH PMSA; Boston-Worcester-Lawrence, MA-NH-ME-CT CMSA	27.0
Milwaukee-Waukesha, WI PMSA; Milwaukee-Racine, WI CMSA	27.0
Ventura, CA PMSA; Los Angeles-Riverside-Orange County, CA CMSA	26.9
Nashville, TN MSA	26.9
Tucson, AZ MSA	26.7
San Luis Obispo-Atascadero-Paso Robles, CA MSA	26.7
Salt Lake City-Ogden, UT MSA	26.5
Boise City, ID MSA	26.5
Charlotte-Gastonia-Rock Hill, NC-SC MSA	26.5
Bangor, ME MSA	26.4
Greenville, NC MSA	26.4
Billings, MT MSA	26.4
Wilmington, NC MSA	26.1
Topeka, KS MSA	26.0
Sioux Falls, SD MSA	25.9
Sacramento, CA PMSA; Sacramento-Yolo, CA CMSA	25.9
Indianapolis, IN MSA	25.8
Bismarck, ND MSA	25.5
Eugene-Springfield, OR MSA	25.5
St. Louis, MO-IL MSA	25.3
Bremerton, WA PMSA; Seattle-Tacoma-Bremerton, WA CMSA	25.3
Cincinnati, OH-KY-IN PMSA; Cincinnati-Hamilton, OH-KY-IN CMSA	25.3
Jersey City, NJ PMSA; New York-Northern New Jersey-Long Island, NY-NJ-CT-PA CMSA	25.3
New London-Norwich, CT-RI MSA	25.1
Phoenix-Mesa, AZ MSA	25.1
Fort Worth-Arlington, TX PMSA; Dallas-Fort Worth, TX CMSA	25.1
Charleston-North Charleston, SC MSA	25.0
Spokane, WA MSA	25.0
Rapid City, SD MSA	25.0
Pocatello, ID MSA	24.9
Baton Rouge, LA MSA	24.9
Los Angeles-Long Beach, CA PMSA; Los Angeles-Riverside-Orange County, CA CMSA	24.9
Orlando, FL MSA	24.8
Little Rock-North Little Rock, AR MSA	24.8
Montgomery, AL MSA	24.7
Wichita, KS MSA	24.7
Birmingham, AL MSA	24.7
Springfield, MA MSA	24.6
Sarasota-Bradenton, FL MSA	24.6
La Crosse, WI-MN MSA	24.6
Fort Lauderdale, FL PMSA; Miami-Fort Lauderdale, FL CMSA	24.5
Asheville, NC MSA	24.5
Oklahoma City, OK MSA	24.4
Lubbock, TX MSA	24.4
Hattiesburg, MS MSA	24.3

Akron, OH PMSA; Cleveland-Akron, OH CMSA	24.3
Fort Walton Beach, FL MSA	24.2
Grand Forks, ND-MN MSA	24.2
Syracuse, NY MSA	24.1
Pittsfield, MA MSA	24.1
Tuscaloosa, AL MSA	24.0
Pittsburgh, PA MSA	23.8
Norfolk-Virginia Beach-Newport News, VA-NC MSA	23.8
Reno, NV MSA	23.7
South Bend, IN MSA	23.6
Providence-Fall River-Warwick, RI-MA MSA	23.6
Melbourne-Titusville-Palm Bay, FL MSA	23.6
Hamilton-Middletown, OH PMSA; Cincinnati-Hamilton, OH-KY-IN CMSA	23.5
Knoxville, TN MSA	23.5
Kalamazoo-Battle Creek, MI MSA	23.5
Cheyenne, WY MSA	23.4
Richland-Kennewick-Pasco, WA MSA	23.3
Cleveland-Lorain-Elyria, OH PMSA; Cleveland-Akron, OH CMSA	23.3
Tulsa, OK MSA	23.2
Buffalo-Niagara Falls, NY MSA	23.2
Savannah, GA MSA	23.2
Waterloo-Cedar Falls, IA MSA	23.0
Grand Rapids-Muskegon-Holland, MI MSA	22.9
Greensboro-Winston-Salem-High Point, NC MSA	22.9
Jacksonville, FL MSA	22.9
Detroit, MI PMSA; Detroit-Ann Arbor-Flint, MI CMSA	22.8
Monroe, LA MSA	22.7
Galveston-Texas City, TX PMSA; Houston-Galveston-Brazoria, TX CMSA	22.7
Memphis, TN-AR-MS MSA	22.7
Vallejo-Fairfield-Napa, CA PMSA; San Francisco-Oakland-San Jose, CA CMSA	22.7
Harrisburg-Lebanon-Carlisle, PA MSA	22.6
New Orleans, LA MSA	22.6
Tyler, TX MSA	22.5
Salinas, CA MSA	22.5
Green Bay, WI MSA	22.5
Roanoke, VA MSA	22.5
Abilene, TX MSA	22.5
San Antonio, TX MSA	22.4
Appleton-Oshkosh-Neenah, WI MSA	22.4
Springfield, MO MSA	22.4
Fayetteville-Springdale-Rogers, AR MSA	22.4
Las Cruces, NM MSA	22.3
Medford-Ashland, OR MSA	22.3
Louisville, KY-IN MSA	22.2
Dayton-Springfield, OH MSA	22.1
Eau Claire, WI MSA	22.1
Newburgh, NY-PA PMSA; New York-Northern New Jersey-Long Island, NY-NJ-CT-PA CMSA	22.1
Binghamton, NY MSA	22.0
Grand Junction, CO MSA	22.0

Chico-Paradise, CA MSA	21.8
Tampa-St. Petersburg-Clearwater, FL MSA	21.7
Miami, FL PMSA; Miami-Fort Lauderdale, FL CMSA	21.7
Brockton, MA PMSA; Boston-Worcester-Lawrence, MA-NH-ME-CT CMSA	21.7
Greeley, CO PMSA; Denver-Boulder-Greeley, CO CMSA	21.6
Toledo, OH MSA	21.6
Pensacola, FL MSA	21.5
Great Falls, MT MSA	21.5
Waterbury, CT PMSA; New York-Northern New Jersey-Long Island, NY-NJ-CT-PA CMSA	21.4
Dubuque, IA MSA	21.3
Allentown-Bethlehem-Easton, PA MSA	21.2
Duluth-Superior, MN-WI MSA	21.2
Peoria-Pekin, IL MSA	21.1
Fort Myers-Cape Coral, FL MSA	21.1
Amarillo, TX MSA	21.0
St. Cloud, MN MSA	21.0
Jonesboro, AR MSA	20.9
Augusta-Aiken, GA-SC MSA	20.9
Erie, PA MSA	20.9
Salem, OR PMSA; Portland-Salem, OR-WA CMSA	20.8
Greenville-Spartanburg-Anderson, SC MSA	20.7
Tacoma, WA PMSA; Seattle-Tacoma-Bremerton, WA CMSA	20.6
Lancaster, PA MSA	20.5
Charleston, WV MSA	20.4
Muncie, IN MSA	20.4
Racine, WI PMSA; Milwaukee-Racine, WI CMSA	20.3
Davenport-Moline-Rock Island, IA-IL MSA	20.3
Jackson, TN MSA	20.1
Casper, WY MSA	20.0
Mobile, AL MSA	19.9
Fort Pierce-Port St. Lucie, FL MSA	19.7
Wichita Falls, TX MSA	19.7
Atlantic-Cape May, NJ PMSA; Philadelphia-Wilmington-Atlantic City, PA-NJ-DE-MD CMSA	19.7
Chattanooga, TN-GA MSA	19.7
Benton Harbor, MI MSA	19.6
Brazoria, TX PMSA; Houston-Galveston-Brazoria, TX CMSA	19.6
Enid, OK MSA	19.6
San Angelo, TX MSA	19.5
Fitchburg-Leominster, MA PMSA; Boston-Worcester-Lawrence, MA-NH-ME-CT CMSA	19.5
Macon, GA MSA	19.5
Fort Wayne, IN MSA	19.4
Lynchburg, VA MSA	19.3
Kenosha, WI PMSA; Chicago-Gary-Kenosha, IL-IN-WI CMSA	19.2
Lawton, OK MSA	19.1
Fayetteville, NC MSA	19.1
Waco, TX MSA	19.1
Shreveport-Bossier City, LA MSA	19.1
Glens Falls, NY MSA	18.9
Myrtle Beach, SC MSA	18.7

Florence, SC MSA	18.7
Dover, DE MSA	18.6
Terre Haute, IN MSA	18.6
Elmira, NY MSA	18.6
Columbus, GA-AL MSA	18.6
Rockford, IL MSA	18.5
Evansville-Henderson, IN-KY MSA	18.5
Reading, PA MSA	18.5
Odessa-Midland, TX MSA	18.4
York, PA MSA	18.4
Pueblo, CO MSA	18.3
Wausau, WI MSA	18.3
Saginaw-Bay City-Midland, MI MSA	18.1
Killeen-Temple, TX MSA	18.1
Daytona Beach, FL MSA	18.0
Sheboygan, WI MSA	17.9
Sioux City, IA-NE MSA	17.9
Corpus Christi, TX MSA	17.8
Utica-Rome, NY MSA	17.7
Gary, IN PMSA; Chicago-Gary-Kenosha, IL-IN-WI CMSA	17.7
Panama City, FL MSA	17.7
Albany, GA MSA	17.7
Punta Gorda, FL MSA	17.6
Biloxi-Gulfport-Pascagoula, MS MSA	17.6
Lafayette, LA MSA	17.5
Scranton-Wilkes-Barre-Hazleton, PA MSA	17.4
Canton-Massillon, OH MSA	17.3
Sharon, PA MSA	17.3
New Bedford, MA PMSA; Boston-Worcester-Lawrence, MA-NH-ME-CT CMSA	17.2
Sherman-Denison, TX MSA	17.2
St. Joseph, MO MSA	17.2
Kokomo, IN MSA	17.1
Owensboro, KY MSA	17.0
Clarksville-Hopkinsville, TN-KY MSA	17.0
Jamestown, NY MSA	16.9
Decatur, IL MSA	16.9
Dothan, AL MSA	16.9
Lake Charles, LA MSA	16.9
Longview-Marshall, TX MSA	16.8
Florence, AL MSA	16.8
Fresno, CA MSA	16.8
Janesville-Beloit, WI MSA	16.7
El Paso, TX MSA	16.6
Johnson City-Kingsport-Bristol, TN-VA MSA	16.6
Redding, CA MSA	16.6
Alexandria, LA MSA	16.5
Las Vegas, NV-AZ MSA	16.4
Joplin, MO MSA	16.4
Riverside-San Bernardino, CA PMSA; Los Angeles-Riverside-Orange County, CA CMSA	16.3
Jackson, MI MSA	16.3

Victoria, TX MSA	16.2
Flint, MI PMSA; Detroit-Ann Arbor-Flint, MI CMSA	16.2
Sumter, SC MSA	15.8
Decatur, AL MSA	15.8
Pine Bluff, AR MSA	15.7
Elkhart-Goshen, IN MSA	15.5
Yakima, WA MSA	15.3
Anniston, AL MSA	15.2
Parkersburg-Marietta, WV-OH MSA	15.2
Youngstown-Warren, OH MSA	15.1
Williamsport, PA MSA	15.1
Texarkana, TX-Texarkana, AR MSA	15.0
Goldsboro, NC MSA	15.0
Kankakee, IL PMSA; Chicago-Gary-Kenosha, IL-IN-WI CMSA	15.0
Lakeland-Winter Haven, FL MSA	14.9
Jacksonville, NC MSA	14.8
Beaumont-Port Arthur, TX MSA	14.7
Wheeling, WV-OH MSA	14.6
Hagerstown, MD PMSA; Washington-Baltimore, DC-MD-VA-WV CMSA	14.6
Stockton-Lodi, CA MSA	14.5
Huntington-Ashland, WV-KY-OH MSA	14.4
Lewiston-Auburn, ME MSA	14.4
Modesto, CA MSA	14.1
Laredo, TX MSA	13.9
Rocky Mount, NC MSA	13.9
Altoona, PA MSA	13.9
Fort Smith, AR-OK MSA	13.8
Ocala, FL MSA	13.7
Hickory-Morganton-Lenoir, NC MSA	13.6
Bakersfield, CA MSA	13.5
Cumberland, MD-WV MSA	13.4
Lima, OH MSA	13.4
Gadsden, AL MSA	13.4
Brownsville-Harlingen-San Benito, TX MSA	13.4
Yuba City, CA MSA	13.2
McAllen-Edinburg-Mission, TX MSA	12.9
Johnstown, PA MSA	12.7
Houma, LA MSA	12.3
Steubenville-Weirton, OH-WV MSA	12.1
Yuma, AZ MSA	11.8
Mansfield, OH MSA	11.8
Vineland-Millville-Bridgeton, NJ PMSA; Philadelphia-Wilmington-Atlantic City, PA-NJ-DE-MD CMSA	11.7
Visalia-Tulare-Porterville, CA MSA	11.5
Danville, VA MSA	11.3
Merced, CA MSA	11.0

MEDIAN HOUSEHOLD INCOME (CENSUS 2000)

MSA	Median Household Income (in $ thousands)
Stamford-Norwalk, CT PMSA; New York-Northern New Jersey-Long Island, NY-NJ-CT-PA CMSA	76,554
San Jose, CA PMSA; San Francisco-Oakland-San Jose, CA CMSA	74,335
Danbury, CT PMSA; New York-Northern New Jersey-Long Island, NY-NJ-CT-PA CMSA	70,173
Nassau-Suffolk, NY PMSA; New York-Northern New Jersey-Long Island, NY-NJ-CT-PA CMSA	68,351
Middlesex-Somerset-Hunterdon, NJ PMSA; New York-Northern New Jersey-Long Island, NY-NJ-CT-PA CMSA	66,731
San Francisco, CA PMSA; San Francisco-Oakland-San Jose, CA CMSA	63,297
Washington, DC-MD-VA-WV PMSA; Washington-Baltimore, DC-MD-VA-WV CMSA	62,216
Nashua, NH PMSA; Boston-Worcester-Lawrence, MA-NH-ME-CT CMSA	60,082
Ventura, CA PMSA; Los Angeles-Riverside-Orange County, CA CMSA	59,666
Bergen-Passaic, NJ PMSA; New York-Northern New Jersey-Long Island, NY-NJ-CT-PA CMSA	59,405
Oakland, CA PMSA; San Francisco-Oakland-San Jose, CA CMSA	59,365
Orange County, CA PMSA; Los Angeles-Riverside-Orange County, CA CMSA	58,820
Lowell, MA-NH PMSA; Boston-Worcester-Lawrence, MA-NH-ME-CT CMSA	57,152
Newark, NJ PMSA; New York-Northern New Jersey-Long Island, NY-NJ-CT-PA CMSA	56,957
Trenton, NJ PMSA; New York-Northern New Jersey-Long Island, NY-NJ-CT-PA CMSA	56,613
Boulder-Longmont, CO PMSA; Denver-Boulder-Greeley, CO CMSA	55,861
Anchorage, AK MSA	55,546
Boston, MA-NH PMSA; Boston-Worcester-Lawrence, MA-NH-ME-CT CMSA	55,183
Ann Arbor, MI PMSA; Detroit-Ann Arbor-Flint, MI CMSA	55,016
Monmouth-Ocean, NJ PMSA; New York-Northern New Jersey-Long Island, NY-NJ-CT-PA CMSA	54,865
Minneapolis-St. Paul, MN-WI MSA	54,304
Bridgeport, CT PMSA; New York-Northern New Jersey-Long Island, NY-NJ-CT-PA CMSA	54,027
Santa Cruz-Watsonville, CA PMSA; San Francisco-Oakland-San Jose, CA CMSA	53,998
Lawrence, MA-NH PMSA; Boston-Worcester-Lawrence, MA-NH-ME-CT CMSA	53,478
Vallejo-Fairfield-Napa, CA PMSA; San Francisco-Oakland-San Jose, CA CMSA	53,431
Dutchess County, NY PMSA; New York-Northern New Jersey-Long Island, NY-NJ-CT-PA CMSA	53,086
Santa Rosa, CA PMSA; San Francisco-Oakland-San Jose, CA CMSA	53,076
Seattle-Bellevue-Everett, WA PMSA; Seattle-Tacoma-Bremerton, WA CMSA	52,804
Hartford, CT MSA	52,188
Wilmington-Newark, DE-MD PMSA; Philadelphia-Wilmington-Atlantic City, PA-NJ-DE-MD CMSA	52,121
Brockton, MA PMSA; Boston-Worcester-Lawrence, MA-NH-ME-CT CMSA	52,058
Atlanta, GA MSA	51,948
Honolulu, HI MSA	51,914
Chicago, IL PMSA; Chicago-Gary-Kenosha, IL-IN-WI CMSA	51,680
Rochester, MN MSA	51,316
Denver, CO PMSA; Denver-Boulder-Greeley, CO CMSA	51,191
Newburgh, NY-PA PMSA; New York-Northern New Jersey-Long Island, NY-NJ-CT-PA CMSA	51,151
Manchester, NH PMSA; Boston-Worcester-Lawrence, MA-NH-ME-CT CMSA	50,410

Baltimore, MD PMSA; Washington-Baltimore, DC-MD-VA-WV CMSA	49,938
New Haven-Meriden, CT PMSA; New York-Northern New Jersey-Long Island, NY-NJ-CT-PA CMSA	49,825
New London-Norwich, CT-RI MSA	49,283
Madison, WI MSA	49,223
Detroit, MI PMSA; Detroit-Ann Arbor-Flint, MI CMSA	49,175
Portsmouth-Rochester, NH-ME PMSA; Boston-Worcester-Lawrence, MA-NH-ME-CT CMSA	49,025
Austin-San Marcos, TX MSA	48,950
Raleigh-Durham-Chapel Hill, NC MSA	48,845
Fort Collins-Loveland, CO MSA	48,655
Brazoria, TX PMSA; Houston-Galveston-Brazoria, TX CMSA	48,632
Salt Lake City-Ogden, UT MSA	48,594
Dallas, TX PMSA; Dallas-Fort Worth, TX CMSA	48,364
Salinas, CA MSA	48,305
Naples, FL MSA	48,289
Racine, WI PMSA; Milwaukee-Racine, WI CMSA	48,059
Worcester, MA-CT PMSA; Boston-Worcester-Lawrence, MA-NH-ME-CT CMSA	47,899
Hamilton-Middletown, OH PMSA; Cincinnati-Hamilton, OH-KY-IN CMSA	47,885
Philadelphia, PA-NJ PMSA; Philadelphia-Wilmington-Atlantic City, PA-NJ-DE-MD CMSA	47,536
Appleton-Oshkosh-Neenah, WI MSA	47,438
Portland-Vancouver, OR-WA PMSA; Portland-Salem, OR-WA CMSA	47,077
San Diego, CA MSA	47,067
Bloomington-Normal, IL MSA	47,021
Olympia, WA PMSA; Seattle-Tacoma-Bremerton, WA CMSA	46,975
Kenosha, WI PMSA; Chicago-Gary-Kenosha, IL-IN-WI CMSA	46,970
Colorado Springs, CO MSA	46,844
Bremerton, WA PMSA; Seattle-Tacoma-Bremerton, WA CMSA	46,840
Richmond-Petersburg, VA MSA	46,800
Burlington, VT MSA	46,732
Santa Barbara-Santa Maria-Lompoc, CA MSA	46,677
Des Moines, IA MSA	46,651
Sacramento, CA PMSA; Sacramento-Yolo, CA CMSA	46,602
Green Bay, WI MSA	46,447
Waterbury, CT PMSA; New York-Northern New Jersey-Long Island, NY-NJ-CT-PA CMSA	46,353
Sheboygan, WI MSA	46,237
Cedar Rapids, IA MSA	46,206
Kansas City, MO-KS MSA	46,193
Charlotte-Gastonia-Rock Hill, NC-SC MSA	46,119
Grand Rapids-Muskegon-Holland, MI MSA	46,116
Barnstable-Yarmouth, MA MSA	46,034
Fort Worth-Arlington, TX PMSA; Dallas-Fort Worth, TX CMSA	45,962
Milwaukee-Waukesha, WI PMSA; Milwaukee-Racine, WI CMSA	45,901
Provo-Orem, UT MSA	45,833
Santa Fe, NM MSA	45,822
Reno, NV MSA	45,815
Indianapolis, IN MSA	45,548
Janesville-Beloit, WI MSA	45,517
Lancaster, PA MSA	45,507
York, PA MSA	45,268

Tacoma, WA PMSA; Seattle-Tacoma-Bremerton, WA CMSA	45,204
Wausau, WI MSA	45,165
West Palm Beach-Boca Raton, FL MSA	45,062
Rockford, IL MSA	44,988
Omaha, NE-IA MSA	44,981
Richland-Kennewick-Pasco, WA MSA	44,886
Columbus, OH MSA	44,782
Phoenix-Mesa, AZ MSA	44,752
Reading, PA MSA	44,714
Portland, ME MSA	44,707
Houston, TX PMSA; Houston-Galveston-Brazoria, TX CMSA	44,655
Gary, IN PMSA; Chicago-Gary-Kenosha, IL-IN-WI CMSA	44,637
Kokomo, IN MSA	44,531
Elkhart-Goshen, IN MSA	44,478
Lansing-East Lansing, MI MSA	44,441
St. Louis, MO-IL MSA	44,437
Charlottesville, VA MSA	44,356
Cincinnati, OH-KY-IN PMSA; Cincinnati-Hamilton, OH-KY-IN CMSA	44,248
Nashville, TN MSA	44,223
Rochester, NY MSA	43,955
Sioux Falls, SD MSA	43,387
Albany-Schenectady-Troy, NY MSA	43,250
Springfield, IL MSA	43,180
Jackson, MI MSA	43,171
Fitchburg-Leominster, MA PMSA; Boston-Worcester-Lawrence, MA-NH-ME-CT CMSA	43,155
Atlantic-Cape May, NJ PMSA; Philadelphia-Wilmington-Atlantic City, PA-NJ-DE-MD CMSA	43,109
Huntsville, AL MSA	43,104
Allentown-Bethlehem-Easton, PA MSA	43,098
Harrisburg-Lebanon-Carlisle, PA MSA	43,022
Peoria-Pekin, IL MSA	42,986
Fort Wayne, IN MSA	42,817
Akron, OH PMSA; Cleveland-Akron, OH CMSA	42,691
Wichita, KS MSA	42,651
Boise City, ID MSA	42,570
Las Vegas, NV-AZ MSA	42,468
Norfolk-Virginia Beach-Newport News, VA-NC MSA	42,448
Jacksonville, FL MSA	42,439
San Luis Obispo-Atascadero-Paso Robles, CA MSA	42,428
Galveston-Texas City, TX PMSA; Houston-Galveston-Brazoria, TX CMSA	42,419
Riverside-San Bernardino, CA PMSA; Los Angeles-Riverside-Orange County, CA CMSA	42,404
Greeley, CO PMSA; Denver-Boulder-Greeley, CO CMSA	42,321
St. Cloud, MN MSA	42,321
Los Angeles-Long Beach, CA PMSA; Los Angeles-Riverside-Orange County, CA CMSA	42,189
Cleveland-Lorain-Elyria, OH PMSA; Cleveland-Akron, OH CMSA	42,089
Flint, MI PMSA; Detroit-Ann Arbor-Flint, MI CMSA	41,951
Corvallis, OR MSA	41,897
Orlando, FL MSA	41,871
Lincoln, NE MSA	41,850
Providence-Fall River-Warwick, RI-MA MSA	41,748

Fort Lauderdale, FL PMSA; Miami-Fort Lauderdale, FL CMSA	41,691
Columbia, SC MSA	41,677
Dayton-Springfield, OH MSA	41,550
Kankakee, IL PMSA; Chicago-Gary-Kenosha, IL-IN-WI CMSA	41,532
Fort Walton Beach, FL MSA	41,474
Stockton-Lodi, CA MSA	41,282
New York, NY PMSA; New York-Northern New Jersey-Long Island, NY-NJ-CT-PA CMSA	41,053
Topeka, KS MSA	40,988
Dover, DE MSA	40,950
Greensboro-Winston-Salem-High Point, NC MSA	40,913
Louisville, KY-IN MSA	40,821
Yolo, CA PMSA; Sacramento-Yolo, CA CMSA	40,769
Springfield, MA MSA	40,740
Kalamazoo-Battle Creek, MI MSA	40,710
Salem, OR PMSA; Portland-Salem, OR-WA CMSA	40,665
Sarasota-Bradenton, FL MSA	40,649
Davenport-Moline-Rock Island, IA-IL MSA	40,621
Hagerstown, MD PMSA; Washington-Baltimore, DC-MD-VA-WV CMSA	40,617
South Bend, IN MSA	40,420
Fort Myers-Cape Coral, FL MSA	40,319
Jersey City, NJ PMSA; New York-Northern New Jersey-Long Island, NY-NJ-CT-PA CMSA	40,293
Memphis, TN-AR-MS MSA	40,201
Bismarck, ND MSA	40,148
Modesto, CA MSA	40,101
Melbourne-Titusville-Palm Bay, FL MSA	40,099
Iowa City, IA MSA	40,060
Bellingham, WA MSA	40,005
Saginaw-Bay City-Midland, MI MSA	39,909
Toledo, OH MSA	39,902
Syracuse, NY MSA	39,750
La Crosse, WI-MN MSA	39,692
Savannah, GA MSA	39,622
Cheyenne, WY MSA	39,607
Dubuque, IA MSA	39,582
Charleston-North Charleston, SC MSA	39,491
Canton-Massillon, OH MSA	39,457
Eau Claire, WI MSA	39,372
Lexington, KY MSA	39,357
Evansville-Henderson, IN-KY MSA	39,307
Roanoke, VA MSA	39,288
Lima, OH MSA	39,284
Birmingham, AL MSA	39,278
Vineland-Millville-Bridgeton, NJ PMSA; Philadelphia-Wilmington-Atlantic City, PA-NJ-DE-MD CMSA	39,150
Little Rock-North Little Rock, AR MSA	39,145
San Antonio, TX MSA	39,140
Albuquerque, NM MSA	39,088
Lafayette, IN MSA	39,072
Jackson, MS MSA	38,887

Victoria, TX MSA	38,732
Fort Pierce-Port St. Lucie, FL MSA	38,724
Wilmington, NC MSA	38,632
Benton Harbor, MI MSA	38,567
Macon, GA MSA	38,565
Sioux City, IA-NE MSA	38,563
Glens Falls, NY MSA	38,526
Pittsfield, MA MSA	38,515
Buffalo-Niagara Falls, NY MSA	38,488
Greenville-Spartanburg-Anderson, SC MSA	38,458
Baton Rouge, LA MSA	38,438
Tulsa, OK MSA	38,261
Augusta-Aiken, GA-SC MSA	38,103
Fargo-Moorhead, ND-MN MSA	38,069
Flagstaff, AZ-UT MSA	37,971
Decatur, IL MSA	37,859
Hickory-Morganton-Lenoir, NC MSA	37,818
Champaign-Urbana, IL MSA	37,780
Montgomery, AL MSA	37,619
Lawrence, KS MSA	37,547
Rapid City, SD MSA	37,485
Columbia, MO MSA	37,485
Pittsburgh, PA MSA	37,467
Fayetteville, NC MSA	37,466
Chattanooga, TN-GA MSA	37,411
Tampa-St. Petersburg-Clearwater, FL MSA	37,406
New Bedford, MA PMSA; Boston-Worcester-Lawrence, MA-NH-ME-CT CMSA	37,368
Fayetteville-Springdale-Rogers, AR MSA	37,322
Spokane, WA MSA	37,308
Waterloo-Cedar Falls, IA MSA	37,266
Sherman-Denison, TX MSA	37,178
Tyler, TX MSA	37,148
Mansfield, OH MSA	37,060
Lynchburg, VA MSA	37,010
Pensacola, FL MSA	36,975
Eugene-Springfield, OR MSA	36,942
Knoxville, TN MSA	36,874
Owensboro, KY MSA	36,813
Oklahoma City, OK MSA	36,797
Tucson, AZ MSA	36,758
Billings, MT MSA	36,727
Pocatello, ID MSA	36,683
Killeen-Temple, TX MSA	36,669
Biloxi-Gulfport-Pascagoula, MS MSA	36,662
Jackson, TN MSA	36,649
Erie, PA MSA	36,627
Casper, WY MSA	36,619
Myrtle Beach, SC MSA	36,470
Medford-Ashland, OR MSA	36,461
Tallahassee, FL MSA	36,441

Elmira, NY MSA	36,415
Punta Gorda, FL MSA	36,379
Binghamton, NY MSA	36,374
Clarksville-Hopkinsville, TN-KY MSA	36,313
Decatur, AL MSA	36,299
Youngstown-Warren, OH MSA	36,255
Asheville, NC MSA	36,179
State College, PA MSA	36,165
Panama City, FL MSA	36,092
Duluth-Superior, MN-WI MSA	36,081
Lakeland-Winter Haven, FL MSA	36,036
Miami, FL PMSA; Miami-Fort Lauderdale, FL CMSA	35,966
Grand Junction, CO MSA	35,864
Bangor, ME MSA	35,837
Corpus Christi, TX MSA	35,773
Daytona Beach, FL MSA	35,722
Amarillo, TX MSA	35,679
St. Joseph, MO MSA	35,675
Beaumont-Port Arthur, TX MSA	35,669
Mobile, AL MSA	35,629
Grand Forks, ND-MN MSA	35,562
Merced, CA MSA	35,532
Bakersfield, CA MSA	35,446
Charleston, WV MSA	35,418
Lake Charles, LA MSA	35,372
New Orleans, LA MSA	35,317
Utica-Rome, NY MSA	35,292
Lewiston-Auburn, ME MSA	35,244
Florence, SC MSA	35,144
Houma, LA MSA	35,089
Fresno, CA MSA	34,960
Albany, GA MSA	34,829
Yakima, WA MSA	34,828
Rocky Mount, NC MSA	34,795
Odessa-Midland, TX MSA	34,773
Sharon, PA MSA	34,666
Springfield, MO MSA	34,661
Muncie, IN MSA	34,659
Yuba City, CA MSA	34,658
Columbus, GA-AL MSA	34,512
Missoula, MT MSA	34,454
Tuscaloosa, AL MSA	34,436
Redding, CA MSA	34,335
Longview-Marshall, TX MSA	34,253
Terre Haute, IN MSA	34,222
Scranton-Wilkes-Barre-Hazleton, PA MSA	34,161
Wichita Falls, TX MSA	34,098
Abilene, TX MSA	34,035
Williamsport, PA MSA	34,016
Visalia-Tulare-Porterville, CA MSA	33,983

Goldsboro, NC MSA	33,942
Lawton, OK MSA	33,867
Jacksonville, NC MSA	33,756
Parkersburg-Marietta, WV-OH MSA	33,696
Waco, TX MSA	33,560
Jamestown, NY MSA	33,458
Dothan, AL MSA	33,455
Athens, GA MSA	33,416
Bloomington, IN MSA	33,311
Sumter, SC MSA	33,278
San Angelo, TX MSA	33,148
Enid, OK MSA	33,006
Great Falls, MT MSA	32,971
Greenville, NC MSA	32,868
Altoona, PA MSA	32,861
Pueblo, CO MSA	32,775
Florence, AL MSA	32,704
Shreveport-Bossier City, LA MSA	32,558
Joplin, MO MSA	32,446
Jonesboro, AR MSA	32,425
Fort Smith, AR-OK MSA	32,399
Texarkana, TX-Texarkana, AR MSA	32,238
Lubbock, TX MSA	32,198
Yuma, AZ MSA	32,182
Monroe, LA MSA	32,047
Steubenville-Weirton, OH-WV MSA	31,982
Ocala, FL MSA	31,944
Chico-Paradise, CA MSA	31,924
Anniston, AL MSA	31,768
Johnson City-Kingsport-Bristol, TN-VA MSA	31,596
Gainesville, FL MSA	31,426
Pine Bluff, AR MSA	31,327
Danville, VA MSA	31,201
Gadsden, AL MSA	31,170
El Paso, TX MSA	31,051
Lafayette, LA MSA	30,998
Hattiesburg, MS MSA	30,981
Auburn-Opelika, AL MSA	30,952
Cumberland, MD-WV MSA	30,916
Johnstown, PA MSA	30,442
Wheeling, WV-OH MSA	30,335
Alexandria, LA MSA	29,856
Las Cruces, NM MSA	29,808
Huntington-Ashland, WV-KY-OH MSA	29,415
Bryan-College Station, TX MSA	29,104
Laredo, TX MSA	28,100
Brownsville-Harlingen-San Benito, TX MSA	26,155
McAllen-Edinburg-Mission, TX MSA	24,863

WEALTHIEST HOUSEHOLDS (CENSUS 2000)

MSA	% of Households with at least $200K income
Stamford-Norwalk, CT PMSA; New York-Northern New Jersey-Long Island, NY-NJ-CT-PA CMSA	17.6
San Francisco, CA PMSA; San Francisco-Oakland-San Jose, CA CMSA	7.9
San Jose, CA PMSA; San Francisco-Oakland-San Jose, CA CMSA	7.8
Danbury, CT PMSA; New York-Northern New Jersey-Long Island, NY-NJ-CT-PA CMSA	7.3
Naples, FL MSA	5.8
Nassau-Suffolk, NY PMSA; New York-Northern New Jersey-Long Island, NY-NJ-CT-PA CMSA	5.8
Bergen-Passaic, NJ PMSA; New York-Northern New Jersey-Long Island, NY-NJ-CT-PA CMSA	5.7
Newark, NJ PMSA; New York-Northern New Jersey-Long Island, NY-NJ-CT-PA CMSA	5.6
Middlesex-Somerset-Hunterdon, NJ PMSA; New York-Northern New Jersey-Long Island, NY-NJ-CT-PA CMSA	5.3
Trenton, NJ PMSA; New York-Northern New Jersey-Long Island, NY-NJ-CT-PA CMSA	5.0
Orange County, CA PMSA; Los Angeles-Riverside-Orange County, CA CMSA	4.8
Oakland, CA PMSA; San Francisco-Oakland-San Jose, CA CMSA	4.7
Boston, MA-NH PMSA; Boston-Worcester-Lawrence, MA-NH-ME-CT CMSA	4.7
Washington, DC-MD-VA-WV PMSA; Washington-Baltimore, DC-MD-VA-WV CMSA	4.7
West Palm Beach-Boca Raton, FL MSA	4.6
Santa Cruz-Watsonville, CA PMSA; San Francisco-Oakland-San Jose, CA CMSA	4.3
Bridgeport, CT PMSA; New York-Northern New Jersey-Long Island, NY-NJ-CT-PA CMSA	4.2
New York, NY PMSA; New York-Northern New Jersey-Long Island, NY-NJ-CT-PA CMSA	4.2
Boulder-Longmont, CO PMSA; Denver-Boulder-Greeley, CO CMSA	4.0
Monmouth-Ocean, NJ PMSA; New York-Northern New Jersey-Long Island, NY-NJ-CT-PA CMSA	4.0
Ventura, CA PMSA; Los Angeles-Riverside-Orange County, CA CMSA	3.9
Chicago, IL PMSA; Chicago-Gary-Kenosha, IL-IN-WI CMSA	3.7
Santa Barbara-Santa Maria-Lompoc, CA MSA	3.7
Lawrence, MA-NH PMSA; Boston-Worcester-Lawrence, MA-NH-ME-CT CMSA	3.7
Dallas, TX PMSA; Dallas-Fort Worth, TX CMSA	3.6
Los Angeles-Long Beach, CA PMSA; Los Angeles-Riverside-Orange County, CA CMSA	3.5
Atlanta, GA MSA	3.4
Seattle-Bellevue-Everett, WA PMSA; Seattle-Tacoma-Bremerton, WA CMSA	3.2
New Haven-Meriden, CT PMSA; New York-Northern New Jersey-Long Island, NY-NJ-CT-PA CMSA	3.1
Santa Rosa, CA PMSA; San Francisco-Oakland-San Jose, CA CMSA	3.1
Ann Arbor, MI PMSA; Detroit-Ann Arbor-Flint, MI CMSA	3.1
Denver, CO PMSA; Denver-Boulder-Greeley, CO CMSA	3.1
Salinas, CA MSA	3.0
Minneapolis-St. Paul, MN-WI MSA	3.0
Houston, TX PMSA; Houston-Galveston-Brazoria, TX CMSA	3.0
Austin-San Marcos, TX MSA	3.0
San Diego, CA MSA	3.0
Philadelphia, PA-NJ PMSA; Philadelphia-Wilmington-Atlantic City, PA-NJ-DE-MD CMSA	3.0
Rochester, MN MSA	2.9
Sarasota-Bradenton, FL MSA	2.9
Hartford, CT MSA	2.8

Nashua, NH PMSA; Boston-Worcester-Lawrence, MA-NH-ME-CT CMSA	2.8
Fort Myers-Cape Coral, FL MSA	2.8
Reno, NV MSA	2.7
Charlotte-Gastonia-Rock Hill, NC-SC MSA	2.7
Miami, FL PMSA; Miami-Fort Lauderdale, FL CMSA	2.7
Portland, ME MSA	2.6
Detroit, MI PMSA; Detroit-Ann Arbor-Flint, MI CMSA	2.6
Baltimore, MD PMSA; Washington-Baltimore, DC-MD-VA-WV CMSA	2.6
Raleigh-Durham-Chapel Hill, NC MSA	2.6
Santa Fe, NM MSA	2.6
Fort Lauderdale, FL PMSA; Miami-Fort Lauderdale, FL CMSA	2.5
Honolulu, HI MSA	2.5
Anchorage, AK MSA	2.5
Cincinnati, OH-KY-IN PMSA; Cincinnati-Hamilton, OH-KY-IN CMSA	2.5
Barnstable-Yarmouth, MA MSA	2.5
Fort Pierce-Port St. Lucie, FL MSA	2.5
Savannah, GA MSA	2.5
Nashville, TN MSA	2.5
Lowell, MA-NH PMSA; Boston-Worcester-Lawrence, MA-NH-ME-CT CMSA	2.4
Phoenix-Mesa, AZ MSA	2.4
Charlottesville, VA MSA	2.4
Wilmington-Newark, DE-MD PMSA; Philadelphia-Wilmington-Atlantic City, PA-NJ-DE-MD CMSA	2.4
Richmond-Petersburg, VA MSA	2.3
Birmingham, AL MSA	2.3
Vallejo-Fairfield-Napa, CA PMSA; San Francisco-Oakland-San Jose, CA CMSA	2.3
Manchester, NH PMSA; Boston-Worcester-Lawrence, MA-NH-ME-CT CMSA	2.3
Fort Worth-Arlington, TX PMSA; Dallas-Fort Worth, TX CMSA	2.3
Memphis, TN-AR-MS MSA	2.3
Portsmouth-Rochester, NH-ME PMSA; Boston-Worcester-Lawrence, MA-NH-ME-CT CMSA	2.3
Iowa City, IA MSA	2.2
Indianapolis, IN MSA	2.2
Jersey City, NJ PMSA; New York-Northern New Jersey-Long Island, NY-NJ-CT-PA CMSA	2.2
Milwaukee-Waukesha, WI PMSA; Milwaukee-Racine, WI CMSA	2.2
St. Louis, MO-IL MSA	2.2
Des Moines, IA MSA	2.2
Portland-Vancouver, OR-WA PMSA; Portland-Salem, OR-WA CMSA	2.2
Kansas City, MO-KS MSA	2.2
Fort Collins-Loveland, CO MSA	2.2
Sacramento, CA PMSA; Sacramento-Yolo, CA CMSA	2.1
Madison, WI MSA	2.1
Dutchess County, NY PMSA; New York-Northern New Jersey-Long Island, NY-NJ-CT-PA CMSA	2.1
Cleveland-Lorain-Elyria, OH PMSA; Cleveland-Akron, OH CMSA	2.1
Jacksonville, FL MSA	2.1
San Luis Obispo-Atascadero-Paso Robles, CA MSA	2.1
Orlando, FL MSA	2.1
Jackson, MS MSA	2.1
Columbus, OH MSA	2.1

Atlantic-Cape May, NJ PMSA; Philadelphia-Wilmington-Atlantic City, PA-NJ-DE-MD CMSA	2.1
Waterbury, CT PMSA; New York-Northern New Jersey-Long Island, NY-NJ-CT-PA CMSA	2.1
Salt Lake City-Ogden, UT MSA	2.0
New London-Norwich, CT-RI MSA	2.0
Galveston-Texas City, TX PMSA; Houston-Galveston-Brazoria, TX CMSA	2.0
Akron, OH PMSA; Cleveland-Akron, OH CMSA	2.0
Corvallis, OR MSA	2.0
Worcester, MA-CT PMSA; Boston-Worcester-Lawrence, MA-NH-ME-CT CMSA	2.0
Lexington, KY MSA	2.0
Las Vegas, NV-AZ MSA	2.0
Omaha, NE-IA MSA	1.9
New Orleans, LA MSA	1.9
Greensboro-Winston-Salem-High Point, NC MSA	1.9
Tampa-St. Petersburg-Clearwater, FL MSA	1.9
Louisville, KY-IN MSA	1.9
Burlington, VT MSA	1.9
Columbia, SC MSA	1.9
Wilmington, NC MSA	1.9
Tyler, TX MSA	1.8
Yolo, CA PMSA; Sacramento-Yolo, CA CMSA	1.8
Springfield, IL MSA	1.8
Gainesville, FL MSA	1.8
Pittsburgh, PA MSA	1.8
Bremerton, WA PMSA; Seattle-Tacoma-Bremerton, WA CMSA	1.8
Charleston-North Charleston, SC MSA	1.8
Bloomington-Normal, IL MSA	1.8
Colorado Springs, CO MSA	1.8
Grand Rapids-Muskegon-Holland, MI MSA	1.8
Tallahassee, FL MSA	1.8
Athens, GA MSA	1.8
Lawrence, KS MSA	1.8
Providence-Fall River-Warwick, RI-MA MSA	1.8
Tulsa, OK MSA	1.7
Tucson, AZ MSA	1.7
Dubuque, IA MSA	1.7
Boise City, ID MSA	1.7
Little Rock-North Little Rock, AR MSA	1.7
San Antonio, TX MSA	1.7
Elkhart-Goshen, IN MSA	1.7
Odessa-Midland, TX MSA	1.7
Rochester, NY MSA	1.7
Greeley, CO PMSA; Denver-Boulder-Greeley, CO CMSA	1.7
Chattanooga, TN-GA MSA	1.7
Jackson, TN MSA	1.7
Medford-Ashland, OR MSA	1.7
Newburgh, NY-PA PMSA; New York-Northern New Jersey-Long Island, NY-NJ-CT-PA CMSA	1.7
Columbia, MO MSA	1.7
Knoxville, TN MSA	1.7

Hamilton-Middletown, OH PMSA; Cincinnati-Hamilton, OH-KY-IN CMSA	1.7
Charleston, WV MSA	1.7
Bryan-College Station, TX MSA	1.7
Albuquerque, NM MSA	1.7
Brockton, MA PMSA; Boston-Worcester-Lawrence, MA-NH-ME-CT CMSA	1.6
Cedar Rapids, IA MSA	1.6
Lansing-East Lansing, MI MSA	1.6
Florence, SC MSA	1.6
Huntsville, AL MSA	1.6
Riverside-San Bernardino, CA PMSA; Los Angeles-Riverside-Orange County, CA CMSA	1.6
Modesto, CA MSA	1.6
Roanoke, VA MSA	1.6
Bellingham, WA MSA	1.6
Harrisburg-Lebanon-Carlisle, PA MSA	1.6
Racine, WI PMSA; Milwaukee-Racine, WI CMSA	1.6
Corpus Christi, TX MSA	1.6
Greenville, NC MSA	1.6
Montgomery, AL MSA	1.6
Albany-Schenectady-Troy, NY MSA	1.6
Benton Harbor, MI MSA	1.6
Hattiesburg, MS MSA	1.6
Waco, TX MSA	1.6
Monroe, LA MSA	1.6
Rockford, IL MSA	1.6
Toledo, OH MSA	1.6
New Bedford, MA PMSA; Boston-Worcester-Lawrence, MA-NH-ME-CT CMSA	1.6
Greenville-Spartanburg-Anderson, SC MSA	1.6
Baton Rouge, LA MSA	1.6
Wausau, WI MSA	1.6
Provo-Orem, UT MSA	1.5
Evansville-Henderson, IN-KY MSA	1.5
Canton-Massillon, OH MSA	1.5
Lubbock, TX MSA	1.5
Eugene-Springfield, OR MSA	1.5
Appleton-Oshkosh-Neenah, WI MSA	1.5
Mobile, AL MSA	1.5
Gary, IN PMSA; Chicago-Gary-Kenosha, IL-IN-WI CMSA	1.5
Tacoma, WA PMSA; Seattle-Tacoma-Bremerton, WA CMSA	1.5
Owensboro, KY MSA	1.5
Albany, GA MSA	1.5
Dayton-Springfield, OH MSA	1.5
Fresno, CA MSA	1.5
Olympia, WA PMSA; Seattle-Tacoma-Bremerton, WA CMSA	1.5
Allentown-Bethlehem-Easton, PA MSA	1.5
Pensacola, FL MSA	1.5
Norfolk-Virginia Beach-Newport News, VA-NC MSA	1.5
Oklahoma City, OK MSA	1.5
Reading, PA MSA	1.5
Shreveport-Bossier City, LA MSA	1.5
Augusta-Aiken, GA-SC MSA	1.5

Fargo-Moorhead, ND-MN MSA	1.5
Fort Wayne, IN MSA	1.5
Alexandria, LA MSA	1.5
Stockton-Lodi, CA MSA	1.5
Asheville, NC MSA	1.5
South Bend, IN MSA	1.5
Punta Gorda, FL MSA	1.5
Lincoln, NE MSA	1.5
Champaign-Urbana, IL MSA	1.5
Springfield, MO MSA	1.5
Peoria-Pekin, IL MSA	1.5
San Angelo, TX MSA	1.5
Muncie, IN MSA	1.5
Amarillo, TX MSA	1.5
Lancaster, PA MSA	1.5
Billings, MT MSA	1.5
Tuscaloosa, AL MSA	1.4
Decatur, IL MSA	1.4
Green Bay, WI MSA	1.4
Fayetteville-Springdale-Rogers, AR MSA	1.4
Fort Walton Beach, FL MSA	1.4
Rapid City, SD MSA	1.4
La Crosse, WI-MN MSA	1.4
Longview-Marshall, TX MSA	1.4
Wichita, KS MSA	1.4
Grand Junction, CO MSA	1.4
Jackson, MI MSA	1.4
Saginaw-Bay City-Midland, MI MSA	1.4
Sioux City, IA-NE MSA	1.4
Victoria, TX MSA	1.4
Syracuse, NY MSA	1.4
Springfield, MA MSA	1.4
Flint, MI PMSA; Detroit-Ann Arbor-Flint, MI CMSA	1.4
Sherman-Denison, TX MSA	1.4
Chico-Paradise, CA MSA	1.4
Kalamazoo-Battle Creek, MI MSA	1.4
Bloomington, IN MSA	1.4
Melbourne-Titusville-Palm Bay, FL MSA	1.4
St. Cloud, MN MSA	1.4
Columbus, GA-AL MSA	1.4
Lakeland-Winter Haven, FL MSA	1.4
Daytona Beach, FL MSA	1.4
Lake Charles, LA MSA	1.3
Sheboygan, WI MSA	1.3
Macon, GA MSA	1.3
Richland-Kennewick-Pasco, WA MSA	1.3
Myrtle Beach, SC MSA	1.3
Lafayette, IN MSA	1.3
Fort Smith, AR-OK MSA	1.3
Brazoria, TX PMSA; Houston-Galveston-Brazoria, TX CMSA	1.3

Visalia-Tulare-Porterville, CA MSA	1.3
State College, PA MSA	1.3
Texarkana, TX-Texarkana, AR MSA	1.3
Pittsfield, MA MSA	1.3
Wichita Falls, TX MSA	1.3
York, PA MSA	1.3
Glens Falls, NY MSA	1.3
Buffalo-Niagara Falls, NY MSA	1.3
Lafayette, LA MSA	1.3
Yakima, WA MSA	1.3
Spokane, WA MSA	1.3
Waterloo-Cedar Falls, IA MSA	1.3
Beaumont-Port Arthur, TX MSA	1.3
Jonesboro, AR MSA	1.3
Redding, CA MSA	1.2
El Paso, TX MSA	1.2
Sioux Falls, SD MSA	1.2
Flagstaff, AZ-UT MSA	1.2
Salem, OR PMSA; Portland-Salem, OR-WA CMSA	1.2
Houma, LA MSA	1.2
Great Falls, MT MSA	1.2
Bismarck, ND MSA	1.2
Kenosha, WI PMSA; Chicago-Gary-Kenosha, IL-IN-WI CMSA	1.2
Vineland-Millville-Bridgeton, NJ PMSA; Philadelphia-Wilmington-Atlantic City, PA-NJ-DE-MD CMSA	1.2
Topeka, KS MSA	1.2
Erie, PA MSA	1.2
Dothan, AL MSA	1.2
Bakersfield, CA MSA	1.2
Lewiston-Auburn, ME MSA	1.2
Hickory-Morganton-Lenoir, NC MSA	1.2
Pueblo, CO MSA	1.2
Biloxi-Gulfport-Pascagoula, MS MSA	1.2
Kankakee, IL PMSA; Chicago-Gary-Kenosha, IL-IN-WI CMSA	1.2
Lima, OH MSA	1.2
Goldsboro, NC MSA	1.2
Johnson City-Kingsport-Bristol, TN-VA MSA	1.2
Bangor, ME MSA	1.2
Lynchburg, VA MSA	1.2
Panama City, FL MSA	1.2
Florence, AL MSA	1.2
Davenport-Moline-Rock Island, IA-IL MSA	1.2
Abilene, TX MSA	1.2
Eau Claire, WI MSA	1.2
Rocky Mount, NC MSA	1.1
Joplin, MO MSA	1.1
St. Joseph, MO MSA	1.1
Casper, WY MSA	1.1
Decatur, AL MSA	1.1
Janesville-Beloit, WI MSA	1.1

Killeen-Temple, TX MSA	1.1
Ocala, FL MSA	1.1
Anniston, AL MSA	1.1
Cheyenne, WY MSA	1.1
Yuma, AZ MSA	1.1
Scranton-Wilkes-Barre-Hazleton, PA MSA	1.1
Sharon, PA MSA	1.1
Binghamton, NY MSA	1.1
Yuba City, CA MSA	1.1
Merced, CA MSA	1.1
Missoula, MT MSA	1.1
Enid, OK MSA	1.0
Elmira, NY MSA	1.0
Wheeling, WV-OH MSA	1.0
Auburn-Opelika, AL MSA	1.0
Fayetteville, NC MSA	1.0
Fitchburg-Leominster, MA PMSA; Boston-Worcester-Lawrence, MA-NH-ME-CT CMSA	1.0
Pocatello, ID MSA	1.0
Laredo, TX MSA	1.0
Brownsville-Harlingen-San Benito, TX MSA	1.0
Youngstown-Warren, OH MSA	1.0
Grand Forks, ND-MN MSA	1.0
Kokomo, IN MSA	1.0
Danville, VA MSA	1.0
Hagerstown, MD PMSA; Washington-Baltimore, DC-MD-VA-WV CMSA	1.0
Sumter, SC MSA	1.0
Clarksville-Hopkinsville, TN-KY MSA	1.0
Williamsport, PA MSA	1.0
McAllen-Edinburg-Mission, TX MSA	0.9
Pine Bluff, AR MSA	0.9
Terre Haute, IN MSA	0.9
Gadsden, AL MSA	0.9
Parkersburg-Marietta, WV-OH MSA	0.9
Utica-Rome, NY MSA	0.9
Jamestown, NY MSA	0.9
Huntington-Ashland, WV-KY-OH MSA	0.9
Johnstown, PA MSA	0.9
Las Cruces, NM MSA	0.9
Mansfield, OH MSA	0.9
Duluth-Superior, MN-WI MSA	0.8
Altoona, PA MSA	0.8
Steubenville-Weirton, OH-WV MSA	0.8
Dover, DE MSA	0.7
Lawton, OK MSA	0.7
Cumberland, MD-WV MSA	0.6
Jacksonville, NC MSA	0.6

METROS BY PRICE GROWTH AS OF 2006

MSA	% chg (2002 to 2005)
Riverside-San Bernardino-Ontario, CA	112.0
Sarasota-Bradenton-Venice, FL	110.5
Cape Coral-Fort Myers, FL	102.0
Palm Bay-Melbourne-Titusville, FL	99.3
Miami-Fort Lauderdale-Miami Beach, FL	92.1
Reno-Sparks, NV	91.0
Las Vegas-Paradise, NV	90.7
Los Angeles-Long Beach-Santa Ana, CA	82.4
Sacramento-Arden-Arcade-Roseville, CA	78.8
Atlantic City, NJ	78.3
Orlando, FL	78.3
Deltona-Daytona Beach-Ormond Beach, FL	77.7
Honolulu, HI	76.1
Washington-Arlington-Alexandria, DC-VA-MD-WV	75.7
Phoenix-Mesa-Scottsdale, AZ	72.0
Baltimore-Towson, MD	71.4
Anaheim-Santa Ana-Irvine, CA	67.7
San Diego-Carlsbad-San Marcos, CA	65.9
Kingston, NY	60.8
Tucson, AZ	58.2
Dover, DE	54.3
Tampa-St.Petersburg-Clearwater, FL	53.8
Glens Falls, NY	53.3
Edison, NJ	52.8
Allentown-Bethlehem-Easton, PA-NJ	51.1
New York-Northern New Jersey-Long Island, NY-NJ-PA	50.4
Jacksonville, FL	48.7
Nassau-Suffolk, NY	48.7
Philadelphia-Camden-Wilmington, PA-NJ-DE-MD	46.6
Norwich-New London, CT	46.4
New Haven-Milford, CT	45.8
Albany-Schenectady-Troy, NY	45.8
Trenton-Ewing, NJ	45.5
Pensacola-Ferry Pass-Brent, FL	44.5
Providence-New Bedford-Fall River, RI-MA	44.3
Reading, PA	44.2
Spokane, WA	43.9
Portland-South Portland-Biddeford, ME	43.3
Barnstable Town, MA	42.5
New York-Wayne-White Plains, NY-NJ	42.3
Richmond, VA	41.9
Gainesville, FL	41.5
Rockford, IL	41.4
Hartford-West Hartford-East Hartford, CT	41.3
Pittsfield, MA	38.9
San Francisco-Oakland-Fremont, CA	38.4
Seattle-Tacoma-Bellevue, WA	38.1
Portland-Vancouver-Beaverton, OR-WA	38.0

Shreveport-Bossier City, LA	37.7
Eugene-Springfield, OR	37.5
Springfield, MA	37.4
Newark-Union, NJ-PA	35.9
Corpus Christi, TX	32.6
Cumberland, MD-WV	31.4
Gulfport-Biloxi, MS	31.1
San Jose-Sunnyvale-Santa Clara, CA	30.9
Farmington, NM	30.6
New Orleans-Metairie-Kenner, LA	28.9
Worcester, MA	28.9
Chicago-Naperville-Joliet, IL	28.8
Syracuse, NY	28.0
Bridgeport-Stamford-Norwalk, CT	28.0
Bismark, ND	27.6
Minneapolis-St. Paul-Bloomington, MN-WI	26.9
Madison, WI	26.6
Albuquerque, NM	26.5
El Paso, TX	25.8
Binghamton, NY	25.4
Baton Rouge, LA	25.1
Mobile, AL	24.5
Little Rock-N. Little Rock, AR	24.3
Peoria, IL	24.2
Milwaukee-Waukesha-West Allis, WI	24.1
Davenport-Moline-Rock Island, IA-IL	24.1
Charleston-North Charleston, SC	23.6
Champaign-Urbana, IL	23.4
Fargo, ND-MN	23.3
Boston-Cambridge-Quincy, MA-NH	23.2
Tallahassee, FL	22.4
Raleigh-Cary, NC	21.7
Knoxville, TN	21.4
Charlotte-Gastonia-Concord, NC-SC	21.3
San Antonio, TX	21.3
Rochester, NY	21.0
Kankakee-Bradley, IL	20.1
Boise City-Nampa, ID	19.3
Saint Louis, MO-IL	18.8
Topeka, KS	18.8
Green Bay, WI	18.5
Chattanooga, TN-GA	17.5
Montgomery, AL	17.3
Salt Lake City, UT	16.9
Beaumont-Port Arthur, TX	16.8
Amarillo, TX	16.5
Waterloo/Cedar Falls, IA	16.4
Colorado Springs, CO	16.4
Sioux Falls, SD	16.4
Yakima, WA	15.7

Lexington-Fayette,KY	15.6
Spartanburg, SC	15.2
Appleton, WI	15.0
Oklahoma City, OK	14.6
Buffalo-Niagara Falls, NY	14.3
Birmingham-Hoover, AL	14.3
Atlanta-Sandy Springs-Marietta, GA	14.1
Kansas City, MO-KS	14.0
Gary-Hammond, IN	13.6
Pittsburgh, PA	13.4
Elmira, NY	13.0
Columbia, SC	13.0
Lansing-E. Lansing, MI	12.5
Lincoln, NE	12.1
Erie, PA	11.9
Des Moines, IA	11.8
Springfield, IL	11.4
Omaha, NE-IA	11.3
Cedar Rapids, IA	10.9
Tulsa, OK	10.8
Charleston, WV	10.4
Decatur, IL	10.3
Wichita, KS	10.1
Grand Rapids, MI	10.0
Greenville, SC	9.7
Boulder, CO	9.7
Kennewick-Richland-Pasco, WA	9.4
Dallas-Fort Worth-Arlington, TX	9.2
Memphis, TN-MS-AR	9.1
Greensboro-High Point, NC	8.8
Cincinnati-Middletown, OH-KY-IN	8.8
Louisville, KY-IN	8.5
Columbus, OH	8.3
Denver-Aurora, CO	8.3
Ft. Wayne, IN	7.8
Houston-Baytown-Sugar Land, TX	7.7
Toledo, OH	7.0
Dayton, OH	6.3
South Bend-Mishawaka, IN	6.2
Indianapolis, IN	6.0
Austin-Round Rock, TX	4.7
Akron, OH	4.5
Kalamazoo-Portage, MI	2.8
Canton-Massillon, OH	−6.2

METROS BY MEDIAN PRICE AS OF 2006

MSA	Median Price (in $ thousands)
San Jose-Sunnyvale-Santa Clara, CA	744.5
San Francisco-Oakland-Fremont, CA	715.7
Anaheim-Santa Ana-Irvine, CA	691.9
San Diego-Carlsbad-San Marcos, CA	604.3
Honolulu, HI	590.0
Los Angeles-Long Beach-Santa Ana, CA	529.0
New York-Wayne-White Plains, NY-NJ	495.2
Bridgeport-Stamford-Norwalk, CT	482.4
Nassau-Suffolk, NY	465.2
New York-Northern New Jersey-Long Island, NY-NJ-PA	445.2
Washington-Arlington-Alexandria, DC-VA-MD-WV	425.8
Newark-Union, NJ-PA	416.8
Boston-Cambridge-Quincy, MA-NH	413.2
Barnstable Town, MA	398.3
Sacramento-Arden-Arcade-Roseville, CA	375.9
Edison, NJ	375.5
Riverside-San Bernardino-Ontario, CA	374.2
Miami-Fort Lauderdale-Miami Beach, FL	370.1
Sarasota-Bradenton-Venice, FL	354.2
Reno-Sparks, NV	349.9
Boulder, CO	348.4
Seattle-Tacoma-Bellevue, WA	316.8
Las Vegas-Paradise, NV	304.7
Providence-New Bedford-Fall River, RI-MA	293.4
Worcester, MA	290.7
New Haven-Milford, CT	279.1
Cape Coral-Fort Myers, FL	269.2
Baltimore-Towson, MD	265.3
Chicago-Naperville-Joliet, IL	264.2
Trenton-Ewing, NJ	261.1
Atlantic City, NJ	256.1
Norwich-New London, CT	255.9
Hartford-West Hartford-East Hartford, CT	253.3
Kingston, NY	251.0
Phoenix-Mesa-Scottsdale, AZ	247.4
Denver-Aurora, CO	247.1
Portland-South Portland-Biddeford, ME	246.6
Portland-Vancouver-Beaverton, OR-WA	244.9
Orlando, FL	243.6
Allentown-Bethlehem-Easton, PA-NJ	243.4
Minneapolis-St. Paul-Bloomington, MN-WI	234.8
Tucson, AZ	231.6
Madison, WI	218.3
Milwaukee-Waukesha-West Allis, WI	215.7
Philadelphia-Camden-Wilmington, PA-NJ-DE-MD	215.3
Palm Bay-Melbourne-Titusville, FL	209.7
Hagerstown-Martinsburg, MD-WV	208.7

Pittsfield, MA	207.3
Colorado Springs, CO	205.9
Tampa-St.Petersburg-Clearwater, FL	205.3
Richmond, VA	201.9
Springfield, MA	201.8
Eugene-Springfield, OR	197.6
Virginia Beach-Norfolk-Newport News, VA-NC	197.2
Charleston-North Charleston, SC	197.0
Raleigh-Cary, NC	194.9
Deltona-Daytona Beach-Ormond Beach, FL	192.5
Gainesville, FL	184.0
Albany-Schenectady-Troy, NY	183.5
Charlotte-Gastonia-Concord, NC-SC	180.9
Dover, DE	180.4
Salem, OR	177.7
Jacksonville, FL	175.2
Salt Lake City, UT	173.9
Albuquerque, NM	169.2
Tallahassee, FL	167.6
Atlanta-Sandy Springs-Marietta, GA	167.2
Austin-Round Rock, TX	163.8
Pensacola-Ferry Pass-Brent, FL	162.1
Nashville-Davidson-Murfreesboro, TN	161.8
Bloomington-Normal, IL	159.2
New Orleans-Metairie-Kenner, LA	159.2
Birmingham-Hoover, AL	157.0
Kansas City, MO-KS	156.7
Spokane, WA	156.4
Farmington, NM	155.1
Green Bay, WI	154.8
Kennewick-Richland-Pasco, WA	154.1
Glens Falls, NY	153.1
Columbus, OH	152.0
Greensboro-High Point, NC	147.8
Dallas-Fort Worth-Arlington, TX	147.6
Boise City-Nampa, ID	147.0
Lexington-Fayette,KY	146.9
Baton Rouge, LA	146.2
Cincinnati-Middletown, OH-KY-IN	145.9
Des Moines, IA	145.5
Greenville, SC	145.4
Knoxville, TN	143.7
Ocala, FL	143.5
Houston-Baytown-Sugar Land, TX	143.0
Lansing-E. Lansing, MI	142.2
Memphis, TN-MS-AR	141.2
Saint Louis, MO-IL	141.0
Cleveland-Elyria-Mentor, OH	138.9
Grand Rapids, MI	137.8
Champaign-Urbana, IL	137.7

Lincoln, NE	137.2
Reading, PA	136.6
Omaha, NE-IA	136.2
Louisville, KY-IN	135.8
Sioux Falls, SD	135.8
Columbia, SC	135.0
Detroit-Warren-Livonia, MI	134.5
San Antonio, TX	133.9
Yakima, WA	133.9
Jackson, MS	133.8
Montgomery, AL	133.3
Fargo, ND-MN	132.8
Chattanooga, TN-GA	131.9
Cedar Rapids, IA	131.8
Gulfport-Biloxi, MS	131.4
Mobile, AL	130.5
Gary-Hammond, IN	129.8
Appleton, WI	129.6
Kankakee-Bradley, IL	127.1
Corpus Christi, TX	125.2
Bismark, ND	124.9
Shreveport-Bossier City, LA	124.3
Indianapolis, IN	123.8
Spartanburg, SC	121.2
Kalamazoo-Portage, MI	121.1
Springfield, MO	121.1
Akron, OH	120.5
Dayton, OH	119.7
Little Rock-N. Little Rock, AR	119.0
Charleston, WV	118.4
Rockford, IL	118.2
Tulsa, OK	118.2
Davenport-Moline-Rock Island, IA-IL	117.9
Toledo, OH	117.3
Pittsburgh, PA	116.1
Oklahoma City, OK	114.7
Rochester, NY	113.5
El Paso, TX	111.8
Syracuse, NY	110.6
Peoria, IL	109.3
Wichita, KS	108.0
Amarillo, TX	107.1
Springfield, IL	106.4
Topeka, KS	105.7
Ft. Wayne, IN	102.3
Canton-Massillon, OH	102.2
Waterloo/Cedar Falls, IA	102.2
Erie, PA	100.0
Buffalo-Niagara Falls, NY	99.0
Beaumont-Port Arthur, TX	98.5

South Bend-Mishawaka, IN	96.6
Binghamton, NY	94.4
Cumberland, MD-WV	87.4
Youngstown-Warren-Boardman, OH-PA	85.6
Decatur, IL	82.1
Elmira, NY	77.1
Danville, IL	67.7

METROS BY AFFORDABILITY INDEX AS OF 2006

MSA	Housing Affordability Index
Danville, IL	305.8
Elmira, NY	291.0
Decatur, IL	287.1
Youngstown-Warren-Boardman, OH-PA	262.8
Ft. Wayne, IN	258.5
South Bend-Mishawaka, IN	257.0
Springfield, IL	253.1
Buffalo-Niagara Falls, NY	252.3
Waterloo/Cedar Falls, IA	246.8
Binghamton, NY	246.7
Rochester, NY	241.9
Topeka, KS	239.8
Wichita, KS	238.2
Cumberland, MD-WV	238.1
Peoria, IL	237.5
Canton-Massillon, OH	233.9
Syracuse, NY	230.6
Erie, PA	228.5
Indianapolis, IN	226.7
Rockford, IL	224.7
Appleton, WI	223.7
Detroit-Warren-Livonia, MI	223.3
Akron, OH	220.9
Beaumont-Port Arthur, TX	220.8
Toledo, OH	218.2
Dayton, OH	217.1
Cedar Rapids, IA	216.0
Kalamazoo-Portage, MI	215.7
Davenport-Moline-Rock Island, IA-IL	215.0
Omaha, NE-IA	207.9
Pittsburgh, PA	207.4
Amarillo, TX	206.8
Fargo, ND-MN	205.6
Lincoln, NE	204.9
Gary-Hammond, IN	203.1
Des Moines, IA	203.0
Oklahoma City, OK	200.2
Little Rock-N. Little Rock, AR	199.8
Saint Louis, MO-IL	198.4
Reading, PA	198.4
Lansing-E. Lansing, MI	198.0
Tulsa, OK	197.2
Spartanburg, SC	194.1
Grand Rapids, MI	193.2
Kankakee-Bradley, IL	192.9
Cleveland-Elyria-Mentor, OH	192.1
Sioux Falls, SD	192.0

Bloomington-Normal, IL	191.9
Cincinnati-Middletown, OH-KY-IN	191.6
Champaign-Urbana, IL	189.7
Columbia, SC	188.8
Dallas-Fort Worth-Arlington, TX	187.9
Louisville, KY-IN	185.1
Columbus, OH	184.2
Charleston, WV	184.1
Austin-Round Rock, TX	183.7
Springfield, MO	183.3
Kansas City, MO-KS	183.0
Houston-Baytown-Sugar Land, TX	182.2
Atlanta-Sandy Springs-Marietta, GA	181.8
Lexington-Fayette,KY	179.1
Green Bay, WI	176.5
Montgomery, AL	173.9
Chattanooga, TN-GA	172.6
Shreveport-Bossier City, LA	170.4
San Antonio, TX	168.7
Greenville, SC	168.6
Boise City-Nampa, ID	168.3
Kennewick-Richland-Pasco, WA	168.1
Memphis, TN-MS-AR	166.5
Greensboro-High Point, NC	164.4
Knoxville, TN	164.0
Corpus Christi, TX	163.9
Baton Rouge, LA	163.3
Nashville-Davidson-Murfreesboro, TN	162.1
Mobile, AL	157.8
Raleigh-Cary, NC	157.1
Salt Lake City, UT	155.2
Albany-Schenectady-Troy, NY	154.4
Jackson, MS	154.4
Birmingham-Hoover, AL	151.8
Charlotte-Gastonia-Concord, NC-SC	151.5
El Paso, TX	151.4
Glens Falls, NY	150.7
Yakima, WA	148.9
Spokane, WA	148.5
Gulfport-Biloxi, MS	148.4
Tallahassee, FL	147.3
Philadelphia-Camden-Wilmington, PA-NJ-DE-MD	145.1
Jacksonville, FL	144.4
Minneapolis-St. Paul-Bloomington, MN-WI	143.8
Richmond, VA	143.5
Madison, WI	141.9
New Orleans-Metairie-Kenner, LA	140.5
Salem, OR	139.4
Albuquerque, NM	138.7
Dover, DE	137.7

Trenton-Ewing, NJ	136.5
Colorado Springs, CO	135.4
Pensacola-Ferry Pass-Brent, FL	134.7
Springfield, MA	134.3
Milwaukee-Waukesha-West Allis, WI	132.6
Hartford-West Hartford-East Hartford, CT	132.3
Ocala, FL	131.7
Virginia Beach-Norfolk-Newport News, VA-NC	131.4
Pittsfield, MA	127.9
Denver-Aurora, CO	127.3
Gainesville, FL	124.7
Charleston-North Charleston, SC	123.7
Farmington, NM	123.3
Norwich-New London, CT	120.7
Eugene-Springfield, OR	120.3
Baltimore-Towson, MD	119.3
Hagerstown-Martinsburg, MD-WV	118.2
Portland-Vancouver-Beaverton, OR-WA	118.0
Palm Bay-Melbourne-Titusville, FL	114.8
Chicago-Naperville-Joliet, IL	113.8
Allentown-Bethlehem-Easton, PA-NJ	113.5
New Haven-Milford, CT	112.2
Tampa-St.Petersburg-Clearwater, FL	111.4
Deltona-Daytona Beach-Ormond Beach, FL	109.8
Portland-South Portland-Biddeford, ME	108.8
Worcester, MA	106.2
Atlantic City, NJ	105.0
Kingston, NY	104.8
Phoenix-Mesa-Scottsdale, AZ	103.4
Boulder, CO	103.2
Orlando, FL	99.2
NY: Edison, NJ	97.1
Providence-New Bedford-Fall River, RI-MA	96.8
Tucson, AZ	95.8
Seattle-Tacoma-Bellevue, WA	91.9
Washington-Arlington-Alexandria, DC-VA-MD-WV	88.8
Cape Coral-Fort Myers, FL	87.5
NY: Newark-Union, NJ-PA	85.4
Las Vegas-Paradise, NV	85.0
NY: Nassau-Suffolk, NY	83.8
Bridgeport-Stamford-Norwalk, CT	82.9
Boston-Cambridge-Quincy, MA-NH	81.1
Reno-Sparks, NV	79.9
Sacramento-Arden-Arcade-Roseville, CA	74.0
Barnstable Town, MA	72.3
Sarasota-Bradenton-Venice, FL	69.2
Riverside-San Bernardino-Ontario, CA	65.2
Miami-Fort Lauderdale-Miami Beach, FL	61.9
San Francisco-Oakland-Fremont, CA	52.0
New York-Wayne-White Plains, NY-NJ	51.1

Honolulu, HI	50.4
Anaheim-Santa Ana-Irvine, CA	48.0
San Diego-Carlsbad-San Marcos, CA	45.7
Los Angeles-Long Beach-Santa Ana, CA	45.1

INDEX